The Cultures of the American New West

NEIL CAMPBELL

EDINBURGH UNIVERSITY PRESS

© Neil Campbell, 2000

Edinburgh University Press Ltd
22 George Square, Edinburgh

Typeset in Monotype Fournier
by Bibliocraft, Dundee, and
printed and bound in Great Britain
by MPG Books Ltd, Bodmin

A CIP record for this book is available
from the British Library

ISBN 0 7486 1176 2 (paperback)

Contents

Acknowledgements

I would like to thank a number of people who have contributed in different ways to this project and to my interest in the American West over a number of years: to George McKay for his support for the initial idea; to Maude Crawford-Odgers' western ideas, books, and friendship; to the generosity of other 'westerners' Mark Klett, Larry Watson; and to the inspiration of Lawrence Clark Powell who years ago replied to a hesitant postgraduate student's letter with the advice that 'the only way to understand the West was to go there' – advice I've taken many times since. For financial support for some of those travels, I'd like to thank the University of Derby research development fund.

Finally, as ever, this is for Jane.

List of Plates

Introduction:
Mapping the New West

*Connection. Invention. Reinvention. This may be the real work of the
West.*   (Apt Russell, 1993: 13)

Culture, Place and Identity

The American West has always been represented as 'new', a place of
immense promise and growth: Native American emergence stories,
European myths of new Eden, settlers' and immigrants' belief in the
dream of the new start in the golden land, the Okies fleeing the Dust
Bowl in the 1930s for California, Kerouac's countercultural road, the
Sunbelt economies' vision of perpetual expansion and wealth, 'New
Age' philosophies and environmentalism's 'last best place', or new
contemporary settlers escaping the cities and beginning lives in the
hinterland. The West was invested with hopes and dreams, with communities rooted in the landscape who simultaneously experienced disappointment and frustration over years of migration and change. In the
Native American history of the West, for example, there was original in-
migration across the Bering Strait to settle the Americas, and within the
West itself, different tribes developed and dispersed with their lands
reoccupied by others. Thus, the Anasazis who built complex settlements
in the Southwest, left their villages in Mesa Verde, moving to Acoma
and the Rio Grande valley, while new settlements grew in their wake.
The hostile and peaceful contacts, exchanges and cultural dialogues that
these migrations created were an early indication of the processes to
become evermore important to the region. Far from static or inward
looking, these Pueblo peoples adapted and learned through their range
of contacts creating communities with complex social rituals that formed
hybrid religions mixing Catholicism and tribal practices that honoured
the land and ancient gods. These elements of newness, dream, migration, change, and adaptation have been constant and abiding themes in

I

the American West, and remain so today. Played out in a variety of diverse landscapes amid equally varied peoples, the West has never been easily defined as geography or sociopolitical region because it has been engaged in dynamic change, with its meaning always being rethought, revised, and contested. The West is, and always has been, many different spaces – real and imagined – plural in every sense, but especially in the mix of cultures that constitute and define the region. Standing in the East looking toward the geographic west, as Frederick Jackson Turner and others did in the mid to late nineteenth century, there was a line, a frontier, that marked the territory of opportunity and became the preferred reading of the region. But for Mexicans annexed to the USA in 1848 after the Mexican-American War, standing in the South looking north, there was another region – not a geographic west – representing oppression and struggle not opportunity. For the Chinese coming literally from the west into California, the journey was east. The point is that the American West is more than geography, it is a complex, unstable signifier that has been given meaning by those who have lived within it, passed through it, conquered it, settled, farmed, militarized, urbanized, and dreamed it. The West is a multicultural, multiaccented, multilayered space whose various cultures exist both separately and in dialogue with all the others that exist around them. I have deliberately used the plural 'cultures' in the title of this study as a reminder that the West is unreadable as a single, identifiable unit of place, but rather exists as many 'systems of meaning' that compete for attention and whose status and significance may change over time. These cultures are contested, with different people imposing different meanings upon them and seeking to emphasize certain aspects and not others. As Doreen Massey has written, 'the notion of place simply as settled, enclosed and internally coherent' has to replaced by the idea of it as 'a meeting place, the location of the intersections of particular bundles of activity spaces, of connections and interrelations, of influences and movements' (Massey and Jess, 1995: 58–9). This is precisely the sense of cultures to be explored in this book. Because the West has been formed by overlapping, interconnecting systems of meaning, including, of course, invasion, conquest, and colonization, it can only be accessed as a series of 'routes' rather than a single 'root' from which all grew. Paul Gilroy (1994) and Stuart Hall (in Massey and Jess, 1995) have expanded on these ideas as a way of seeing culture in late modernity where notions of 'roots' or essential identity rooted in place and commonly shared by all are less recognizable than a more fluid, mixed sense of culture born out of exchange, movement, relations, and hybridization. However, too often, the West has been seen more narrowly as the 'root-place' for American Exceptionalism, the space in which the nation was forged and its 'character' created in contact with the landscape and indigenous peoples.

As early as 1888 William Thayer wrote a guide called the *Marvels of the New West* in which he celebrated its 'remarkable growth' and the 'marvels' of nature, enterprise, agriculture, and settlement that he found there all combined in a unified and coherent vision of the future. Amid the industrializing West, Thayer wrote of 'marvels', mixing images of natural awe and wonder with those of technology and human ingenuity (quoted in Riebsame et al, 1997). This marriage of pragmatic, practical development and the capacity to dream fuse together to create an example of the way the West can be viewed as a space of paradox, a geographical Imaginary filled up with often contradictory desires to match the incipient nation's own complex cultural profile. In the West there was room for all these layers of meaning, all the differences of individuals and their reasons for being in the region, and because of this it became rapidly associated with America-as-nation. This version of American identity has immense ideological weight for embedded in it is the sense of a melting down of differences into a new thing, a composite American self, formed out of the rejection of European values, a westward journey, and contact with the rigours of climate, geology, and indigenous populations. Out of migration and movement comes a new rooted identity as the focus for the epic narrative that gave coherence and authority to the westward urge of nation-building, and provided America with its own creation myth. As Slotkin has written, 'myth-making ... is simultaneously a psychological and a social activity ... its function is to reconcile and unite ... individualities into a collective identity' (Slotkin, 1973: 8). However, just as the notion of a geographic West is an unstable concept, so too is this idea of national beginnings rooted in the Frontier which apparently proceeded with efficient order across the landscape. The simple neatness of this concept reveals its mythic structure, for what it glosses over are the very complex relations discussed earlier that actually existed in the various spaces of the West. The need for a national origin story occluded the recognition of the true nature of the historical processes being played out across the region and sought only to reduce these to a managed set of images and stories that would become the West's official history.

Stuart Hall's discussion of 'cultural identity' is a useful exploration of the problems of a too neat linkage between the American West and the concept of national identity. Hall warns against an essentialist position in which everything looks back to a point at which the identity was formed and whole, but which has subsequently been altered and corrupted. At this point of origin there is a unity, a 'oneness' linking all together. Instead, Hall favours a view of identity which acknowledges 'critical points of deep and significant difference' which constitute 'what we have become' (Hall, in Rutherford, 1990: 225):

> Cultural identity . . . is a matter of 'becoming' as well as 'being'. It belongs to the future as much as to the past . . . Cultural identities come from somewhere, have histories. But like everything which is historical, they undergo constant transformation . . . subject to the 'play' of history, culture and power . . . It is not once-and-for-all. It is not a fixed origin to which we can make some final and absolute Return . . . It has its histories – and histories have their real, material and symbolic effects . . . It is always constructed through memory, fantasy, narrative and myth. (ibid.: 225–6)

Hall's analysis ensures a different consideration under which the West might be seen as a space of complex interactions rather than 'a straight, unbroken line, from some fixed origin' (ibid.: 226). Hence, there is continuity within the 'identity' of the American West but also, simultaneously, *discontinuity* – migration, imperialism, ethnic dispute, violent intervention, and cultural exchange. In this sense, 'difference, therefore, persists – in and alongside continuity' (ibid.: 227). Within the histories of the American West there are always points of coherence for all – relations with the land, for example – but also the significant 'play' of difference, as Hall terms it, suggesting instability, movement, and 'the lack of any final resolution' (ibid.: 228). Hall suggestively comments that any attempt to represent these relations could not rely on a conventional 'binary structure' such as 'past/present' or 'them/us' because the 'boundaries are re-sited' (ibid.). In so doing, Hall refers to Derrida's concept of '*différance*' which deliberately echoes differ *and* defer in order to indicate that difference is critical and yet within it is the persistent chain of other meanings into the future (hence deferred) and back into the past, seen in the 'trace' contained in the word (differ*a*nce). The outcome is the rejection of binary fixtures which seek to stabilize meanings, in favour of a fluid concept of difference, deferral, and incompleteness. Hall applies these ideas to an understanding of a 'New World' cultural identity which rejects the old sense of a rooted, fixed essence, defined by binary thinking such as 'us/them' or, in the case of the American West, between 'East/West', and favours instead what he terms the 'diasporic':

> the recognition of a necessary heterogeneity and diversity; by a conception of 'identity' which lives with and through, not despite, difference; by hybridity. Diaspora identities are those constantly producing and reproducing themselves anew, through transformation and difference. (ibid.: 235)

The sense of identity and place worked through in these ideas is constituted within the representations produced by those within its cultural formations. Cultures are created by a whole body of ideas, struggles, and representations, and, therefore, need to be analyzed as 'routes', movements, and processes of change. As Raymond Williams wrote in 1961, culture is 'the study of relationships between elements in a whole way of life. The analysis of culture is the attempt to discover the nature of the organization which is the complex of these relationships' (Williams, 1965: 63). It is with these definitions and debates in mind that this study of the New West begins.

The New West: 'an agglomerative space'

In 1992 Wilbur Jacobs spoke of the West as a place that 'floats on the map, almost like a puddle of mercury. The sub-puddles, spinning around, have so many socioeconomic, political, environmental, and cultural eddies that they are almost impossible to control when we try to write a coherent account' (quoted in Milner, 1996: 49). Cultural theory provides tools by which we might understand how a region can be viewed productively in these terms, for it defines the New West as a complex, multifaceted, cultural text. As Roland Barthes wrote:

> To interpret a text is not to give it a (more or less justified, more or less free) meaning, but on the contrary to appreciate what *plural* constitutes it . . . the networks are many and interact, without any one of them being able to surpass the rest; this text is a galaxy of signifiers, not a structure of signifieds; it has no beginning; it is reversible; we gain access to it by several entrances, none of which can be authoritavely declared to be the main one; the codes it

mobilizes extend *as far as the eye can reach*, they are indeterminable. (Barthes, 1975: 5–6)

The West-as-text is multilayered, 'an agglomerative space' (ibid.: 7) where 'everything signifies ceaselessly and several times, but without being delegated to *a great final ensemble, to an ultimate structure*' (ibid.: 12 – my emphasis). The 'ultimate structure' or metanarrative, in terms of the West, has been a series of dominant stories or myths told over time and endowed with massive cultural power, such as the Promised Land, Manifest Destiny, Turner's frontier thesis, each of which sought to encompass and define the West. Taken together and over time, these myths contribute to the construction of a discourse that defines the West in the consciousness:

> Discourse ... defines and produces the objects of our knowledge. It governs the way that a topic can be meaningfully talked about and reasoned about. It also influences how ideas are put into practice and used to regulate the conduct of others ... [it] 'rules in' certain ways of talking about a topic, defining an acceptable way to talk, write, conduct oneself, so also, by definition, it 'rules out', limits and restricts other ways of talking, of conducting ourselves in relation to the topic or constructing knowledge about it. (Hall, 1997: 44)

This mythic discourse, produced by selective history, literature, visual arts, and popular culture, constructs an ideological framework or grid that authorizes and privileges the dominant stories of the West. Such myths have to be examined closely because they distort by naturalizing history, hollowing it out into a neat, closed, unambiguous process. Barthes writes that myth 'abolishes the complexity of human acts ... it does away with dialectics ... organizes a world which is without contradictions because it is without depth, a world wide open and wallowing in the evident ...' (Barthes, 1973: 143). The effect of this myth-making is to stifle human diversity, narrow the limits of achievement, and 'depoliticize' the world, creating 'a realm which has purged itself of ambiguity and alternative possibility' (ibid.). William H. Truettner summarized the ideological implications of myth in relation to the West in an essay for the art exhibition *The West As America* (1991) which controversially revisioned the West as a place of conquest and imperialism:

Myth functions to control history, to shape it in text or image as an ordained sequence of events. The world is rendered pure in the process; complexity and contradictions give way to order, clarity, and direction. Myth, then, can be understood as an abstract shelter restricting debate. But myth can also function as ideology – as an abstraction broadly defining the belief system of a particular group or society ... When viewed through a new perspective, images often yield this agenda – one taken for granted and therefore never acknowledged by nineteenth century viewers. (Truettner, 1991: 40)

The Turner Legacy

In political rhetoric, guidebooks, dime novels, and visual arts, these ideological myths gained influence in their definition of the West. By the time Frederick Jackson Turner delivered his 'The Significance of the Frontier in American History' in 1893, to mark the closing of the frontier, many of these myths had become solidified and embedded into his historiography. Turner's thesis became 'the central story of American history' despite (or because) of the fact that it was 'ethnocentric and nationalistic' (Limerick, 1987: 20, 21), offering a final statement on the inevitable progress westward and its formative influence upon the creation of an American character.

Turner, speaking at the Columbian Exposition in 1893, claimed he could 'read' America 'like a huge page ... Line by line ... from West to East [to] find the record of social evolution' (Turner, in Milner, 1989: 6–7). Onto this page, Turner inscribed his version of history, marking out his concept of the West as the key to American development. As Trachtenberg has written:

The nation needed ... a coherent, integrated story of its beginnings and its development. Connectedness, wholeness, unity: these narrative virtues, with their implied telos of closure, of a justifying meaning at the end of the tale, Turner would now embody in the language of historical interpretation. And an interpretation not merely accurate according to the canons of historical writing but serviceable according to the needs of politics and culture ... (Trachtenberg, 1982: 13)

For Turner the West created American character itself and became the site where the process that formed the nation as a whole could be revealed. His 'blank' Western page filled up with the tenets of

Americanism, forged by the notions of Western expansion and frontier values, while it ignored or nullified the other histories that were already there. Turner finds no space for women or ethnic groups, and Native Americans appear only to be dismissed as 'the slender paths of aboriginal intercourse' superseded by 'the complex mazes of modern commercial lines' (Turner, in Milner, 1989: 8).

For Patricia Nelson Limerick, a key figure in the revisionist New Western History, Turner provided America with 'a creation myth – a tale explaining where its [white] members came from and why they are special, chosen by providence for a special destiny' (1987: 322). This was a myth of character formed on the frontier, of the primacy of colonial English settlement, of racial destiny, and of the rightness of expansionism. In her foreword to the exhibition *The West As America*, Elizabeth Broun underlined these points and recognized the need to see beyond Turner:

> Today, a century after America's creation myth was ushered into the world, we struggle with its inadequacies and insensitivities . . . [and] we can see *the large realities that lay to either side of this artificially straight line*, finding there a new perspective on our past and future. (in Truettner, 1991: ix – my emphasis)

The 'straight line' of Turner's frontier omits the stories on 'either side' and instead constructed an official narrative which was centrist and reflective of the dominant beliefs and values of the time: white, male, and imperialist. A characteristic of the New West, a post-Turnerian West, is the interruption and challenging of this epic narrative by a host of significant revisions from 'either side of this artificially straight line'. As Elliot West has written:

> Life is not 'straighter' here [in the West]. The way of understanding the West is never by clean lines but by indirection and by webs of changing connections among people, plants, institutions, animals, politics, soil, weather, ambitions, and perceptions. (West 1995: 166)

West recognizes the growing dissatisfaction with the reductionist ideological myths of the American West and how they were indicative of a wider American Cold War mentality desperate to hold onto old certainities about identity, race, and national order. However, the times were changing with the impact of postcolonialism, civil rights, the women's movement, and the growth of postmodern theory and cultural studies. It was in the light of these broad cultural shifts that the New West also emerged as an economic and cultural space, benefitting from the Cold War growth in the military economy and the expansion of the so-called Sunbelt and becoming influential as a political base and cultural region (see Chapter 4). In this climate, old explanations and histories came under scrutiny with Americans looking again, or revising, their long-held and often paradoxical views about the West. The mythic space of the West, for so long summed up by the Turner thesis, John Wayne films, the Marlboro Man, and Ansel Adams' pristine wilderness, was being revised by those concerned to represent a fuller, more complex portrait of the region. Revision is a key term in the interrogation of myth, opening the way for the kind of multiplicitous discourses of the New West that this book will examine:

> Re-vision – the act of looking back, of seeing with fresh eyes, of entering an old text from a new critical direction ... it is an act of survival ... Until we can know the assumptions in which we are drenched we cannot know ourselves. (Rich, 1993: 167)

Thus, to look again at the West is not just an academic game, but a political act concerned with survival, especially for all those previously omitted or silenced in the old histories. It is, therefore, vital to discuss the New West in relation to the wider context of changing values and critical alliances known broadly as postmodernism, for it is largely in this post–1950s world that it entered prominently into the cultural debates within the USA. The voices of women, ethnic Americans, and the marginalized play a very significant part in this process of cultural revision, broadening the discourse through which the West is defined and expressed.

To comprehend the context of these changes more fully, it is worth examining how many of the voices of the New West are proposing a fundamental critique of conventional representations, within history, geography, literature, the visual arts, and popular culture, offering an interdisciplinary alternative that reframes the West as the kind of multilayered, 'agglomerative space'.

New Histories: Bakhtin, Benjamin, and Foucault

The mythic framework that constructed and maintained the West as an American Imaginary, articulated core values of individualism, success, industriousness, masculinity, and a possessive attitude to the land, creating a powerful monomyth for identity. Its authority was immense, functioning to hold out other voices and points of view, replacing dialogue with monologue. In Bakhtinian terms, the idea of monologism helps us to understand how these stories of the West circulated and controlled debate: 'Monologue manages without the other, and therefore to some degree materializes all reality. Monologue pretends to be the *ultimate word*. It closes down the represented world and represented persons' (Bakhtin, 1997: 293). Myths are monologic, reducing alternatives and the complex relations of history to simple statements, images, or concepts. Instead of the representation of the West as a dialogic zone of contact and encounter where interaction and dialogue take place at all levels, myth presented a frozen, one-dimensional idealization of space.

Bakhtin felt that the world was polyphonic – many voiced – writing 'I hear voices in everything and dialogic relations among them' (Bakhtin, 1990b: 169), and his work was based on the belief that all things are formed in contact with others (human and nonhuman), endlessly engaged in dialogues which connect us to webs and networks of meaning and belief. 'Life by its very nature is dialogic. To live means to participate in dialogue: to ask questions, to heed, to respond, to agree, and so forth' (Bakhtin, 1997: 293).

Dialogism means a perpetual interchange, an 'interillumination' across a *space* of contacts, encounters, and relations through which individuals and cultures are formed. As Holquist puts it, dialogic relations are where 'differences – while still remaining different – serve as the building blocks of simultaneity' and dialogism 'is present in exchanges at all levels – between words in language, people in society, organisms in ecosystems, and even between processes in the natural world' (Holquist, 1991: 40, 41). This sense of being and becoming, of life itself as a dialogue – echoed in Hall and Massey's sense of contemporary cultures (see earlier) – is a way of interpreting the lived space of the West as a complex web of interconnections, competing discourses, and different 'voices' that together constitute the region. Bakhtin's approach acknowledges the contradictory, the unfinished and the 'multi-accented' (Bakhtin, 1997: 15) as central to the process of constitution, and ultimately as its very strength and vitality. These things exist simultaneously within space in 'coexistence and interaction' – and this is what Bakhtin admires in Dostoevsky who was able 'to see many and varied things where others saw one and the same thing.

Where others saw a single thought, he was able to find and feel out two thoughts . . .' (ibid.: 28, 30). Within dialogue, Bakhtin 'heard both the loud, recognized, reigning voices of the epoch . . . as well as voices still weak, ideas not yet fully emerged, latent ideas . . . and ideas that were just beginning to ripen, embryos of future worldviews' (ibid.: 90).

What defines polyphony is hybrid space stressing simultaneity, co-existence, and interaction: 'to *juxtapose* and *counterpose* . . . to see every-thing as coexisting, to perceive and show all things side by side and simultaneous, as if they existed in space and not in time . . . (ibid.: 28). Through this emerges a new approach to cultural relations rejecting myth, monologue, and linear narrative in favour of a more varied, sophisticated recognition of genuine interaction and contact. In exam-ining the West, such an approach breaks down the boundaries con-structed by narrow historiographical studies, dime novel stereotypes, and romantic visualizations of landscape and human action, by intro-ducing new discourses in dialogue with the old.

The attack on Turner's monologic method has often been overstated in order to provide a launching pad for what became known as New Western History (see later), when in fact Turner himself saw his own work as a heroic rejection of 'the Great Man histories' of Europe and as an effort to relocate the common man within the frame of history (see Klein, 1997). Turner's interest in local documents, the reconstruction of everyday working lives, statistics, and concepts of culture have led others to produce new histories which broaden further our sense of the West. But, of course, Turner omitted much and did follow a slavish, linear perspective that obscured, often by poetic generalization, the complex relations in the West. Despite his interest in the common man, his historiographical technique was wedded to cause and effect and sweeping explanatory tropes: glaciation, arterial flows, waves, germs, and seeds. In this respect, his thesis shares much with a particular form of monologue described by Bakhtin – the literary epic – defined as a genre 'walled off absolutely from all subsequent times . . . as closed as a circle; everything is finished, already over . . . [with] no place . . . for any open-endedness, indecision, indeterminacy' (Bakhtin, 1990a: 16). The epic has everything 'fused into a single inseparable whole' (ibid.) that can only be questioned by 'the arrival . . . of an active polyglossia and interillumina-tion of languages' (ibid.: 17) which erode the single, inseparable whole through the introduction of contrary perspectives. This change is related to the 'dialogic relations and hybrid combinations' which define 'a zone of contact' in which the old epic distance is 'surmounted' and new relations established by a 'new positioning' (ibid.: 28). As we will see, it is precisely this kind of revision that ushers in the New West by eroding the inflexible, epic narrative of the frontier myth.

Although epic in tone and ambition, Turner's historical method is traditional historicism within which

> history is construed as an absolutist and homogeneous evolutionary march ... unfolding and creating itself through the dialectical in-corporation of otherness, culminating in a total or totalitarian self-realisation ... all the contradictory and heterogeneous aspects of histories – including the history of the oppressed and colonised – are reconciliable with, or reducible to, historicist methods. (Williams and Chrisman, 1993: 9)

Walter Benjamin argues that this kind of history writing provides a seamless continuum in need of disruption by alternative histories, or 'historical materialism'. Historicism connects events in a linear se-quence of inevitable progress across time, just as Turner had in his vision of the frontier West, whereas Benjamin interrogates the monu-mental, mythic, history and unsettles the order and conformity inherent within it, creating 'a science of history whose subject matter is not a tangle of purely factual details, but consists rather of the numbered group of threads that represent the weft of the past as it feeds into the warp of the present' (Benjamin, 1997: 362).

Benjamin's sense of historical 'textuality' is suited to the earlier discussion of the West as a complex, multilayered text, since if History is a spatial weaving of textures (Latin, *texere*, *textum*: to weave), overlaid, interwoven, even fraying at the edges, it would be a 'mistake' 'to equate this weft with the mere nexus of causation', for it is 'thoroughly dialectical, and threads may have been lost for centuries that the present course of history erratically, inconspicuously picks up again' (ibid.: 362). The task of the historian (or cultural worker) is, therefore, to explore these threads and textures, not necessarily to unravel and reshape them into an entirely new fabric, or into a linear arrangement like Turner's thesis. To do so, argues Benjamin, is to 'remake' history's complex, multiple stories as a linear cause and effect, as 'the epic dimension of history' (ibid.: 352).

Applied to the West, historical materialism intrudes and unsettles traditional history creating juxtapositions, fragments, and discontinuities like an interdisciplinary revisionist 'montage'. It excavates secret histories so that the epic, monumental history embodied in myth, in Turner, and in the unproblematized acceptance of a sense of Manifest Destiny are challenged and deharmonized.

Bakhtin and Benjamin's antimythography and their search for alternative methodologies are amplifed in the work of many postmodern cultural critics like Derrida, Lyotard, Jameson, and Bhabha, seeking ways to move beyond mythic or binary frames which organized the world into structures and patterns so as to define and explain its complex, often contradictory, relations. The postmodern critique of Michel Foucault, sharing many of these doubts about conventional history, wanted to include space as a factor in a broader definition of history because it was traditionally seen as empty and without meaning, or reduced to a single, one-dimensionality, such as Western landscape signifying monumental purity or natural beauty and wonder. Foucault offers another way of looking at space as heterogeneous, multiple, and textured, telling many histories across sites of relations and networks of meaning. Whereas conventional historicism's attention to time and its search for pattern and order, has excluded space as worthy of study and tended to concentrate upon overarching narratives, Foucault's approach works in the margins, listening to the voices that Bakhtin and Benjamin celebrated. It is in these previously silenced zones that a 'new history' finds its focus; 'where "borderline", "borrowed", or "rejected" phenomena can be perceived' and related to 'supposed or posited totalities ...', bringing to them 'the corrective' and '*bringing forth differences* relative to continuities' (de Certeau, 1988a: 79).

Foucault argued against 'traditional history' and for 'effective history' where discontinuity and interruption deprived 'the self of the reassuring stability of life and nature' and offered instead the desire to 'uproot ... traditional foundations and relentlessly disrupt ... pretended continuity' (1993: 154). Foucault's phrase describing history as 'a profusion of entangled events' is closer to the New West representation being discussed in this book, and his point that 'the true historical sense confirms our existence among countless lost events' (ibid.) helps explain the fascination with rediscovery and revision of the apparently 'lost events' and voices of the West previously 'silenced' by Turner and others. The 'postcolonial' nature of New Western representation has taken up these subaltern voices to assert difference and counter the claims of a traditional, linear, and often mythic history (see Allmendinger, 1998). Thus, 'new history' has a maxim: 'Nothing must escape it and, more importantly, nothing must be excluded' (ibid.: 157).

Earlier modes of history bar 'access to the actual intensities and creations of life' (Foucault, 1993: 161) and must be countered by what Foucault terms a 'genealogy' that 'disturbs what was previously considered immobile . . . fragments what was thought unified . . . shows the heterogeneity of what was imagined consistent with itself' (in Mahon, 1992: 108). In the upsetting carnivalization of 'traditional history' what is unmasked is its false unity now superseded by the 'plural' histories where 'countless spirits dispute . . . numerous systems intersect and compete [and] . . . a complex system of distinct and multiple elements, unable to be mastered by the powers of synthesis' are revealed (Foucault, 1993: 161). For Foucault, as we have seen, this 'complex system' had to include the spatial dimension with the historical and social all crossing and interconnecting with one another in the construction of histories.

Active forgetting is the enemy of genealogy, for like Benjamin and Bakhtin, Foucault is interested in what he terms 'subjugated knowledges', those 'historical contents that have been buried and disguised in a functionalist coherence or formal systemisation' (Foucault, 1980: 81). The new history rejects this 'coherence' and looks within it to reclaim and to restate the 'subjugated' and to voice 'disqualified' knowledges 'located low down on the hierarchy, beneath the required level of cognition' (ibid.: 82). These hidden and secret histories, 'parallel and marginal . . . delinquent . . . particular, local, regional knowledge, a differential knowledge incapable of unanimity' (ibid.) permit a new form of critical and effective history to emerge in dialogue with the 'centralising powers' (ibid.) that enframe and fix 'history' or 'knowledge'.

These theories of myth, history, and monologue show a ferment of critique circulating in Europe and America in the post 1960s around questions of representation, power, and authority. Added to the political climate of civil rights and the counterculture, this intellectual questioning created an atmosphere in which discussions of the New West found a more receptive and engaged audience. It was not a sudden change, but rather a process of reflection through which earlier representations were revisited as well as new texts created. Neither was the discussion confined to a single discipline, such as history, for on a number of fronts and through a new commitment to interdisciplinarity, the New West became the focus and stimulus for inventive and significant studies across a whole range of texts.

New Western Representation

The focus for a reassessment of the West in American and global culture has tended to fall on what became known as New Western History, a name coined from the 1989 symposium 'Trails: Towards a New Western History' in Santa Fe organized by Patricia Nelson Limerick. Her book *The Legacy of Conquest* (1987) became its founding text, followed by others by Cronon, Worster, and White, with the aim to revise regional history from multiple viewpoints such as the marginalized, the colonized, and the conquered. This 'new history' starts from the premise that Turner's version of the West was misguided, reductionist, and exclusive; as Limerick puts it:

> Turner, in 1893, seemed to have the field of Western American History fully coralled, unified under the concept 'frontier' . . . In fact, the apparently unifying concept of the frontier had arbitrary limits that *excluded more than they contained.* (Limerick, 1987: 21)

As we have seen, at the root of postmodern theory is, according to Lyotard, an 'incredulity to grand narratives' or a belief that they hide more than they explain. As Limerick suggests, Turner's 'corral' defines America by exclusion, measuring its resilient 'character' in opposition to Native Americans, the land, and by little or no reference to women or ethnic groups. New Western History formalized these criticisms and used them as an opening up of the discipline to wider perspectives, including environmental history, ethnic history, and women's history. As Limerick wrote, 'In rethinking Western history, we gain the freedom to think of the West as a place – as many complicated environments . . .' (Limerick 1987: 26).

However, 'rethinking' and critique were not the exclusive domain of New Western History, for as I will argue throughout the chapters of this book, any consideration of the New West shows that many disciplines were re-examining the nature of the region. There has been constant critique across disciplines, some of which have been ignored or undervalued as 'popular' and, therefore, as not serious. However, many of these 'subjugated knowledges' have engaged with the West in ways far more varied and complex than these judgements might suggest. For example, years before Limerick, photography was challenging its own

'Turner', Ansel Adams, whose myths of 'picturesque sublime' were being undone and questioned by the revisionary 'New Topographics' exhibition (1975) or the Rephotographic Survey Project begun in the mid 1980s (see Chapter 2). Similarly, American literature had been questioning the mythic West and resisting it through multiple cultural voices over a long period of time (see Robinson, 1998). Wallace Stegner, for example, believed that 'the West had been oversold as the Garden of the World' and '[g]rowth is something that has always been a gleam in the eyes of Western boosters; but growth is exactly what the West does not need and cannot stand' (in Holthaus et al., 1991: 222). Stegner's family history was rooted in the boosterism and exploitation of the West: 'the big chance, the ground floor, the inside track', and yet, writes Stegner, in the end there are too many 'suckers' who fell for the dream and ignored the reality of the land. Through his own family history, he sees through the national rhetoric of dream and frontier: 'Rainbows flowered for my father in every sky he looked at; he was led by pillars of fire and cloud . . . he died broke and friendless in a fleabag Western motel . . .', and it became the novel *Big Rock Candy Mountain*, 'the common man's dream of something for nothing' (ibid.: 223–4).

Cultural studies and the new histories of Foucault, Benjamin, and Bakhtin emphasize the need to look beyond the 'monumental' and the 'epic' and to see in the popular and in all variety of representations sources of debate and understanding. The idea that it is the preserve of 'proper history' to interrogate seriously the American West is to reduce the complex nature of the region and to exclude, once again, many of the cultural voices that New Western History claimed to champion. If, as I stated earlier, culture is plural, multilayered, and constructed of 'relationships between elements in a whole way of life', then surely it can only be analyzed through an approach which is itself multivocal, multicultural, and multiperspectival (see Kellner, 1995, and Campbell and Kean, 1997).

New Approaches

Rather than one version opposing another, or claim and counterclaim trapping the mind into a familiar way of thinking that postmodernism questions, there has been an increasingly diverse and influential cross-cultural call for a new approach entirely. The old binary thinking wherein the world is divided 'and/or', 'them/us', 'North/South', 'male/female', etc. is too inflexible and merely creates hierarchies, antagonism, and entrenched positions. Many aspects of the New Western History, for all its innovative thinking, was too dismissive of Turner, and too willing to claim that its position was the 'right' one to adopt. The outcome of Bakhtin's rejection of monologue was a preference for dialogue, or the perpetual exchange between 'sides' so that fixed positions were countered by the contact zone in which the ideas (speech) mingled and crossed. This 'space between' occurs in various ways in New Western representation as a consequence of the desire to break out of the binarism that has for so long defined and divided the West itself. Wallace Stegner, for example, rejected a strict position in favour or against the old or the new versions of the West, preferring to believe in a 'third way or a middle trail' which 'salvages a useful past through a critical analysis that does not succumb to mystification'. The 'third way' is an example of 'keep[ing] both eyes open', allowing explorations of the West that would not exclude other disciplines, but actively encourage productive, critical dialogues between them (Frisk, in Robinson, 1998: 26).

Annette Kolodny's 'Letting Go Our Grand Obsessions: Notes Toward a New Literary History of the American Frontiers' demonstrates this approach, setting out to 'reconceive what we mean by "history" when we address literary history and to reconceptualize what we mean by "frontier" when we intend the Americas' (1992: 2). Her intention is to develop a 'more inclusive interdisciplinarity' that is not bound by chronology or 'continuity', but recognizes the concept of 'frontier' 'as a locus of first cultural contact, circumscribed by a particular physical terrain in the process of change *because of* the forms that contact takes, all of it inscribed by the collisions and interpenetrations of language' (ibid.: 3). Rejecting Turner, Kolodny argues that 'both geography and chronology must be viewed as fluid and ongoing, or as a continuously unfolding palimpsest' in which '[h]ybridized forms and tropes constitute the focus of textual analysis, and the resultant attentiveness to "code switching" radically alters our understanding of style and aesthetics' (ibid.: 9). One example is Gloria Anzaldúa whose work 'code switches' across languages, cultural terrains, and histories to create a hybrid text which engages the reader in a multilayered experience akin to the kind of space that Kolodny defines as the West (see Chapter 3).

Kolodny's 'frontier' is 'that liminal landscape of changing meanings on which distinct human cultures first encounter one another's 'otherness' and appropriate, accommodate, or domesticate it through language ... [in an] inherently unstable locus of ... environmental transitions and cultural interpenetrations ...' (ibid.: 9–10). In this she echoes the work of Mary-Louise Pratt who has written of the cultural 'contact zone' of the frontier as a space 'where disparate cultures meet, clash and grapple with each other' – often in violence and conquest – and in so doing, establish relations of 'copresence, interaction, interlocking understandings and practices' (Pratt, 1995: 6–7). Part of this process of contact might be 'transculturation' whereby one group absorbs and uses aspects of the other group's culture and vice versa in a form of dialogical exchange. This in turn may create a form of hybridization, as the two cultures negotiate across the contact zone in what Pratt terms 'mutual appropriation' (ibid.: 80). Kolodny's approach asserts the 'multilingual, polyvocal, and the newly intertextual and multicultural' as characteristics of the 'frontier' texts as opposed to the 'univocal and monolingual, defining origins by what later became the tropes of the dominant or conquering language' (ibid.: 12). Clearly, her purpose is to open up the frontier as a defining tool of 'white' mainstream history in order to re-represent the more complex relations that existed within the West. These kinds of negotiations and exchanges, points of contact, and dialogue characterize the New West and are examined throughout this book as a means by which we might arrive at a sense of the shifting identity of this region

A New Spatial Geo-history

Living in the West, and teaching in California, Edward Soja has become a great promoter of postmodern critical geography in which spatiality, historicality, and sociality are combined as a 'trialectics'. In *Postmodern Geographies* (1989) and *Thirdspace* (1996) he has developed, after Foucault, John Berger, and Henri Lefebvre (as well as Mandel and Jameson) both his own genealogy of the new geography and contributed to a whole new way of interpreting space and place. His ideas interconnect with critiques of history and myth that we have already examined, and provide a further element in our critical tools for a study of the New West. Soja saw in Lefebvre a theorist suspicious of 'the dangers of reductive 'totalizations' ...' (Soja, 1989: 48) whose primary interest was in the way space was marginalized in critical theory: 'socially mystified ... hidden from critical view under thick veils of illusion and ideology' (ibid.: 50). And yet, like Foucault, Lefebvre knew that space had to be reclaimed for analysis: 'This dialectised, conflictive space is where the reproduction of the relations of production is achieved. It is this space that produces reproduction, by introducing into it its multiple contradictions' (cited in Soja, 1989: 50). As I have argued about the New West, space could not be totalized, nor formulated into a reduced 'unitary' meaning, for it embodied the complex patterns and textures of many interwoven discourses. Victor Burgin has written of the relationship between Lefebvre and Soja, and explains that the former is concerned with (a) 'spatial practice . . . the material expression of social relations in space', (b) 'representations of space . . . those conceptual abstractions that may inform the actual configuration of such spatial practices', and (c) 'representational space . . . space as appropriated by the imagination' (Burgin, 1996: 27). Lefebvre's three categories recognize 'there can be no question of choosing one form of attention to the exclusion of the other' (ibid.: 28) because they interrelate and occur together. Burgin calls it the 'simultaneous imbrication of the physical and the psychological' which characterizes Lefebvre's conceptualization of space. What Burgin and Soja see here in Lefebvre is vital as a new critical approach to the study of the New West, for what he recognized is that space is constructed and produced through a variety of practices: 'mental space and social realities are *in reality* inseparable' (ibid.: 28). They are simultaneous and imbricated (overlapping), comingling to create a 'hybrid space, at once material and psychical . . . in which [we] . . . *actually live and act*' (ibid.: 29). We do not dwell in two separate worlds, one real and one imagined; they constantly bleed into each other – we cross between both – and perhaps occupy the space between, 'a "between" formed only in the simultaneous presence of the two' (ibid.: 185) – a third space. This idea of 'third space' returns us to the earlier discussion of postmodernism's collapsing of binaries and the possibility of moving beyond this particular way of thinking.

The significance of this to a study of American Western space should now be stated, if it is not already clear. Lefebvre, channelled through Soja, is concerned with the 'misplacing' of space, its veiling and invisibility despite its everpresence in writings and representations. They argue its ideological presence has, in fact, always been absent from analysis and replaced by the idea of space as 'setting', as 'first nature', or as an ahistorical ideal. What emerges is space as asocial, uncomplex, depoliticized – 'mythic' in the Barthesian sense discussed earlier. Hence, a new history, a new geography, a new revisioning of space must address these concerns:

Space is not a scientific object removed from ideology and politics; it has always been political and strategic. If space has an air of neutrality and indifference with regard to its contents and thus seems to be 'purely' formal, the epitome of rational abstraction, it is precisely because it has been occupied and used, and has already been the focus of past processes whose traces are not always evident on the landscape. *Space has been shaped and molded from historical and natural elements*, but this has been a political process. Space is political and ideological. It is a product literally filled with ideologies. (Lefebvre, cited in Soja, 1989: 80 – my emphasis)

A new spatial, cultural geohistory of the American West gathers the 'traces', the artefacts, and the fragments in order to articulate, not a unified and totalizing story but one in which many voices speak, many, often contradictory, histories are told, and many ideologies cross, coexist, and collide. All these forces construct the New West's dense and distinct histories into a 'texture' that is as complex to represent as it is to read. My contention is that New Western cultural representations examined in this book construct this 'texture' and seek to find modes of articulation and speculation that offer approximations towards its understanding. These different works, as we shall see later, resist the tendency to provide a one dimensional, closed reading of the West, preferring instead to see 'the simultaneity and interwoven complexity of the social, the historical, and the spatial, their inseparability and interdependence' (Soja, 1996: 3). Thus it is hard to envisage, as I stated earlier, *the* American West, but only *Wests* – plural, multidimensional, imbricated, and contradictory.

The New West as 'Thirdspace'

Edward Soja, borrowing from Lefebvre, defines 'thirding' as the activity of resistance to any binary reductionism and the tendency to oppose in an 'either/or' mode of thinking. He proposes the 'both/and' option in which many aspects coexist, contest within the same shared space/ texture – or what he terms 'thirdspace' (Soja, 1996: 4). This is a 'recombinatorial and radically open perspective ... "thirding-as-Othering" ... [which] respond[s] to all binarisms, to any attempt to confine thought and political action to only two alternatives, by interjecting an-Other set of choices' (ibid.). Hence binarism is not in itself rejected or dismissed but is 'restructured,' or as I shall add, *dialogized*, so as to create a third, dynamic perspective. Thus space, as Lefebvre realized, is not adequately defined by such statements as 'real, material space' or 'imagined, illusory space', because our experience of it is precisely a combination or dialogized mixture of these effects. We feel, think, dream, sense, know, act in, and exist in space, and as such experience it as a complex, multifaceted texture of the 'real-and-imagined', Hence in the representation of these spaces one is often faced with images that appear to contradict, or to present thresholds, border areas, and hybrid, liminal zones. It is in such spaces that the breaking down of the binaries and the recombinations take place most evidently. In the imbricated other-places where things change and flow we are made most aware of the 'trialectics of spatiality' (Soja, 1996: 10): the perceived space, the conceived space, and the lived space. This is a way of seeing the spaces of the New West, since for so long there has been a binary thinking defining the region as myth and reality, true and false, utopia and dystopia, when, in fact, it has always existed as both a region and more than region, as imagined, dream-space as well as real, material space. It is in the confluence of these different, but connected, views of the West that it remains a powerful and meaningful idea within the American psyche.

In order for space to be read in this way, however, one has to reject a purely linear narrative of history and recognize that things happen simultaneously. Soja is radical in his questioning of linear, progressive views of narrative and history, claiming stories can no longer be told 'sequentially unfolding in time' as if 'an infinitely small part of a straight line', but instead 'as an infinitely small part of an infinite number of lines ... the result of our constantly having to take into account the simultaneity and extension of events and possibilities' (John Berger, cited in Soja, 1989: 22). The complex interweavings of histories could not be fairly represented as a 'timeline':

> Simultaneities intervene, extending our point of view outward in an infinite number of lines connecting the subject to a whole world of comparable instances, complicating the temporal flow of meaning, short-circuiting the fabulous stringing-out of 'one damned thing after another'. (Soja, 1989: 23)

The reduction of history and its representations to myth are challenged here, not the concept or importance of history itself. Soja's application of Lefebvre's theory is a productive rethinking of how to analyze Western space and enables us to theorize and develop many of the approaches suggested by prominent Western critics. Echoing Kolodny, Pratt, and others discussed earlier, Limerick calls for a 'rendezvous theory' of the West rather than one where 'a multi-sided convergence of people' was reduced to a 'two-sided frontier', turning the history of the West into an 'edited version' (in Udall et al., 1990: 41). Native American Paula Gunn Allen writes of the 'confluential' history of the West where differences 'do not fuse into one, nor do they remain entirely separate', but engage in 'a variety of modes of interchange' (Gunn Allen, in Wrobel and Steiner, 1997: 345). New Western historian Richard White's 'relational outlook' interprets Western space in these terms, seeing 'a series of relationships established within that place inevitably changed over time' (in Limerick et al., 1991: 36). In examining these relational tensions he recognizes differences in power and influence, connected to class, race, and gender, accepts diversity and the coexistence and contest between forces, ways of seeing, and groups, and provides a helpful tool for analyzing the reality of a complex region like the West. Within this dynamic space of relations, simultaneity is a factor as is contradiction and change:

> The whole relational logic of the New Western History forces attention to movement, to contact, to exchange. The West – like all of us – is the product of relationships, either brief or prolonged. It is an historically derived, contingent place where one thing leads to another ... [but] The trails in this West seem more a maze than a simple line from one point to another ... to a land and people constantly in the midst of reinvention and reshaping. (ibid.: 39)

The relational West White defines summarizes many of the key arguments made in this introduction and points the way to the discussions in the following chapters that emphasize not the 'simple line' but the 'maze' as an approach to the New West. Kerwin Lee Klein writes that to represent the West, one must get beyond the binaries of tragic/comic, dark/light, new/old in order to 'tell both stories, for each calls forth the other ... [and] these tales have written us, as we have written them ... We are all these equations, this is what dialogue is, and we will find our new selves – as our precursors found theirs – in these shifting frontiers' (Klein, 1997: 12). Above all, these positions and approaches might help us to gather up a sense of the New West which is not exclusive, but problematic and multiple, putting back the richness of its history rather than the one dimensionality of myth. As Klein suggests, it is a 'dialogue' across 'shifting frontiers' that still might have the capacity to project a sense of identity most suited to living in a complex age and equipping us for a more honest future.

From Theory to Practice – 'The story's told/Turn the page': Cormac McCarthy's Border Trilogy

The popularity of Cormac McCarthy's border trilogy both with academics and with the public is a clue to the lasting interest in the significance of the West within the American cultural Imaginary. The trilogy charts the formation of the New West between the 1900s and 2002, from the remains of the Old West to the atomic bomb at the Trinity test site, to a post-millennial future, with its characters journeying endlessly back and forth across the West and into Mexico. I want to examine briefly the fascination that these complex novels hold for readers and how they might be seen as archetypal New West texts. McCarthy's final book of the trilogy, *Cities of the Plain* (1998), begins in 1952 as the West undergoes its postwar shocks of change, and yet this becomes a deep background for his two central characters, Billy Parham and John Grady Cole, to play out the final stages of the journeys traced through the previous two novels of the trilogy, *All The Pretty Horses* (1992) and *The Crossing* (1994). They exist in a strange limbo between the Old West and the inevitability of the New, holding onto the events and stories that structure and determine their pasts and their futures. The novel's 'country had gone from the oil lamp and the horse and buggy to jet planes and the atomic bomb', and it is in this space of rapid change and uncertainty that McCarthy explores the New West (1998: 106). McCarthy's West is a borderlands, both geographically, but also metaphorically, a space for physical and philosophical migration, where issues of life and death, myth and reality, dream and actuality intersect and cross like his characters in its landscapes. As the USA changes, Mexico takes on greater significance as emblematic of some lost time or imagined 'Old West'. In *Cities of the Plain*, discussing the old times, Billy Parham says 'if there's anything left of this life it's down there ... It's another world' where people 'went back ... after somethin' (1998: 218). McCarthy suggests the 'outlaw' West of old times, now signified by Mexico, is like the mythic Imaginary, a space outside time where life is a series of unfinished quests and unattainable goals. It is 'a thing now extinct among

[Americans]. A thing for which perhaps they no longer even have a name' (1998: 249).

John Grady Cole is ironically described as 'the all-american cowboy' (ibid.: 4), immediately locating him ambiguously within a mythic tradition, just as the novel itself simultaneously suggests a world of cowboys *and* nuclear industries living side by side. On the border, real and imagined worlds coexist, and as one crosses and recrosses the landscape of real space and imagined space, the layers become porous until they fuse. Within this textual space, McCarthy's characters search for something to ground their lives in, they engage in quests of epic proportion seeking horses, wolves, women who might, in some way, help them to validate their own existence in a rapidly changing environment. McCarthy's borderland space relates to many of the ideas discussed in this introduction and throughout this study, for his fictional territory is the liminal space called forth by Kolodny's essay and furthermore, creates both a complex genealogy of the New West and also a spatial geohistory like that theorized by Soja. Stephen Tatum makes the point that McCarthy, like Soja, is concerned with space as a 'construct resulting from the intersection of geography with geology, with social and economic forces – and with human desires ... ', and through this creates 'topographies of transition' where established histories and traditions are brought under question in some way (Tatum, 1998: 315). For Tatum, McCarthy's topographies 'create paradoxical space and in the process force a reconsideration of borders and boundaries' (ibid.: 318). Tatum's analysis relates to my earlier comments on 'thirdspace', since the 'paradoxical' topography outlined here is another version of this 'in-between' that partakes of all oppositions, is marked by them all, while intervening in the 'natural', truth-making processes of culture. Homi Bhabha writes that '[s]uch an intervention ... challenges our sense of the histotrical identity of culture as a homogenizing, unifying force, authenticated by the originary Past, kept alive in the national tradition of the People' (Bhabha, 1994: 37). Hence, within the American 'nation' the West's mythic significance as 'originary Past' and its relation to ideas of essentialist 'identity' are challenged as 'oppositions' enter into the cultural space in which earlier meanings had been created. No longer convinced that the first story is the only story, a new space emerges – 'thirdspace' – in which a broader range of voices are heard, old hierarchies are questioned and notions of origin, cultural power, and innate stability are displaced. Fundamentally, this 'thirdspace' is the '*in-between* space – that carries the burden of the meaning of culture' as a space of hybridity, translation, and negotiation where 'we may elude the politics of polarity and emerge as the others of our selves' (ibid.: 38–9). As I argue throughout, hybridity is a space of contacts, where other positions emerge, new concepts generate from the crossing over between existing histories, but all the various elements, discourses, or traces remain within the emergent forms.

McCarthy's crossings and his use of migration and movement make him a very 'Western' writer engaged with issues of 'thirdspace', hybridity, and changing cultural identity, but equally his fiction is haunted by the past. Repeatedly in his work there is a powerful sense of loss, often bound up with the endless quest of his characters to regain something, to hunt it down and capture it, or to salvage it in some way. These gestures symbolize the psychic dislocation that marks the West as a space haunted by a mythic past and yet torn between a desire to relive those myths, and to move beyond them entirely into an equally impossible 'real' world. As Hall writes, 'this "return to the beginning" is like the imaginary in Lacan – it can neither be fulfilled nor requited, and hence is the beginning of the symbolic of representation, the infinitely renewable source of desire, memory, myth, search, discovery' (in Rutherford, 1990: 236). McCarthy's Western space embodies this sense of shifting patterns as the inevitable 'real-and-imagined' territory in which his characters construct their identities. They may long for a simpler reality, for a fixed and absolute sense of the past, of the self, and of the world, but the novels consistently debate these matters of being, presenting a more varied and complex set of options. Hence, in the first novel, we find: 'There aint but one truth, said John Grady. The truth is what happened. It aint what come out of somebody's mouth' (McCarthy, 1993: 168). Yet the authority of 'one truth' is always under question and the stories people tell structure the worlds his characters inhabit. As Hall writes, identity is constituted within representation, that is, it is not a given, a fixed and essential thing. Thus 'stories' – and all representative practices – do not merely reflect an identity that already exists 'out there', but are able to constitute us as subjects. Representation is not a 'second-order mirror held up to reflect what already exists' (ibid.: 236) but creates spaces for new subjectivities to emerge, to be debated and imagined within a notion of cultural identity which rejects fixed essences (myths of identity) to which we can make a return, is multilayered and made of histories real, material, and imagined. Thus, '[t]he past continues to speak to us ... through memory, fantasy, narrative and myth' and cultural identities are made 'within the discourses of history and culture' (ibid.: 226). This is a dialogical process of exchange and crossing over through which old certainties will erode. Hence, later in the same novel, John Grady, as a result of journeying, is less certain of 'truth': 'Where is your country? he said. I dont know, said John Grady. I dont know where it is. *I dont know what happens to country.*' (ibid.: 299 – my emphasis). His 'nation', his 'place', his sense of himself are all part of 'the world that was rushing away' (ibid.: 301), the same world his father spoke of when he told him 'that the country would never be the same. People dont feel safe no more ... We're like the Comanches was two hundred years ago' (ibid.: 25–6). By *Cities of the Plain*, we are told that to hold onto one story is 'irrational passion' since, 'Men have in their minds a picture of how the world will be ... but there is one world that will never be and that is the world they dream of' (1998: 134).

The landscapes of McCarthy's trilogy reflect the characters' own position in-between worlds, as in *All the Pretty Horses* where 'They led the horses up through a midden of old truckdoors and transmissions and castoff motorparts behind the cafe and they watered them at a metal tank used for locating leaks in innertubes' (1993: 32). This surreal, incongruous mixing of Old and New mirrors John Grady's own journey outward in search of an idea of the past, of a West of 'pretty horses', truth and rugged acts of self-definition. In an effort to find a 'map' of his own identity, to fix his position, purpose and role in the world and in the West, John Grady goes to Mexico in search of the old stories that he imagines will give him these truths and coordinates of identity. To live out the mythic past as the active present is a means of self-definition for him, of mapping himself into a frame of certainty by holding onto romantic notions of self, of tragic love (in both *All the Pretty Horses* and *Cities of the Plain*) and honour. However, as McCarthy's work shows, identity is not easily mapped, for like the landscape itself, it changes and is changed constantly, and the romance of the past can be deceptive. In *The Crossing*, an old man tells Billy Parham that

> Between their acts and their ceremonies lies the world and in this world the storms blow and the trees twist in the wind and all the animals that God has made go to and fro yet this world men do not see. They see the acts of their own hands or they see that which they

name and call out to one another but the world between is invisible to them. (1995: 46)

The invisible 'world between' exists beyond the static fixing of myth, a more fluid, changing world of process and motion ('to and fro') like the migratory crossings of the novels McCarthy writes to bring his characters (and readers) into contact with this very space, the 'border-lands' I discussed earlier. In this 'thirdspace', 'everything is necessary. Every least thing . . . Nothing can be dispensed with. Nothing despised. Because the seams are hid from us . . . in the tale itself and the tale has no abode or place of being except in the telling only and there it lives' (ibid.: 143). Thus in stories are constructed the full richness of life, and only in them can the 'between world' be traced, and the unmappable, unfixed, and multiple be 'told'. The effort to 'know' the story, to close the tale, is like the effort to know the country, the landscapes of the West – impossible. The search is unending, like the story, its meanings revealed only by the journey itself and never by the destination. The West, like those lives that seek to uncover it, is, as poststructuralists would say, a chain of signifiers, deferred endlesssly in the telling, one only leading to another. Everyone has stories to tell throughout McCarthy's work, but as much as the tellers and the listeners long for them to be as clear as myths, they rarely are. Hence, Quijada says, 'The corrido [ballad or 'poor man's history'] tells all and it tells nothing' (ibid.: 386). Yet Billy longs, like John Grady, for the 'true history' (ibid.: 404), only to be told that this too is a collection of stories, an 'argument between counterclaimants' (ibid.: 411).

By *Cities of the Plain*, McCarthy's West spirals between the old stories told by old men and the efforts of those, like Billy and John Grady, to live in the increasingly diminishing landscapes of that pre-vious world. John Grady dreams of some stability, of marriage, of a home, and of love – and it is all wrapped up in a final quest to save the Mexican prostitute he loves from her pimp, Eduardo. In their own ways, these dreams are illusory, belonging to some bygone age that probably never existed, like that spoken of in the 'old waddies' stories that punctuate the novel, but which provide the basis for John Grady's identity. However, McCarthy's West is always changing, epitomized by the land itself: 'this country aint the same. Nor anything in it. The war changed everthing', and the ever-present city whose 'aura of lights' can be seen forty miles away (1998: 78). What exists is the New West symbolized by military encroachment on the land, just as McCarthy suggested at the end of *The Crossing* with Billy's witnessing of the atomic bomb at Trinity with 'no sun and ... no dawn ...', only its 'inexplicable darkness' (1995: 425–6).

McCarthy's novels, accessible and yet complex and philosophical, create a picture of the coming of the New West which is signified as a hybrid space where differences meet in almost surreal combinations where 'beauty and loss are one' (1998: 71). As the trilogy closes with Billy journeying once more, McCarthy produces some powerful, elusive images. Sleeping by the roadside, for example, Billy sees 'the pale and naked concrete pillars of an east-west onramp ... curving away, clustered and rising without pediment like the ruins of some older order standing in the dusk' (ibid.: 289), as if he is gazing upon the 'older order' he has longed for and sought out throughout the trilogy now reduced to concrete ruins hovering over the desert landscape, unfinished and going nowhere. The effect of this wild mixing of loss and beauty, dream and horror, is like the 'framed photograph' he describes at the conclusion of *Cities of the Plain*: 'printed from a glass plate *broken* into five pieces' where 'certain ancestors were puzzled back together in a study that *cohered with its own slightly skewed geometry*. Apportioning some *third* or separate meaning to each of the figures seated there' (ibid.: 290 – my emphases). As with this image, so with the trilogy, McCarthy's West has a 'skewed geometry', a coherence drawn from fragments creating a 'third ... meaning' or thirdspace from the collision of people's dreams and lived experience, their real and imagined worlds. Finally, McCarthy's vision of the New West is as complex and multiple as postmodernism allows, and summed up in the first and (almost) last words of the trilogy. 'The candleflame and the image of the candleflame caught in the pierglass twisted and righted when he entered the hall and again when he shut the door' (McCarthy, 1993: 3) suggests the shimmering real and reflected images that define the worlds his characters inhabit and move between. While at its end, Billy's body has ironically become as marked as the landscapes he has crossed in search of some sense of identity and origin, constructing for others 'a map enough for men to read ... to make a landscape. To make a world' (ibid.: 291). However, it may be as another passage suggests, that any map, whether on the body or like that the storyteller dreamed, is multiple: 'It looked like different things. There were different perspectives one could take' (ibid.: 269) and as much as we might wish that it reveals every direction, it does not for there are things which cannot be mapped, 'that which we have no way to show' (ibid.: 273). The traditional map is a form of closed narrative in which all is controlled and plotted, but in McCarthy's new mapping of the West there are inconsistencies, gaps, and questions in the narrative making it an 'immappable world' (ibid.: 288). As he writes, 'Where all is known no narrative is possible' (ibid.: 277) and in this resides a vision of the New West as an unfinished, unfinishable story constantly awaiting new narratives and new maps from which to construct its future.

Conclusion

Writing in 1987, two years after McCarthy had written his first western, *Blood Meridian*, Gerald Haslam recognized there was 'a new West built on the old ... Without rejecting the past, westerners are no longer trapped in it ... [but] recreating it to include previously ignored realities while rejecting illusions previously cherished', and quotes Wallace Stegner, as I did earlier in this chapter, about the need to 'rig up ... a line between past and present', commenting that 'Writers are rigging the line, and a few are even extending it into the future. Rediscovering the West, they are discovering themselves' (in Golden Taylor et al., 1987: 1024–5). Haslam saw the need and the importance of what this book argues, the identification of the New West as a network of 'lines' between past and present, crossing different groups, ethnicities, genders – not to create a fixed, singular notion of the West, but on the contrary to emphasize its heterogeneity and its hybrid, relational texture. To achieve this requires a new mapping: simultaneous, dialogical, sensitive to diverse histories and voices, and to the relations that exist between them.

Haslam, like McCarthy and others, championed a 're-storying' of the West, an idea that I borrow from Gary Nabhan (in Nabhan and Klett, 1994), with its two strong connotations: (a) the sense of creating new stories to counter and displace the mythic ones that have, for so long, framed the vision of the West in the minds and imaginations of the world, and (b) the sense of *restoring*, healing and regenerating the diverse cultures of the West as meaningful, relevant voices within both national and global cultures. A third meaning that I would add is that through stories, through all representations and modes of expression, the West is articulated as a 'thirdspace' where cultures collide, fuse, and interrelate and where the new mapping might be achieved. As Terry Tempest Williams has written:

A story keeps things known. It is the umbilical cord that connects us to the past, present, and future. A story allows us to envision the possibility of things. It draws on the power of memory and imagination. It awakens us to our surroundings. It reminds us of who we are and where the source of the power lies ... the earth is a storied landscape. (Williams, in Holthaus et al., 1991: 51)

It is the different stories, from wherever they come, that define the New West and it is the purpose of this book to discuss some of their sources, meanings, and significance, for, as Gary Nabhan, like Cormac McCarthy, knows, 'The stories will outlast us' (Nabhan and Klett, 1994: 193).

CHAPTER I

Landscapes of the New West

Land and the West

The landscapes of the New West are the constructions of imagination and dream, as much as they are the material consequences of geography, settlement, agriculture, extraction, and environmental damage. Humanity created landscape when it invested it with meanings, desires, fears, beliefs, and significations, and so to see it as 'fixed, dead, undialectical' (Soja, 1989: 11) and outside of historical processes is to be reductionist and to perpetuate myths that inevitably favour certain ideological positions. The 'natural' has always been 'cultural' and so it is through representation – speech, writing, art, photography – that we perceive landscape. Within a discussion of the American West, ideological readings of space have always been part of the way the environment has been interpreted, with a close consideration of how different people and communities have imagined, settled, used, and abused their landscapes.

European images of the West predated its encounter and envisaged a land of promise where 'nature's bounty was endless, happiness was certain, and death was banished forever' in 'a magic otherworld' fulfilling 'a yearning for a land of laughter, of peace, and of life eternal . . . located to the west of the man who wondered where it was' (Baritz, 1961: 618, 619). Mixing the Christian vision of a new Eden, a Promised Land of new beginnings, and the symbolism of the golden land, the West became fixed as a place of Utopian opportunity drawing people towards its rich promise of success and wealth both spiritual and material. The attraction of the Turner thesis (see Introduction) was its expansion of these earlier images of land and promise into a new language of historiographical certainty.

Another significant image of the West, was the association of the land with the feminine. For Turner, the frontier that forged American national identity excluded women and yet its rhetoric often referred to the feminine, to the 'virgin land' (see Nash Smith, 1950; Kolodny, 1975,

1984), with space as 'other', unknowable, to be discovered and penetrated, or as a place of motherly comfort from which a new nation could be born and nurtured by the 'fresh, green breast of the new world' (Fitzgerald, 1976: 187). *The Great Gatsby* is a 'miniature of American history itself, with its pastoral longings both to return to and to master the beautiful and bountiful femininity of the new continent' (Kolodny, 1975: 139). Thus the land was often defined by contradictory responses, both linked to the feminine: land as desirable conquest and as motherly comfort.

The conquest of the West was often expressed in masculinist images of sexual violence exploring the 'psychosexual dynamic' whereby 'the material and the erotic were to be harmoniously intermingled' (Kolodny, 1984: 3, 4) in male language. The land-as-feminine provided a repetitive image of the West as a place of male protection, possession, and assault, in which the woman was passively held as fantasy or ideal. Frank Norris's 1901 novel *The Octopus* describes the earth as female and the technology as male:

> It was the long stroking caress, vigorous, male, powerful, for which the Earth seemed panting. The heroic embrace of a multitude of iron hands, gripping deep into the brown, warm flesh of the land ... so robust as to be almost an assault, so violent as to be veritably brutal ... the elemental Male and Female, locked in a colossal embrace ... untamed, savage, natural, sublime. (quoted in Merchant, 1995: 43)

Enacted here is the mythic narrative of the West as 'male energy subduing female nature, taming the wild ... recreating the garden lost by Eve' (ibid.) and making a landscape fit for settlement. Ironically, the Earth Mother is raped in order to assert a male power that will, in turn, promote the land for the civilizing goodness of women to live upon it as a garden. Nature as Eve has to be tamed in order that Nurturing Eve can be re-established and such a cruel paradox underlines why feminism has provided such an important impetus to the rethinking of Western history and geography. The 'natural', taken-for-granted images of land-as-woman were central to the mythology that had to be examined and countered before the land could be experienced in a more even-handed, reciprocal manner.

By the late twentieth century, the dreams of the Golden West and its dominant regime of representation have been challenged from a variety of positions (economic, gender, environmental, ethnic), and its validity as a definition of true Americanness denied. Some argue that all that remains of this first hope is a dystopic 'junkyard of dreams' (Davis, 1990: 435), epitomized by Los Angeles and its sprawl with a landscape 'beyond Blade Runner':

> The mile-high neo-Mayan pyramid of the Tyrell Corporation drips acid rain on the mongrel masses in the teeming giza far below. Enormous neon images float like clouds above fetid, hyperviolent streets, while a voice intones advertisements for extraterrestrial suburban living in 'Off World'. (Davis, 1998b: 359)

The advertisement speaks of a 'golden land of opportunity' where people can 'begin again', in a new frontier of the 'Off World' colonies, no longer escaping the East, but the cities of the West in 2019 with its 'ethnocentric anxieties about multiculturalism run amok' (ibid.: 361). For Davis, this is no more than romance, 'not so much the future of the city as the ghost of past imaginations' (ibid.) because the 'Blade Runner' landscape is nothing compared to the hierarchized sprawl and suburban badlands already present in LA. Davis's dark vision of the West is apocalyptic on a Biblical scale – riots, earthquakes, floods, and 'ecocide', related to 'the false expectations [imposed] on the environment' and its endless capacity to service the dreams of its inhabitants (Davis, 1993; 1998: 9). Water, energy, real estate are all bound up with the myths of the Land of Sunshine and the expectations that there is an endless supply of them all, when in truth they are increasingly scarce.

Issues in Environmentalism

Davis's 'noir' vision of the West is the consequence of the careless predation and poor resource management that transformed a space of boundless possibility into one of possession and inventive but invasive capitalism. New Eden was not compatible with the reality of Manifest Destiny, immigration, and expansionism, and like the Native Americans who inhabited the land, would have to be swept aside in pursuit of progress, or remodelled as myth. As Wallace Stegner has written, 'From the very beginning, Americans approached the West not as the Children of Israel approached the Land of Canaan ... but as Egyptian grave robbers might approach the tomb of a pharoah' (in Holthaus et al., 1991: 227), extracting its natural resources carelessly and with no sense of limitation.

Thus water, the scarcest resource in the arid West, has been a constant issue in the region, and its exploitation has become central to the environmentalists' calls for change and reform. In the West, it is often said, water flows uphill toward money since irrigation plans, dams, and reservoirs have moved water thousands of miles to the thirsty, expanding urban centres of the New West. Reisner's *Cadillac Desert* (1986) charts this history of water in the West, the struggles over irrigation and the consequences of water depletion, damming, and rerouting on agriculture, wildlife, and fisheries. By 1936 the US was building the four largest dams in the world: Hoover, Shasta, Bonneville, and Grand Coulee, but the creation of the Glen Canyon Dam and Lake Powell (1963) on the Utah/Arizona border became a rallying point for environmental protest. Edward Abbey wrote his 'Down the River' essay as a eulogy for the lost canyon flooded by the dam and the group Earth First! came to public attention as a result of their protests against it. The failure to prevent the dam led to a greater determination to stop plans to dam the Grand Canyon in what Reisner calls the movement's 'coming of age' (ibid.: 285). Led by David Brower of the Sierra Club, who later formed Friends of the Earth, the campaign forced Congress to vote against the dams in 1968. The rapidity and scale of the projects undertaken in the West to divert and conserve water created the problems; 'we overreached ourselves', writes Reisner (ibid.: 486) because in setting out to help the small farmers in the West, the policies created large, rich ones who over-farmed and produced gluts of food. As Reisner says, 'We set out to make the future of the American West secure; what we really did was make ourselves rich and our descendants insecure' (ibid.).

Water is just one of the issues surrounding the rapid development of the West in the postwar era. Indeed the whole relationship between local and federal control of projects became an increasing source of debate in the West from the 1930s. The West's proud individualism and suspicion of 'big government' controls sits uncomfortably with the reality of the federal programmes that exist everywhere in the region. Almost half of the eleven western states are federally owned land (East of the Rockies, no more than 13 per cent of a state is federal land), with a mixture of uses: National Parks, forests, Bureau of Land Management holdings, wildlife refuges, military lands, bomb testing grounds (83 per cent of Nevada, 62 per cent of Idaho and 33–50 per cent of other western states).

With the vast projects to supply water and energy, the federal government and its agencies (such as the Bureau of Land Management and National Rivers Authority) became a major source of revenue and power in the West, creating what some have termed the 'era of western empire building' (Gottlieb, in Rothman, 1998b: 188; Wiley and Gottlieb, 1982). The New West grew out of the rise of a resource-based western capitalism, combining federal projects and private companies, epitomized by the Western Energy Supply and Transmission (WEST) coalition of utility companies across the West who planned grids of power plants across the Colorado Plateau, and by the militarization of the western economy. These expansions led to rapid developments of new urban centres to support the projects with services and labour, which in turn required water and energy (see Chapter 4). This spiral of expansion characterized the growth of the West in the postwar years led by the Six Companies (Utah Construction, Bechtel, Kaiser, Morrison-Knudsen, J-F Shea, Macdonald-Kahn and Pacific Bridge) whose consortium won federal contracts and became multinationals with enormous influence. The scale of the projects and the growing importance of the Pacific Basin as the source of new trading markets added to the wealth of these companies who had developed with the blessing of federal money during the Cold War.

The militarization of the West is most noticeable through the nuclear industries mining uranium, building and testing bombs, and dumping their waste products from Los Alamos, New Mexico to Hanford, Washington. The effects in terms of land and air pollution on the 'downwinders' who lived in proximity to the test sites, to the Native peoples whose land was taken for the sites, and on the lasting damage to the ecosystems of the West are still far from clear, but Kuletz (1998) defines the region as an example of 'deterritoriality', meaning a national sacrifice zone where land has been practically abandoned. No longer a Promised Land, it suited the various agencies to redefine parts of the West as a 'wasteland' or uninhabited emptiness, to 'write the Indians out of the picture' and define the land as 'the vast nothingness' into which a new nuclear script could be inscribed (ibid.: 186). This nuclear script erased Native American presence and accessed their lands, beginning in the 1940s in the Navajoan desert where uranium was mined for the Los Alamos atomic bombs. This 'environmental racism' (ibid.: 12) ignored alternative visions of land as the sacred geographies of Native peoples and assumed that western science was superior.

White settlements, like St George, Utah, 'downwinded' after the first nuclear detonation took place in Mormon City, Nevada in 1951, were another consequence of this 'internal colonialism' described in Carole Gallagher's *America Ground Zero* (1993), where birth defects, leukemia clusters and chilling memories of family sickness, haunt the land and the 170,000 people exposed to contamination within a 250-mile radius of the test site (in Davis, 1993). However, the 'X-Files' style cover-ups of this 'secret nuclear war' against American people (red and white) has meant that facts about radiation levels and long-term effects are only now being fully recognized.

A recent controversial nuclear issue has been over the Yucca Mountain high-level nuclear waste storage repository to be built into a sacred mountain of the Southern Paiute and Western Shoshone tribes. Seeing this 'site' through the eyes of Native Americans transforms it from 'empty' wasteland to sacred space with a 'web of meanings' (Kuletz, 1998: 137), and in a perverse way reminds us of the often bizarre diversity of the West. These areas of land in Nevada and Utah – Zone Two – are a series of overlapping sites and perspectives: sacred native lands, nuclear dumps, airforce bases, wildlife refuges, small towns and tourist centres, federal and local government, all demonstrating the complex interactions of the New West. It is symbolic of this diversity that Yucca Mountain – 'sacred *and* expendable' (ibid.: 139) – is only 100 miles northeast of Las Vegas, one of the fasting growing cities in the US, whose own 'natural-resource infrastructure' has been long depleted and whose 'ecological "footprint" now covers all of southern Nevada and adjacent parts of California and Arizona', using excessive amounts of water it cannot generate and power created by mining the Black Mesa (Davis, in Rothman, 1998: 55). However, in this multilayered New West, road signs around Yucca Mountain mix the official history of the Nevada Test Site, a town sign for Pahrump declaring it 'the heart of the new old west', graffitti against nuclear war and contamination, and the ever-present signs of Native existence. Its cultural maps are complex, interconnected and relational: 'Yucca Mountain exists within vastly different worlds simultaneously ... [with] different positions of power as narratives ... all ... influenced by political events'. Yet these differences 'overlap and intersect' (Kuletz, 1998: 142) raising important questions about how the West is defined and used by various inhabitants and how these perspectives can be coexistent. Within all this diversity, there are political struggles and conflict, oppositions and divisions constituted in the different interpretations, or readings, of landscape and space. The attitudes to land embodied in Native thought – its alternative geography – insist upon an intersubjective relationship manifested in rituals and stories, which is secondary in western scientific thinking where the human is at the centre of things. For the Southern Paiute, Yucca Mountain is part of 'The Storied Land', bound up in the lived experience of people and place: 'Our history is in the Creator's belongings; the rocks and the mountains, the springs and in all living things' (Shoshone, quoted in Kuletz, 1998: 211). In the abuse of Western lands by extractive and nuclear industries, the old stories that still run through the earth, sky, and water have been restricted or erased, rewritten in the language of official history according to the scripts of self-justification. The intersubjective stories have been reduced to new myths of the West as 'national sacrifice zone', shifted from dialogue to monologue, away from reciprocity to consumption and production.

These diverse views mapped on the landscape have brought alliances of protest, reiterating once more the historical nature of the West as a place of encounter, a meeting place for differences. Here, questions over environment have brought together religious groups, anti-nuclear protesters, and Native Americans over water use, nuclear industries, and pollution, responding to issues with a diversity characteristic of the place itself. From Native Americans' struggles over land rights, to the Earth First! monkeywrenchers who wanted direct action to halt the ecological damage, to the New Age philosophies burgeoning in the New West, to ecocritics, there have emerged alliances with strong attachments to place and to what Aldo Leopold in 1949 called the 'land ethic'. Leopold believed ethics should be extended to a 'third element', humanity's relationships with all around them and to 'enlarge … the boundaries of the community to include soils, waters, plants, and animals, or collectively: the land', effecting a shift from 'conqueror of the land-community to plain member and citizen of it' (Leopold, 1970: 238–40). Leopold's 'third element' echoes the 'thirdspace' that provides a vision of the New West as 'a constantly shifting and changing milieu of ideas, events, appearances, and meanings … [reflecting] the simultaneity and interwoven complexity of the social, historical, and the spatial, their inseparability and interdependence' (Soja, 1996: 2–3). This 'thirdness' defines a Western space in which human and nature interact and exchange in a multitude of ways reminiscent of Evernden's definition of ecology as 'interrelatedness', but not 'casual connectedness', rather 'intermingling ... "a delicate interpenetration" ...' (in Glotfelty and Fromm, 1996: 93). Ecocriticism, as I shall discuss later, is an important development out of these kinds of alliances and political struggles.

Native Americans and the Land

Within Native American cultures, however, elements of nature, plants, animals, and the land itself have always been sacred, bound up in an intricate web of relationships with all living things, including humankind. A Navaho religious creation story relates that

> one morning long ago a lone man awoke, face to the sun, emerging from the soil. Only his head was visible, the rest of his body not yet being fashioned ... the rays of the sun hardened the face of the earth and strengthened the man ... from this man sprang the Lakota nation ... We are of the soil and the soil is of us. (Luther Standing Bear, in Turner, 1977: 125–6)

Paula Gunn Allen writes: 'We are the land, and the land is mother to us all ... that is the fundamental idea that permeates American Indian life' (Gunn Allen, 1992: 119). Thus land cannot become property any more than your own body could be, for 'the land is not really a place, separate from ourselves', nor is it 'an ever-dead other that supplies us with a sense of ego-identity by virtue of our contrast to its perceived nonbeing' (Gunn Allen, 1992: 119). Rejecting the land as 'other' to be manipulated or possessed for self-aggrandisement, 'the earth *is* being' (ibid.: 119) and 'the elements of nature (plants and animals chiefly) are relatives and ... the processes of nature are sacred' (Toelken, in Milner, 1996: 253). As a rule, nature is seen as beyond human control and part of a set of negotiative relations and agreements between 'relatives' within a whole. As Black Elk said, 'all our power came to us from the sacred hoop of the nation ... The flowering tree was the the living center of the hoop, and the circle of the four quarters nourished it' (in Nash, 1990: 14).

Stories, not ownership or possession, gave coherent identity to the people through the 'sacred hoop' or circle of being, which is 'not physical, but it is dynamic and alive ... It ... moves and knows, and all the life forms we recognize – animals, plants, rocks, winds – partake of this greater life' (Gunn Allen, 1992: 56, 60). As Louise Erdrich has written:

Everything seemed to be one piece. The air, our faces, . . . the ghostly
sky . . . All of a piece. As if the sky were a pattern of nerves and our
thought and memories traveled across it. As if the sky were one
gigantic memory for us all. (Erdrich, 1984: 34)

In contrast, many Anglo-Americans came to the West 'as possessive
individuals pursuing private dreams, trying to fence in their portion of
the whole', and as a result, 'the white settlers thought about the land as
they thought about each other, in simplifying, fragmenting terms'
(Worster, 1994: 14, 15). As Sitting Bull said, 'healthy feet can hear
the very heart of Holy Earth', but the white invaders had 'a love of
possession [which] is a disease with them' seeking to grasp the 'heart'
and make it theirs: 'They claim this mother of ours, the earth, for their
own and fence their neighbours away; they deface her with their
buildings and their refuse' (in Turner, 1977: 255).

Sitting Bull echoes contemporary ecologists showing the influence
of Native American thought on the changing attitudes to the Western
environment. Indeed, Kuletz argues that 'intersubjectivity' – direct
communication between the human and nonhuman worlds (Kuletz,
1998: 225) – deriving from Native ideas is a helpful notion of new
ecology indicating a shared sense of place where humans are 'both
separate and part of [nature] at one and the same time . . . they are
interconstitutive, they make each other . . . they are not static, unchanging, and dualistically separated from one another' (ibid.: 227).
This resembles Bakhtin's notion of dialogue (see Introduction) exem-
plified in the specific intersubjectivity between people and the land,
'a matrix of mutually reinforced perceptions' (ibid.: 228) in which
relations go on simultaneously. David Abram (1996) has recently
analyzed the human disconnection from the land, arguing that 'Language for oral peoples is not a human invention but a gift of the land
itself' and to deny this relation is to 'cut ourselves off from the deep
meanings . . . severing our language from that which supports and
sustains it' (1996: 263).

Activists and writers like Gary Snyder show the direct impact of
these ideas, blended with Thoreau and Eastern religions, in *Turtle
Island* (1974) and *Earth House Hold* (1969) where he writes of becoming a 'gentle steward of the earth's community of being' (1974: 91)
amid times of pollution, waste, radiation and overpopulation, warning
that

a culture that alienates itself from the very ground of its own being – from the wilderness outside (that is to say, wild nature, the wild, self-contained, self-informing ecosystems) and from that other wilderness, the wilderness within – is doomed to a very destructive behavior, ultimately perhaps self-destructive behavior. (ibid.: 106)

Abram writes that 'A story that makes sense is one that stirs the senses from their slumber, one that opens the eyes and ears to their real surroundings, tuning the tongue to the actual tastes in the air and sending chills of recognition along the surface of the skin' (Abram, 1996: 265). Snyder's language is about awakening and reconnecting the human to the land by calling for a 'total transformation' so as 'to change our culture . . . [to] a new ecologically-sensitive harmony-oriented wild-minded scientific-spiritual culture' (Snyder, 1974: 99). In part philosophical, Snyder also wants practical change based on 'local politics', 'stewardship', and 'diversity' in which self and community grow together using the best of 'nature-related cultures' and 'imaginative extensions of science' (ibid.: 102). In this way, America can be rethought, as the Hopi and Navajo might, as 'Turtle Island', a place that incorporates all living things and where 'Anglos, Black people, Chicanos, and others beached up on these shores all share such views at the deepest levels of their old cultural traditions' (ibid.: Introductory Note). Without romanticizing the Native American, Snyder believes there is much to learn from them, as from other groups, in order to create a new community of fusion, between peoples and between them and nature. Snyder claims this all came from his 'double vision of the West, seeing it *simultaneously* from the Native American angle and from the white settler angle' (O'Grady, 1998: 280 – my emphasis).

Snyder's eclectic, hybrid environmental ideas, his 'ethnopoetics', provide alternatives to the dominant notions of the land as possession and as conquest, preferring to view it as home territory and to establish new concepts of ecological balance embodied in the idea of *bioregionalism*, connecting humanity and nature to transcend nation and view America 'place by place' according to biogeography, watersheds, and other natural connections. Such ideas challenge humanity to be 're-inhabitory', that is, to see themselves within place over a long period of time in 'a search for the sustainable sophisticated mix of economic practices that would enable people to live regionally and yet learn from and contribute to a planetary society' (Snyder, 1995: 247). Thus, faced with the inertia of a bar in Farmington, New Mexico, 'like ... a High School dance in the fifties', playing Merle Haggard amid the 'horseplay' of 'cowboys', he connects the mythic machismo with the possession of the land, the 'cancer', 'the foul breeze', and the 'landseekers' who cry 'To the land,/Spread your legs' (Snyder, 1974: 18). This assault on the earth isn't the 'real work' for Snyder, for that is about a different relationship to place, based on respect and mutualism learned from Native cultures:

> I would like,
> with a sense of helpful order,
> with respect for laws
> of nature,
> to help my land
> with a burn. a hot clean
> burn.
> (Snyder, 1974: 19)

Snyder's spiritual ecology, drawing upon Native traditions and Eastern religion, provides a new mapping for the West, where the 'ultimate democracy' comes from a relationship with all that is around us. For Snyder, unlike Mike Davis, this hybrid mapping of an ecological vision for the New West, is not one of doom, 'but a world in which computer technicians might walk in autumn with migrating elk' (ibid.: 280).

Whether through the expansionism of Manifest Destiny or the New West's redevelopment, there is a danger of reducing the land to one dimension: as resource, as settlement, as tourism, as wilderness, and so on. Snyder and others committed to change in the West call for a 'sustainable and sophisticated mix' between modified current usage and their alternatives, 'the balance between cosmopolitan pluralism and deep local consciousness' (Snyder, 1990: 42). Although having a variety of different standpoints on the land, ranging from the extreme environmentalism of Earth First! to the the Sierra Club, and from Native American land rights activists to ecofeminists and conservationists, there is a growing sense that the West cannot be encompassed by one definition or use, but has to be seen both as a diverse space and responded to with multiple sensitivities and perspectives.

New Western Cultural Geography

The human relationship to the land and the re-evaluation of its representation can also be seen in the development of cultural geography which 'is about the diversity and plurality of life in all its variegated richness; about how the world, spaces and places are interpreted and used by people; and how those places help to perpetuate the culture' (Crang, 1998: 3). Applied to the West, this approach to the lived experience of space and the relations between humanity and land discourages reductionism and enables landscape to be 'read' as a complex, multilayered construction mixing memory and desire, myth and reality, but always revealing ideology. Take, for example, this passage by Simon Schama:

> Though the parking is almost as big as the park and there are bears rooting among the McDonald's cartons, we still imagine Yosemite the way Albert Bierstadt painted it or Carleton Watkins and Ansel Adams photographed it: with no trace of human presence. But of course the very act of identifying (not to mention photographing) the place presupposes our presence, and along with us all the heavy cultural backpacks that we lug with us on the trail. (Schama, 1995: 7)

Schama's *Landscape and Memory* rejects trite binary oppositions of nature/culture, civilization/wilderness, and demands to be shelved 'between optimism and pessimism' as 'an excavation below our conventional sight-level' to see landscape as a complex mixture of human desires and 'imprinted with our tenacious, inescapable obsessions' (ibid.: 19, 14). To see the West within this frame of reference rejects any essential meaning and redefines it as part of a larger set of relations, with a living, complex 'history':

> Nature is part of culture. When our physical surroundings are sold to us as 'natural' . . . we should pay close attention. Our experience of the natural world . . . is always mediated. It is always shaped by rhetorical constructs like photography, industry, advertising, and aesthetics, as well, as by institutions like religion, tourism and education. (Wilson, 1992: 12)

Schama and Wilson develop out of a tradition of cultural geography rooted in the work of John Brinckerhoff Jackson and D. W. Meinig. In 1960, Jackson, working in the West, wrote 'there is a constant action

and reaction between ourselves and this environment ... the world
surrounding us affects every aspect of our being ... [and] we are
participants in it (Jackson, 1960: 1–2).

In Meinig's *The Interpretation of Ordinary Landscapes* (1976), a
seminal work of cultural geography, Jackson and W. G. Hoskins are
nominated as the fathers of the movement which argued that 'landscape
displays us as cultures' (1976: 3) in complex relations:

> We regard all landscapes as symbolic, as expressions of cultural
> values, social behaviour, and individual actions worked upon parti-
> cular localities over a span of time. *Every landscape is an accumulation*,
> and its study may be undertaken as formal history, methodically
> defining the making of the landscape from the past to the present ...
> every landscape is a code, and its study may be undertaken as a
> deciphering of meaning, of the cultural and social significance of
> ordinary but diagnostic features. (ibid.: 6 – my emphasis)

Jackson focused on the expressive and varied landscapes of the
everyday -'vernacular' landscape – from suburban home to trailer park
to highway, and wrote that 'a landscape, like a language, is the field of
perpetual conflict and compromise between what is established by
authority and what the vernacular insists upon preferring' (Jackson,
1984: 148). Jackson was interested in the cultural landscape or 'nearly
everything that we can see when we go outdoors' (Pierce Lewis, in
Meinig, 1976: 12), rather than the officially sanctioned geography that
often neglected the vernacular. In studying such landscapes, Jackson
and others began to delve into 'our unwitting autobiography ... [with]
All our cultural warts and blemishes ... there, and our glories too ...'
(ibid.). The field was opened to include those cultural and material
elements once de-emphasized as irrelevant for they were 'messy and
disorganized, like a book with pages missing, torn and smudged; a book
whose copy has been edited and re-edited by people with illegible
handwriting' (Lewis, in Meinig, 1976: 12). Here was the challenge for
Jackson, to read and 'to understand the landscape in living terms' (ibid.:
224), as an engaged participant rather than a scientifically removed
objective observer. For Jackson the land was 'not something to look at
but to live in; and not alone but with other people' (ibid.: 228).

As Native Americans already knew, and New Western historians
and photographers would later assert, the West was dynamic, relational
space, not essential and fixed, and Jackson's influence was crucial to the

development of alternative ways of seeing its landscape, breaking down
old notions of essences held in the natural world with no relationship to
humanity:

> [Landscape] is really no more than a collection, a system of man-
> made spaces on the surface of the earth. Whatever its shape or size it
> is *never* simply a natural space, a feature of the natural environment; it
> is *always* artificial, *always* synthetic, *always* subject to sudden and
> unpredictable change. We create them and need them because every
> landscape is the place where we establish our own human organiza-
> tion of space and time. (Jackson, 1984: 156)

Developing from the work of Jackson, with the impact of European
cultural studies, landscape could now be seen as multiple, ideological
space where human, natural, man-made, quotidian, 'low' and 'high'
were all included in its field. Equally, landscape was not an objective
truth 'out there' to be surveyed and recorded but historical and
dynamic, full of unfixed, contradictory meanings.

Jackson had 'no liking for the cultural anarchy preached by the
radical environmentalists' (Jackson, 1994: vii) because they were 'anti-
urban, antitechnological, antipeople, antihistory ... all urging us to
worship nature' and 'return to origins, to the pretechnological purity of
the past, to a static social order, [as] the only way to go' (ibid.: 88). Such
a return for Jackson was an impossible nostalgia ignoring the coexistence of nature and humanity constructed in a series of 'temporary
contact[s] with nature' of visits, journeys, moments, recreations juxtaposed with their everyday lives (ibid.: 89). For Jackson and later
cultural and 'postmodern' geographers, like Soja, the issue is how to
tell multiple stories of the landscape so that 'inclusiveness' is emphasized. One way is the realization that 'we do not live in an abstract
framework of geometric spatial relationships; we live in a world of
meaning' where 'places are ... combinations of the material and mental
and cannot be reduced to either' (Cresswell, 1996: 13). For Jackson, the
grand narrative of the Western landscape is a pretence and what counts
is the 'plurality of cultures and the multiplicity of landscapes ... [that]
reject[ ] a unitary view of culture as the artistic and intellectual product
of an elite, asserting the value of popular culture both in its own terms
and as an implicit challenge to dominant values' (P. Jackson, 1995: 1).
The geography of the American West *must* include a diverse, heterogeneous mix of pueblo and porch, highway and hieroglyph, trailer park

and national park, and cannot be fixated upon a narrow definition of landscape as Eden or monumental wilderness.

If the West is defined only by the latter, 'the human life ... disappears to the exclusive benefit of its monuments' and complex relations become 'types' and 'essences', 'reduced to a ... nice neat commedia dell'arte, whose improbable typology serves to mask the real spectacle of conditions ... ' (Barthes, 1973: 75). 'To select only monuments suppresses at one stroke the reality of the land and that of its people, it accounts for nothing of the present, that is, nothing historical' (ibid.) and its overwhelming effect is the opposite of its stated intention to describe the landscape. Barthes' warning is clear: the environment includes the human and so representations of it have to record and acknowledge our presence. To do otherwise is duplicitous and reductive. A landscape signified by its monuments – its great mountains, deserts, 'sights' – is only telling a partial story. Cultural geography teaches us to see the complex landscapes of the New West as more than monuments, and to see the environment, in all its forms, as dynamic and alive within the context of human-natural relations.

Environmental History and Ecocriticism

Cultural geography reappraised humanistically lived experience and became one of a number of interdisciplinary areas that advanced the productive rethinking of the American West. Alongside feminism, environmentalism, and cultural geography, the growth in environmental history offered 'an earth's-eye view of the past. It addresse[d] the many ways in which humans have interacted with the natural environment over time' (Merchant, 1993: 1). Worster sees environmental history as a significant and intrinsic part of the New Western History (see Introduction), and has written that:

> This new history rejects the common assumption that human experience has been exempt from natural constraints, that people are a separate and uniquely special species, that the ecological consequences of our past deeds can be ignored. (Worster, 1990: 1088)

He further claims that 'older history' saw humanity as 'not truly part of the planet' (ibid.) and that environmental history aimed to 'deepen our understanding of how humans have been affected by their natural environment through time, and ... how they have affected that environment and with what results' (ibid.: 1089). One area of concern for the 'new' historian is humanity's complex 'dialogue with nature': 'People are continually constructing cognitive maps of the world around them' and these create 'patterns of human perception, ideology, and value' that need to be identified and analyzed (ibid.: 1091). The environment had to be restored to the story of the West, not as nostalgic myth or gendered possession, but as a space of complex, multifaceted correspondences with 'an outer ecological' history and an 'inner cultural history' (Worster, 1992: 230–1). The latter is a landscape 'of daydreams and fantasies, of visions and nostalgia' all of which have constructed 'the Western mind ... full of such fleeting, jumbled bits of memory and romance' (ibid.: 233). The 'new history' must acknowledge the West as a

> place of rapid change, repeated dislocation, and surreal discontinu-
> ities, a place in which time has often seemed to break completely
> apart ... a land in which the same man, as a boy, might have watched
> Billy the Kid ride through town on his way to a shootout, and, as an
> old timer, watched a radioactive mushroom cloud rise ominously on
> the horizon. (ibid.)

The land and the dialogue between it and its inhabitants is crucial to this 'new' history because 'westerners have long been conversing with the landscape as well as with each other, and their imaginations have been altered by that conversation beyond easy telling' (ibid.: 234–5). Environmental history begins to analyse the 'intersubjectivity' of humanity and nature and the varied juxtapositions of people and place making it 'a conversation going on in several languages at once' (Worster, 1992: 232).

Ecocritism is the study of the relationship between representation and the physical environment, examining the ways by which literature, art, film, or photography might define this dialogue. Initially, it has been most prevalent in literary studies, following, according to Glotfelty (1996), a course similar to that of feminist criticism: examining how nature is represented, or how there has been a long tradition of nature writing in America and finally developing a broader theoretical and philosophical framework. Ecocriticism is becoming a broad church concerned as it is with 'interdependent communities, integrated systems, and strong connections amongst constituent parts' (ibid.: xx) and prepared to explore a variety of disciplines and interdisciplinary approaches as a methodology. It has brought to the study of the New West, as my other examples have too, a developing awareness that in order to analyze and understand the complex, diverse nature of the region one must adopt a multifaceted critical stance. As Evernden writes, ecocritism is rooted in 'interrelatedness' defined as a 'genuine intermingling of parts of the ecosystem ... [with] no discrete entities' (in Glotfelty and Fromm, 1996: 93), a definition of particular relevance to the American West. In the following sections, I examine two writers, Edward Abbey and Terry Tempest Williams, and a photographer Richard Misrach whose work, in different ways, are ecocritical and concerned with the interrelatedness of human and nonhuman. Their work blends and fuses the various strands of thought and practice discussed in this chapter and epitomizes the variety and diversity necessary to any representation of the New West.

Landscape Stories 1: Edward Abbey's Paradoxical New West

In 1983, firmly established as an eco-guru, Abbey wrote that 'the entire American West – property of all Americans, home of the wild things, last strong-hold of the Ghost Dancers – lies under massive assault by the industrial armies of Government and Greed' (Abbey, 1984: xvi). Almost thirty years before, in his novel *Brave Cowboy* (1957) – filmed as *Lonely Are the Brave* (see Chapter 2) – there is a clear division between worlds:

> Horse and man passed other signs and stigmata of life; the petroglyph of a wild turkey chiselled in the stone, a pair of tin cans riddled with bullet holes of various calibre, brass cartridge shells, an empty sardine can dissolving in rust. They were nearing civilization. (Abbey, 1962: 13)

The signs of Native American culture inscribed in the desert are ironically contrasted with the remnants and markings of 'civilization' – garbage and violence. For Abbey, the battle lines are clear as his 'brave cowboy', Jack Burns, rides out of the desert: the urban sprawl with its 'continuous droning roar, the commingled vibrations of ten thousand automobiles, trucks, tractors, air-planes, locomotives, television receivers ...' (ibid.: 14), or the silent world of nature beyond.

Abbey's *Desert Solitaire: A Season in the Wilderness* (first 1968) develops ecological themes by examining how humans relate to the environment, like Jack Burns, in paradoxical ways. Beginning with a series of warnings to the reader about the problems of reading the text, Abbey sees language as 'a mighty loose net' adding that the book 'fails to engage and reveal the patterns of unifying relationships which form the true underlying reality of existence' because 'I must confess that I know nothing whatever about true underlying reality, having never met any' (Abbey, 1992: xii, xiii). Abbey's earlier sense of a lost pristine West is returned to as 'elegy' in *Desert Solitaire*, a book built on the premise that 'most of what I write of in this book is already gone or going under fast' (ibid.: xiv). His words, however inadequate he believes them to be, will simultaneously tantalize the reader with the promise of the wilderness while denying us the opportunity to enjoy it in reality, for ourselves. This is the conceit at the heart of Abbey's duality: his denial of our rights to share his emotive experience of the land. Reyner Banham, echoing J. B. Jackson's concern about radical ecologists, is critical of Abbey as a 'desert loner' (Banham, 1982: 57) and writes of the 'familiar exclusivism that powers so much American conservation-politics – "I got here first, now legislate them bums out of my backyard" . . .' (ibid.) as a strand of 'mythic' thinking about the West. Banham argues that such 'purists' (ibid.: 97) 'love the desert without people' and claim it is part of a 'seamless web of the desert ecology, [with a] . . . balanced relationship of the different species that "share" the desert', and yet 'the speaker's own part in that sharing gets little mention [and he] never identifies himself as part of the seamless web' (ibid.: 58). This tension is central to Abbey's work surfacing in the inconsistencies of *Desert Solitaire*.

The divide between nature and culture, mankind and the wilderness, and Abbey's professed role as preserver of the divide is often suspect. For example, early on in *Desert Solitaire* looking out upon the land, he admits to a desire 'to know it all, possess it all . . . as a man desires a beautiful woman', while also claiming to 'evade for a while the clamor and filth and confusion of the cultural apparatus' and 'to confront, immediately and directly . . . the bare bones of existence' (Abbey, 1992: 5, 6). Ultimately, he seeks a place where 'the naked self merges with a non-human world and yet somehow survives still intact, individual, separate. Paradox and bedrock' (ibid.). Paradox indeed! How can he be merged and separate? How can he both possess the land and be outside the 'cultural apparatus' which is the source of so much environmental 'possession' and exploitation? Knowingly or not, Abbey states the heart of the problem of the New West – how can one live there, or visit there, and yet not leave a mark upon the place? He articulates this paradox very well later when he looks in a register box near Millard Canyon to

find the words '"Keep the tourists out", [written by] some tourist from
Salt Lake City ... As fellow tourists we heartily agree' (ibid.: 252).
These paradoxes and inconsistencies represent a man confronting in
public his own responses and struggles with being human and loving
the West in the late twentieth century. For in the contradictions – as
complex as the West itself – we are invited to participate in a dialogue
with Abbey, to 'acknowledge that he is not always right or always fair'
and that one was always 'arguing with him' (Wendell Berry, in Hepworth and McNamee, 1996: 7). Abbey's work is 'straddling a faultline'
(ibid.: 25) that the author himself recognized in his own writings and
experience: 'I'd like to have the best of both worlds. The wilderness and
urban civilization' (ibid.: 141).

In a bizarre section, Abbey describes how he kills a rabbit with a
stone as an 'experiment', a self-inflicted initiation ceremony into the
kind of 'nature' in which 'we are kindred all of us, killer and victim,
predator and prey' (Abbey, 1992: 34). Having killed the rabbit and left it
for 'vultures and maggots', he feels the 'energy and spirit' of the rabbit
has passed 'to my soul', making him no longer 'a stranger from another
world', but part of 'this one'. The telling last comment reinforces the
division everpresent in Abbey's work between two worlds, the one
where humans dwell and that of the natural forces of land and animals:
'out there is a different world, older and greater and deeper by far than
ours, a world which surrounds and sustains the little world of men as
sea and sky surround and sustain a ship' (ibid.: 37). Yet the sustaining
wilderness invokes at the same time

a justified not merely sentimental nostalgia for the lost America our
forefathers knew ... the past and the unknown, the womb of earth
from which we all emerged ... something lost and something remote
and at the same time intimate ... buried in our blood and nerves ...
beyond us and without limit ... The romantic view, while not the
whole truth, is a necessary part of the whole truth. (ibid.: 167)

Abbey's 'truth' includes 'rattlesnakes and Gila monsters ... bacteria
and bear ... disease and death and the rotting of the flesh', and it is 'here
and now, the actual, tangible, dogmatically real earth on which we
stand' (ibid.: 167). As a 'necessity', we cannot deny ourselves the
wilderness for to do so would be like 'civilization ... cutting itself
off from its origins and betraying the principle of civilization itself'
(ibid.: 169).

Worster has termed 'the Western Paradox' the tension between 'two dreams ... tugging at our feelings: one of a life in the past, the other in the future' (Worster, 1992: 81). The 'life in the past' is the West's 'true promise of freedom' (ibid.: 83) proffered by the land as pristine and untainted, but always alongside it is the marriage to technology: to irrigation, railways, roads, nuclear plants, and factories. 'Both dreams have something attractive to offer', and so we struggle with 'wisdom and intelligence' to reconcile them knowing 'that there can be no perfect reconciliation nor any that will suit for all time. This is a struggle that will go on as long as there are people wanting to dwell in this place' (ibid.: 90).

Worster suggests that 'the way to deal with any paradox is to find a way to transcend it' with a 'new vision' drawn from both 'dreams' offering a plan of 'how we can occupy this place without consuming it or letting it consume us' (ibid.: 90). *Desert Solitaire*'s final section, 'Bedrock and Paradox', acknowledges these contradictions by mapping a territory which is multilayered and complex. Facing his imminent 'return to civilization', the pull of the city is powerful – 'I long for the view of the jolly, rosy faces on 42nd Street ...' – but he sees that 'Balance, that's the secret ... The best of both worlds' (Abbey, 1992: 265). He moves across two worlds, between the polar extremes, from Hoboken to Moab, East to West, and yet knows his words are 'human vanity' and that the 'finest quality' of the West is 'the indifference manifest to our presence, our absence, our coming, our staying or our going. Whether we live or die is a matter of absolutely no concern whatsoever to the desert' (ibid.: 267). Speaking from his 'valley of paradox' (ibid.: 268), he cannot 'transcend' it, as Worster suggests, but instead voices, what is for him, the reassuring spirit of the place: 'All things are in motion, all is in process, nothing abides, nothing will ever change in this eternal moment' (ibid.).

Abbey, perhaps unknowingly, stumbles on the dilemma of a place in which the inevitable dynamic of motion, process, and change coexists in a land where tranquility, serenity, and staticity appears still possible. How might these poles be transcended or collapsed? It is Abbey's problem of the binary experience restated. What he instinctively knows is that the only way is *both*, not one or the other, but 'balance' or mingling across the boundaries that he for so long straddles. At the end of his novel *Brave Cowboy*, the two worlds or 'dreams' collide literally on the highway, when Jack Burns and his horse are hit my a truck, which has been tracked by the reader throughout the novel. It is associated with the the urban machine, Worster's 'hydraulic West' (1992: 29) – a world that Burns enters at the opening of the novel, 'chrome-plated, neonized, red-brick' (Abbey, 1962: 34), full of 'diesel monsters' with air 'conditioned for human consumption and reconsumption by tireless electrical engines pumping ammonia through coils of copper tubing' (ibid.). Against this, Burns, who escapes the human-machine of prison for the space of the desert and the mountains, is associated with the land through hunting knowledge and ritual which make him feel 'a whole and living creature, a man again and not a derelict stumbling through a mechanical world he could not understand' (ibid.: 155). In Abbey's simple construction of opposites, the individualist, 'brave cowboy' formed by the land is contrasted to Johnson, the institutionalized policeman to whom the same land is an 'irrational bulk and complexity ... a great ugly eruption of granite, not only meaningless but malignant ... a piece of sheer insolence' with an 'absurd, exasperating lack of purpose or utility' (ibid.: 190). The inevitable metaphorical and literal collision of these positions is the only solution for Abbey. Burns must die along, one assumes, with his particular view of environment, while triumphant are the 'great four lane highway ... steel, rubber ... the fury of men and women immured in engines' (ibid.: 224). The final irony is that these survivors who 'utilize' the land are themselves 'immured' or walled in and imprisoned by their technology while Burns is dead but 'all right' (ibid.), merging with the 'near-silent world' (ibid.: 155).

In our urgent need to find a balance between the kind of extremes that Abbey recorded, Barry Lopez argues we have 'to listen to the land' and enter into a productive dialogue with it since 'interdependence is simply a good and wise habit of mind' (Lopez, 1992: 19). We should expect nothing, but 'approach the land as we would a person, by opening an intelligent conversation', and remember that in itself it is 'more complex even than language' (ibid.: 36–7). This is not a simplistic recasting of older 'wilderness values' or the desire of a Jack Burns (or a Huck Finn, in Lopez's example) 'to light out for the Territory', but a genuine effort to 'discover the lineaments of cooperation' (ibid.: 49) with the environment. Human life, with all its 'dark flaws' (ibid.: 51) must be a significant part of this cooperative dialogue searching out a ground on which to stand hopefully rather than in eco-despair. Unlike Abbey's 'immured' voyeurs at the conclusion of *Brave Cowboy*, Lopez encourages us to not 'become the prisoners of our own minds' trapped in 'despair', for we can 'step onto wounded ground' (ibid.: 53) and see things differently, and act together to make the 'monumental adjustment' (ibid.: 58) that is required.

Abbey's *The Monkey Wrench Gang* (1975) appears to advocate 'ecotage' or the destruction of the trappings of technological culture to avenge its despoilation of the Western environment. Taken up by the Earth First! movement, the novel is rather more ambivalent than it is often given credit for. It does speak clearly of environmental scars, waste, and destruction, but does it through a range of oddball characters who must cast some doubt on the intention of the author. In a world gone mad only the mad can answer back. Their speeches are often on the edge of sanity: '"We are caught", continued the good doctor, "in the iron treads of a technological juggernaut. A mindless machine. With a breeder reactor for a heart"' (Abbey, 1976: 61). In this they echo their progenitor Ned Ludd: 'They called him a lunatic but he saw the enemy clearly' (ibid.: 65). Abbey's prose draws a powerful visual portrait of the damaged West: 'the tin-can tumbleweed community of the roadside ecology', 'a smudge of poisoned air overhung his homeland', and 'the blazing cities feed on the defenseless interior' (ibid.: 14, 15, 24), but the desire within the destructive eco-politics is one at odds with the views of Lopez and Tempest Williams (see later). In the novel, Abbey's characters desire an imagined lost West:

> The great golden light of the setting sun streamed across the sky, glowing upon the clouds and the mountains. Almost all the country within their view was roadless, uninhabited, a wilderness. They meant to keep it that way. They sure meant to try. *Keep it like it was.* (ibid.: 77)

And they institute an apocalyptic means to achieve it, imagining a time 'when cities are gone . . . when sunflowers push up through the concrete and asphalt of the forgotten interstate freeways . . . when the glass-aluminium skyscraper tombs of Phoenix Arizona barely show above the sand dunes' (ibid.: 100–1). Their aim is to destroy 'that phosphorescent putrefying glory . . . called Down Town, Night Time, Wonderville, U.S.A.' (ibid.: 161). As Zakin argues, Abbey 'created a new kind of nature writing' (1995: 135) with a hard-edged refusal to be sucked into a nostalgia for 'babbling brooks and heavenly birdsong' (ibid.: 136), and yet one full of contradictions. Here, she claims, was a writer who believed in biocentrism, 'the idea that nature, not humanity, is the measure of all things' (ibid.), in whose writings nature was often 'off its pedestal' (ibid.); and a man who rejected romantic views of nature and yet was still riddled by a 'sense of loss' (ibid.: 182) for a vision of a more perfect past. Zakin argues that Abbey's loss was conveyed as 'rage' – an emotion he passed on to his followers in the Earth First! environmental movement – who ultimately demanded the impossible: 'to go back and make it right. All of it' (ibid.: 182). Thus Hayduke's fantasy in *The Monkey Wrench Gang* is to 'roam the sagebrush canyonlands in freedom ... by the light of a reborn moon' (1976: 101) revealing again the constant presence of images of romantic yearning for a lost time in Abbey's work.

The paradox of *Desert Solitaire* and Abbey's dialogue with his own split self, straddling two worlds, is less apparent in *The Monkey Wrench Gang* where a more direct path is presented through his eco-warrior characters. In isolation the novel misrepresents Abbey's complex struggle and paints an oversimplified portrait of environmental issues. The novel is a provocation, a call to arms, an extreme example of one approach to the same collision faced by Jack Burns at the conclusion of *Brave Cowboy*. As Terry Tempest Wiliams has written, Abbey was a 'human being of complex paradox and passion who lured us out of complacency again and again' (in Hepworth and McNamee, 1996: 201), and the novel was a further strategy to be used in this process. In a less poetic manner, Dave Foreman of Earth First! called Abbey 'the Mudhead Kachina of the environmental movement ... a trickster farting in polite company. Pissing on overblown egos, making a caricature of himself and laughing at himself' (ibid.: 249). This is surely what Abbey meant when he said that his work was 'outrageous and provocative,' aimed to 'startle people ... to wake up people ... [but with] no desire to to simply soothe or please' (Abbey, quoted in Slovic, 1992: 100). The provocations in Abbey's work are contained in its contradictions and its irritating inconsistencies, all part of his project to force his readers 'to abandon secure mental ruts' (ibid.).

Landscape Stories 2:
Terry Tempest Williams – 'a vision that includes'

Terry Tempest Williams has acknowledged her debt to Abbey who 'embodies the sacred rage in regard to the land' (in Regan, 1996: 1), and yet her work links the politics of environmentalism to spirituality and to gender in different ways. She writes, 'we are in flux ... we are rethinking who we are and where we live and how we want to be' (Siporin, 1996: 108) and this is reflected in new ways of telling since 'the old stories [of the West] don't work for us anymore. So it's a shattering of the mythologies, the mythology of the cowboy, of the rugged individualist, of using the land simply for one's economy ...' (ibid.). In Williams's work, as in other contemporary 'environmental writers' like Barry Lopez, Rick Bass, and Ann Zwinger, no single genre is sufficient to encompass the complex West, and so she blends natural history, storytelling, ancestral memory, eco-politics, and other forms to articulate a new 'relationship to place' (ibid.) born out of New Western hybridity, combining local knowledge (she is a naturalist by profession), personal and regional history, environmentalism, and a widening sense of gender and national politics. She endorses Elliot West's comment that:

> Stories have power. Western history has been shaped not only by exchanges among people, land, and animals and by evolving institutions like the family. Each part of the West is also what it is because of the stories people have told about it. (West, 1995: 127)

Williams has said that 'it's only in the act of telling and receiving stories that we will be healed as a nation in terms of our relationship to place, where we can truly move with any sort of compassionate intelligence' (Siporin, 1996: 110). For her, 'we must tell a story that bypasses the rhetoric and pierces the heart' (in Regan, 1996: 2).

Refuge (1991) is full of stories of people and place, but is also a revisioning of writing itself, an attempt to draw together previously separate strands of expressions and representations of the West and its people to create a book which is simultaneously about the land (the Great Salt Lake, Utah), natural history (the bird and wildlife of the area), the elements (water levels, floods, droughts, the desert), the deaths of Williams's mother and grandmother to cancer, spirituality (as a non-orthodox Mormon), and an awareness of the politics of land use in the West (nuclear test sites in Utah and Nevada). Yet the parts do not describe the overall interminglings of the text, as Williams writes herself:

> What attracts me to the Great Basin archaeology is putting all the pieces together, the complexity of the parts creating the whole.

Artifacts alone have never interested me. It's the stratigraphy that speaks. The human stories are told within the layers of sediments. (Williams, 1992: 184)

Williams's own writing is 'stratigraphic' in this sense, concerning itself with the layers of meaning that constitute her experience of the West, and her work seeks to articulate and interconnect these 'pieces' into a vision of the 'whole'. This corresponds to her summary of the New West as the opposite of 'monoculture', 'an unbelievably complex set of cultures' with 'disparate voices' (Siporin, 1996: 109). Writers can create 'bridges on which we can move on to the next era' (ibid.) through a relationship to the earth and to each other, where 'There is no separation between the interior landscape and the eternal landscape. The story is the bridge between them' (in Regan 1996: 2). In *Refuge*, Williams explains how she has stepped outside the strict codes of Mormonism – 'rewriting my genealogy' (Williams, 1992: 241) – in order to see the Holy Ghost as feminine, but significantly, this is also true of her writing about the West. The old established story ('mythology') or 'writing' cannot articulate the West as she knows it, for it serves only to reduce its complexities, but through personal experience she revisions public history, through the disease in her body she re-examines the politics of land use in the West, and through the land she enlarges her spirituality. Hence the map's 'blank spot' (ibid.: 242) where the nuclear sites hide provoke her 'rewriting' of history as a refutation of the blankness showing that in these official silences there is much to be told. As with so much New Western representation – like Misrach's photographs (discussed later) – the secret histories of the land and the people are told to counter the 'blank spots'.

Williams's work links land to gender for as a Mormon woman she has had to step outside the dominant story and the controlling voice of patriarchy in order to make her view known. She connects her writing with the tradition of feminism that has related itself to the earth and to the erasure of the earth's voice in a predominantly male defined culture of the West. Speaking up for oneself and feeling the connection of that self to the land means that Williams's work coheres around key themes 'of family ... and relationship to place ... gender, geography, and culture' (Siporin, 1996: 108). Her writing shares its impetus with Virginia Woolf and the French feminist Hélène Cixous who 'speak out of the body' (ibid.: 103) and with the philosophy of ecofeminism. Ecofeminism links the subjugation of environment and women with the power of patriarchy and its binary and hierarchical way of describing reality.

For Williams the natural and familial history of place with all its secrets are bound up with the land – the West – and the relationship is articulated, explored, and changed through the stories told about it. 'The birds and I share a natural history. It is a matter of rootedness, of living inside a place for so long that the mind and imagination fuse' (Williams, 1992: 21): 'I am desert. I am mountains. I am Great Salt Lake ... We are no more or less than the life that surrounds us' (ibid.: 29). This connectedness is both real and mystical, which for Williams are inseparable: 'All of life drums and beats, at once, sustaining a rhythm audible only to the spirit' (ibid.: 85), and related to the wider cycles of nature (see 137–9) and gender. In a key essay, Williams calls this the 'erotics of place' – 'Loving the land and dreaming it' (Williams, 1995: 85) – whereby the body and the land are in 'dialogue' as part of an essential 'process of redefining our relationship toward the land' (ibid.: 86). She develops this 'erotics', echoing the visual sensuality of the paintings of Georgia O'Keeffe, in *Desert Quartet: An Erotic Landscape* (1995), writing of a fusion with nature:

> My left hand reaches for the frog dangling between my breasts like a withered heart, beating inside me, inside the river. We are moving downstream. Water. Water music. Blue notes, white notes, my body mixes with the body of the water like jazz, the currents like jazz. I too am free to improvise. (Williams and Frank, 1995: 24)

She writes that 'the things that concern me are relationships. Women, health, and the environment – no separation' (Siporin, 1996: 104). Out of this intimacy and recognition, she believes 'a politics of place is emerging ... rooted in empathy in which we extend our notion of community ... We call to the land – and the land calls back' (ibid.: 86–7), in what she terms, with an important pun, an 'Echo System,' that is, an ecosystem created by the dialogue of humanity and nature and rejecting binary thought. As she writes:

> The fact of the land, the health of the land, the health of the women in the land are all related ... that is how I approach environmental issues. It's not abstraction. Wilderness is not an abstraction, it's not an idea it's a place ... the health of the earth is the health of its inhabitants. (Siporin, 1996: 104)

At the end of *Refuge*, Nancy Holt's 'Sun Tunnels' desert installation becomes symbolic of Williams's feelings about land and self, embodying the gnostic teaching that 'what is inside of you is what is outside of you' and that 'Refuge is not a place outside myself' (Williams, 1992: 267) but is precisely the meeting of the inside and outside. The 'Sun Tunnels' echo the human voice and the sound of the land, connecting them together as bodies. Williams contrasts this with Karl Momem's 'Metaphor', a sculpture rising out of the desert like a 'small phallus' with its shadow a 'mushroom cloud' (ibid.: 127). Momem perpetuates the vision of a masculine West and marks it with his steel phallus signifying control and ownership, whereas the 'Sun Tunnels' are feminine, tranquil, and holistic, folded into the earth and air. Williams's writing, like 'Sun Tunnels', connects body and earth using stories as 'bridges' articulating the links between the present and the 'sense of the ancestral', forming 'a vision that includes a strong sense of the animal ... a wild response ... remembering what we're connected to' (Siporin, 1996: 110).

This is how 'a poetics of place translates to a politics of place' (ibid.: 112) for women are 'wedded to wilderness' (Williams, 1995: 140) and know its 'secret narratives' (ibid.: 117). Women cannot separate environmental issues from health issues, for they are all connected in the politics of the New West which is about 'regional diversity' and 'disparate voices' (in Holthaus et al., 1991: 51). Women, whose stories have been traditionally silenced in the West, like so many other vibrant western voices, cannot be ignored for to do so would perpetuate the kind of centralized views that defined the maps with blank spots and the land as empty. Williams's writing echoes the Native American oral traditions of storytelling, explored in her book *Pieces of White Shell* (1997), yet develops a form which is hybrid, truly New Western in its willingness to blur the boundaries between cultures and customs. She writes of the 'mutuality of stories' which connect different peoples who share the landscapes of the West and therefore are constantly in contact with similar basic needs and desires. Such common ground reminds Williams of the 'spirit of place' and 'the human necessity to realize itself through community, which is in direct correspondence to the land' (ibid.: 56). It is in stories that these relationships are conveyed, and for Williams, there can be no single, dominant overarching story, but as many stories as there are peoples to tell them. As we have seen earlier, the West is a complex texture of stories and this is an image favoured by Williams too: 'the tension and strength woven together through regional diversity; the warp dressed by individual communities and the weft created by the landscape that binds us' (ibid.: 57).

She refutes 'monoculture' and prefers the heteroglossic textures of the West, for 'stories give us residency' by linking us to 'the landscape of many' (ibid.: 58) while emphasizing and restating our own rooted-ness, our own belonging and our own inclusion in a community of all things. Ultimately, Williams suggests that living in the West is about accommodation, about learning to live with and respecting the land, to be in relations (*erotics*) with it. She tells of her grandfather's belief that all stories ever told are present in the universe and that 'when we are sitting on the land, walking in the land ... there are stories there that can be retrieved, both from the distant past [and] maybe even from the future' (Siporin, 1996: 107). In this image lies Williams's faith in the persistence of the human-natural relations as long as we are prepared to listen, prepared to care, and prepared to love: 'Listen / Below us. / Above us. / Inside us. / Come. This is all there is' (Williams and Frank, 1995: 58).

Landscape Stories 3: Richard Misrach's Photography

Williams wrote a short essay on Richard Misrach's photography in 1996 in which she praised his work for revealing 'the open wound in the landscapes and lives' of the West and for showing 'what is on the ground and what is buried in our history' (Williams, 1996: 187). Misrach's work deals with 'the real desert ... stained and trampled, franchised and fenced, burned, flooded, grazed, mined, exploited, and laid waste,' and yet it retains 'great visual beauty' (Banham, in Misrach, 1988: 1). For Banham, Misrach represents the West differ-ently, for 'we try to block out these manifestations of our presence, and lift up our eyes unto the hills beyond – hoping that they, at least, will still look something like the work of Ansel Adams. They don't, of course ...' (ibid.) (see Chapter 2). Banham pleads for an open reading of the landscape acknowledging diversity and contradiction, breaking away from the mind-set that 'discriminate[s] clearly between D and not-D, that which is deserted and without people, and that which is peopled and therefore cannot be desert' (ibid.: 2). Hence his descrip-tion in *Scenes in America Deserta* of the 'deep satisfactions of the sunset ... [or] the stripes of morning mist across the Little Cowhole

Mountain' *and* alongside it 'a Didion landscape of moral anorexia, collapsed Chevrolets, and mountains of beer cans' (Banham, 1982: 167). His reference to Joan Didion recalls her description of California: 'The lemon groves are sunken, down a three- or four-foot retaining wall, so that one looks directly into their dense foliage, too lush, unsettingly glossy, the greenery of nightmare; the fallen eucalyptus bark is too dusty, a place for snakes to breed' (Didion, 1985: 20–1).

Misrach's photographs capture these Didion landscapes but on a grander scale, involving not just the trash of everyday life, but the military nuclear dumps of the state. For Davis, Misrach's photographs are a 'frontal attack on the hegemony of Ansel Adams, the dead pope of the "Sierra Club School" of Nature-as-God photography' (Davis, 1993: 52) whose awesome photographs of nature in the West have been seen as a final statement of environmental wellbeing. The 'New Western Photography' (see Chapter 2) of Robert Adams, Mark Klett, Misrach, and others suggest otherwise and have 'rudely deconstructed this myth of the virginal, if imperilled nature [and] have rejected Adams' Manichean division between "sacred" and "profane" landscape . . .', presenting instead an 'alternative iconography' (ibid.: 57–8) of the West as complex lived space. They are 'resurveying' the West's cultural landscape, just as it had been originally in the 1870s, in part to demonstrate change and destruction and more generally, as with all revisioning processes, to alert people to what lies behind the official versions of events. As Merry Forresta has put it, 'the present challenge lies in making photographs that address the myths of landscape in ways that make sense out of contemporary experience' (Forresta et al., 1992: 39), which necessarily includes the use of the land for military purposes as well as for a toxic dump.

Misrach's photographs acknowledge the West as a 'simulacrum', 'thoroughly mediated' by Westerns, television, and Ansel Adams (in Holthaus et al., 1991: 135) so that the 'primary experience' has disappeared behind 'perfect unsullied pearls of wilderness . . . perpetuating a myth that keeps people from looking at the truth about what we have done to the wilderness' (in Tucker, 1996: 16).

This simulacrum is the starting point for Misrach's major project *The Desert Cantos*, which is a complex intervention in the 'cultural myth' of the West: a myth about cowboys, masculinity, heroism, violence, and conquest amid the untamed wilderness. His photographs are

an attempt to provide an alternative, more accurate way of understanding the West. They show a land not of open spaces and wilderness
– of loners subsisting on the earth's natural bounty, and heroic efforts
to 'civilize' the West – but a land used by military and government
agencies for the development of weapons of mass destruction . . . where
natural resources are poisoned . . . and where symbolic acts of violence
with a gun portray a culture gone berserk . . . (Misrach, 1992: n.p.)

Misrach's 'alternative' is confrontational, direct, and shocking, as
well as aesthetically beautiful and intense, and from this deliberate
mixture he conjures a dialogue between the viewer and the landscape.
The effect is not the one-dimensional awe of Ansel Adams, but a
darker, anti-mythic questioning with his use of contradictions creating a
complex historical 'cultural dialogue' (ibid.). He says, '[t]he "redemp-
tive" qualities of dark poetry lie in an ability to rupture existing myths
and paradigms' (ibid.). As in Williams's work, redemption and healing
are significant factors for Misrach, but it comes only out of the
destruction of the old assumptions and is bound up with the other
functions he attributes to his work, 'interpreting unsettling truths . . .
bearing witness, and . . . sounding an alarm' (ibid). Misrach's political
activism informs his photographs showing a land constantly being
altered ('man-mauled'), flourishing, and under threat, beautiful and
horrible simultaneously. His images shift from close up details of dead
animals, bombs, graffiti, to more 'conventional' landscapes in which the
first impression is of vastness, geology, horizon, and yet at a closer look
contain disturbing elements, references to something 'unnatual' amid all
this nature: the colour of a crater's water (see Plate 1), a shell casing, a
submerged road sign. These fragments reveal the secret histories in his
photographs like the work of Gallagher and Kuletz discussed earlier.
The apparently normal landscape juxtaposed with a warning about
contamination of the soil alters our perception – indeed, ironically, the
camera has lied to us, showing nature, but nature poisoned. The eery
emptinesses mask the dangers within, like the now empty aircraft
hangars and bombing ranges of Nevada and Utah each telling a story
about the landscape of the West as terrifying, surreal, dreamlike, and
endlessly fascinating. Misrach's work reminds us that the West has been
used and imagined as many things and all of them have to be con-
fronted, recorded, and analyzed, for the greatest deceit is to ignore them
and retreat into the map's 'blank spot'.

Plate 1 Richard Misrach, *Bomb Crater and Destroyed Convoy, 1986.* (San Francisco Museum of Modern Art. Purchased through a gift of the Judy Kay Memorial Fund.)

Conclusion

These diverse examples of the Western lands, their use and abuse, have deliberately resisted any single approach, since the histories of the landscape are in themselves complex and multiple. A recognition of these complexities and the general suspicions about the old mythologies have given rise to a number of new political bodies in the West, such as the so-called 'watershed coalitions', forming alliances between divergent groups frustrated by the federal-local decision-making inertia, coming together in order to find specific, consensual solutions to the problems of resource and land use in the West. They 'consciously seek to incorporate ideals of both the Old and the New West' (Riebsame et al., 1997: 146). Equally true has been the alliances formed around environmental issues and the ways in which Native thought and intersubjectivity has been influential on Anglo-Americans engaged in rethinking attitudes to the land. Kuletz writes that seeing the West through indigenous eyes alongside the traditional scientific perspective and 'moving from one view to the other' can assist in 'opening intellectual horizons onto the diversity of knowledge about place and nature' (Kuletz, 1998: 285). A key element in this process is the recognition that the land is not an alien Other to be controlled and manipulated as though humanity had no place within it, but alternatively that there is a need to relearn the necessity of intersubjectivity, reciprocity, and mutualism – what Terry Tempest Williams calls the 'erotics of place' – in a 'fundamental redefinition' of the 'relationship between the human and nonhuman' (ibid.: 290), closer to Aldo Leopold's 'land ethic' or the 'ethics of place' defined as 'People are here and have rights, but Place is here and has rights, and the law must balance the two' (Hornby, in Holthaus et al., 1991: 122). Perhaps, then, the landscapes of the New West will truly reflect the need to view geography as more than possession, production, and development potential, and more as a real and imagined multi-layered space in which humanity and nature coexist, in dialogue, across time.

CHAPTER 2

Visualizing the New West

Revisiting the Nineteenth-Century Tradition

Early visual images of the West came from painters like those of the Hudson River School led by Thomas Cole (1801–48) whose work blended detailed landscapes with moral themes, juxtaposing harmoniously pristine wilderness and settlement as in his *The Ox Bow* (1836), presenting America as an Eden of possibility. He wrote that 'the most distinctive ... characteristic of American scenery is its wildness ... those scenes of solitude from which the hand of nature has never been lifted, affect the mind with a more deep toned emotion than aught which the hand of man has touched' (quoted in Phillips et al., 1996: 15). Deborah Bright writes that in this tradition

> landscape has been appropriated ... as proof of the timeless virtues of a Nature that transcends history ... [but] Landscape is not the open field of ideological neutrality ... it is a historical construction that can be viewed as a record of the material facts of our social reality and what we have made of them. (in Bolton, 1989: 140)

Cole's followers, Asher Durand and Frederic Church, developed the Edenic mood, and artists like Thomas Moran and Albert Bierstadt perpetuated it with images of the West as transcendent, monumental, sacred spaces drawing on the 'picturesque' tradition whereby idealized images represented the land as a timeless Arcadia, and the 'sublime' tradition with the land seen as awesome and terrifying (see Mills, 1997). The 'natural' wonders of the land are ideological, representing God's design, wonder, terror, sacred space, and revelation, the very myths a contemporary photographer like Richard Misrach (see Chapter 1) self-consciously engages with in his *Canto XVI: The Paintings* (including Thomas Cole's 'The Garden of Eden', 1827–8) introduced with these words:

Along with the railroads came art. While the train has become an obvious symbol of the 'conquest' of America, art has also played its role in the dissemination of European values. If one looks at the paintings not as art but as cultural artifacts, their lexicon of values becomes readily apparent. (in Tucker, 1996: 160)

By rephotographing the original paintings Misrach intervenes in the reception of the 'classic' image, forcing them to be reconsidered while their Eurocentric ideologies of landscape, class, gender, and race are displayed ironically in gilded frames and sold at high prices in the art market. In Bright's words, 'history' is no longer 'transcended' or elided by the dominant energies of nature, but engaged with directly as ideology and power. It was to this revisioning of painting that the exhibition *The West as America* turned in 1991, causing a national scandal because many saw it as un-American in its insistence upon notions of myth, conquest, imperialism, and violence as the significant elements in the expansion of the nation westward.

Misrach's 'lexicon of values' recur in early photographers who travelled with painters as part of the Land Surveys sent west to record and report on the landscape. As Mark Klett has written:

Standing before the landscape with a camera is like looking into a mirror. The landscape reflects our own image, but so much of what we know, and what we think we know about the land has come through someone else's lens. The challenge is to work through this history as much as it is to be absorbed into it. (Klett, 1992: 164)

Nineteenth-century photography was partly a tool of Manifest Destiny and of expansion in the hands of the Survey photographers whose images were seen as indisputable evidence of the potentiality of the West for development, settlement, and investment. Snyder (in Mitchell, 1994: 189) calls this 'invitational' photography, presenting nature as Edenic *and* in harmony with industrial incursions into it via railroads and mining, thus encouraging immigration and settlement. These images reinforced painterly impressions of the West as signs of nature's power and humanity's control, of majesty and spirit, as testament to America's exceptionalism, its meaning and destiny as 'nature's nation'. Photography's scientific approach also put the land at a distance making it appear alien, to be conquered and tamed for human use.

This photo-nationalism is only one aspect of these works which can represent far greater diversity and ambiguity about the West. The photographs of Timothy O'Sullivan (employed by the King expeditions 1867–70, 1872, and Wheeler 1871 and 1873–4 to the Far West) show technology intruding into nature, reminding us that the photograph is representation, constructed by human action without a God's eye view of the sublime beauty of nature. O'Sullivan prefigures later photography's restlessness and ambivalence towards the landscapes of the West as in *Sand Dunes, Carson Desert*, 1868 (see Plate 2): 'The photograph depicts depiction itself – not "nature" as a pure essence, something that can be measured and mapped with godlike objectivity, but a scene already altered by these very acts' (Trachtenberg, 1989: 159–60). The tracks in the sand and the wagon register the presence of the human and the machine in the conquest of the West. O'Sullivan is self-reflexive, recording explicit relations between land and humanity and 'allowing the history and meaning of Western surveys ... to reveal their contradictions' (ibid.: 289) and not hide behind the sublime and

Plate 2 Timothy O'Sullivan, *Sand Dunes, Carson Desert, Nevada, 1868* – *U.S. Geological Exploration of the 40th parallel (King Survey)*, Plate 9. (US Geological Survey.)

Plate 3 Timothy O'Sullivan, *Rock Carved by Drifting Sand, Below Fortification Rock, Arizona, 1871.* (San Francisco Museum of Modern Art. Gift of Randi and Bob Fisher.)

distant images of the land. O'Sullivan's *Rock Carved by Drifting Sand, Below Fortification Rock, Arizona,* 1871 (see Plate 3) reveals this contradiction by juxtaposing the land with its human uses, the debris of the traveller alongside the eroded rock. In a single frame, O'Sullivan's photographic dialogue interrelates human time and geological time, the near and the far, the sharp foreground and the distant, unfocused horizon, in a way that provokes questions and suggests a rather more complex notion of the West than is often claimed for Survey photographers. It's no surprise that Ansel Adams found these photographs 'technically deficient, but nonetheless surrealistic and disturbing' (in Mitchell, 1994: 192) because the epic, pristine Eden of Adams' work is here juxtaposed with human traces.

During the 1980s books by Dingus (1982), Snyder (1981), and Hales (1988) reappraised the Survey photographers arguing for greater ambiguity in their portrayals of the West. For example, Hales reviewed William Henry Jackson (1843–1942) and found examples such as *Study Among the Rocks of Echo Canyon* (1869) (see Plate 4) which unsettled the

Plate 4 William Henry Jackson, *Study Among the Rocks of Echo Canyon, 1869, Plate 34.* (US Geological Survey.)

painterly West with 'a complex, unresolved relationship within the picture itself' between nature coexisting 'at the same time [with] ... man's presence in the same sphere, unthreatened' (Hales, 1988: 57–8). Wrestling with representing simultaneity, Jackson was the first 'divergence from a purely propagandist boosting of the West' (ibid.: 63) capable of recording subtle changes, like tourism and environmental damage, in 'a vision of interlocking, interdependent relations among the various elements, nature and human, now resident in the region' (ibid.: 151). Together, these works show the growing awareness that nineteenth-century photography was not always fully engaged in the project of Manifest Destiny and was developing critical and reflective techniques later extended by twentieth-century landscape photographers. However, the towering presence of Ansel Adams in the representation of the West cannot be overlooked, for it is in his work that the picturesque tradition continued to define the landscape, even of the twentieth-century West, as pristine and wild.

The Ansel Adams Tradition

Rebecca Solnit calls Ansel Adams (1902–84) 'the Great Oedipal father of American Landscape Photography ... an obstacle nearly every Western photographer has to find a way past' (Solnit, 1993: 15) because he represented an ideal, sublime wilderness of transcendent, aesthetic monuments. Adams believed in the unity and magic of the land and his photographs drew upon Stieglitz's concept of 'the equivalent' to emphasize the correspondence (equivalence) between the image and the emotion felt. Yet there is little human presence in his images, despite the massive rise in population, urbanism, and tourism that dominated the New West, for they represented an idealized, preserved, uninhabited landscape. Adams provided a grand photographic narrative of clarity, distance and austere, eternal values in every image, like *Winter Sunrise* (1944), which 'suggests a more agreeable past [to] ... remind us that, with a revived dignity and reverence for the earth, more of the world might look like this again (Adams, 1983: 165). For Adams, landscape is salvation, the West-as-Eden, a virginal land lost to time and to humanity, preserved only in the timeless wonder of the natural world and his photographs. Nature is a supreme order, coherent and, most importantly, beyond history and, therefore, mythic in Barthes' sense. *Moonrise, Hernandez*, 1941, for example, 'is a romantic/emotional moment in time' (ibid.: 43) but in analyzing the image there is a great distance between viewer and landscape, heightened by the stark perfection of the print, and the only human presence is in fact an absence – the graveyard (see Plate 5). Adams's work denies dialogue with the land by holding it at bay, framed in pristine perfection like 'photography made to celebrate photography ... whole, conclusive, final – each glorious print ... a complete and clear answer' (Stupich in Dawson et al., 1993: 95).

Adams's monologues are of epic scale, and as Bakhtin wrote, the epic tradition has a very particular purpose: to bolster a national epic past, to create a national tradition, and to project 'an absolute epic distance [that] separates the epic from contemporary reality' (Bakhtin, 1990a: 13). Adams' work, like the paintings of Bierstadt and Moran, are 'already ready defined and real ... already finished, a congealed and half-moribund genre' (ibid.: 14) defining a myth of the West where, 'In the past, everything is good: all the really good things (i.e., the "first" real things) occur *only* in this past. The epic absolute past is the single source and beginning of everything good for all later times as well' (ibid.: 15). In Adams's work, there is no place for any 'openendedness,

Plate 5 Ansel Adams, *Moonrise, Hernandez, New Mexico, 1941*. (CORBIS/Ansel Adams Publishing Rights Trust.)

indecision, indeterminacy ... no loopholes in it through which we glimpse the future; it suffices unto itself ...' (ibid.: 16) and is blind to the developing West all around. Bakhtin could almost be describing Adams's West when he writes that, 'The epic world is constructed in *the zone of an absolute distanced image*, beyond the sphere of possible contact with the developing, incomplete and therefore re-thinking and re-evaluating present' (ibid.: 17 – my emphasis).

This sense of contact, development, and incompleteness are all facets of the postmodern work of New Western Photography, as we shall see, and run contrary to Adams's modernist desire for order, pattern, and meaning. His suspicion of change is typical of a profound and persistent nostalgia for some imagined, lost time embodied in the very landscapes his photographs sought to fix and preserve.

However, some contemporaries, like Laura Gilpin (1891–1979), were seeking an alternative discourse through which to visualize the West that prefigured New Western photography. Gilpin's *The Rio Grande: River*

Of Destiny (1949), for example, juxtaposes text and photographs to convey the antithesis of a static, preserved landscape devoid of humanity. With the river as subject, Gilpin rejected the boundaries of politics, opting instead for a fluid bioregion with a 'rich history', 'from its depth and from its surface', a landscape of 'great changes', a unique 'blending of peoples' all living 'side by side' (Gilpin, 1949: xi–xii). Her West contained the 'traces' of many cultures, Native American, Spanish, Anglo all written on the landscape she photographed and, taken as a whole, the book records even-handedly a developing postwar multicultural West. Even at its most epic, Gilpin's work refers to the interaction of the people and the place, in a text of cultural geography admired by J. B. Jackson (see Chapter 1) 'not merely as a photogenic natural phenomenon, but as a force that has created *a whole pattern of living* . . . something more than picturesque' (quoted in Sandweiss, 1987: 67 – my emphasis). Her work represents a changing landscape of cities, industry, oil fields, highways, dams, and modern tourism integrating with the traditional uses of the land. Gilpin ushers in the New West under the dark shadow of the atomic bomb, tested in this area with its 'towering mushroom cloud of smoke' (Gilpin, 1949: 125) just 200 miles south of the boomtown of Santa Fe. Adopting metaphors of the atomic age, Gilpin described her work as cultural, relational, and positive: 'A related atom is the building stone of nature. A lone human being is the destroyer of values; a related human being is the builder of individual and social peace' (quoted in Davidov, 1998: 140). Her work portrays historical continuity and change, tinged by romance and nostalgia, but unlike Adams's work, she is much more willing to examine human presence and relations within the West. Her paired photographs, her interest in the 'whole pattern of life' and in the interaction between people and place contrast with Adams and prefigure the cultural work of the next generation. She wrote of the 'haunting tenacity' of landscape as it revealed multiple layers of history, for 'there was no true wilderness in the Southwest, no area that had remained untouched by more than a thousand years of human settlement . . . sometimes [it] provided a nurturing landscape, sometimes a hostile one' (quoted in Sandweiss, 1987: 67, 72). Her work presents radical, gendered revisioning of history, linking her body with the land in a relational empathy providing both an alternative to Adams's epic grandeur and to the romantic, painterly work of other contemporaries. Davidov calls this Gilpin's 'intersubjective' (1998: 113) quality, sharing something of the Native American perception moving between conventional representations and striving for a 'thirdspace' where 'encounter [is] an exchange between self and other in which the voice of the other is heard' (Davidov, 1998: 139). In Gilpin's West, identity is bound up with the land seen as a complex, multidimensional space, both 'depth' and 'surface', in a manner that intimates a more postmodern sense of self as fluid and in process and prefigures the coming generation of photographers stepping out from the shadow of Ansel Adams and prepared to see the New West with new eyes.

New Topographics and the Rephotography Survey Project

Two projects in the 1970s demonstrate the changing attitudes to visualizing the West, showing dialogues taking place with both the nineteenth-century Survey tradition and the authority of Ansel Adams. The 'New Topographics' Exhibition in 1975 at the Eastman House in New York referred back to the surveys of the nineteenth century and the documentary traditions of the 1930s (Walker Evans, Dorothea Lange), but the images were unemotional, flat and appeared everyday, aspiring to 'neutrality' with a 'disembodied eye', capturing the non-heroic spaces that Ansel Adams and others avoided. Having much in common with new cultural geography (see Chapter 1), Robert Adams, a key exhibitor, developed landscape aesthetics in a postmodern context by eschewing Ansel Adams's aestheticism and his 'grand narrative' of sublimity, in favour of 'micronarratives' representing the quotidian landscapes of the New West, blending imposing vistas with the proximate realities of the changing region (see Plate 6). In *The New West* (1975), Robert Adams explained that his images were an effort 'to see the facts without blinking … the whole geography, natural and man-made, to experience a peace' and to see the 'absolutely persistent beauty' that existed through it all (Adams, 1975: xi–xii), and later went further, writing that photographers should see nature as including humanity, for if not, he warned, it would simply perpetuate myths and the 'national misunderstanding of space' (Adams, 1985: 7). The New Topographics, especially the work of Robert Adams, Lewis Baltz, and Joe Deal, defined the New West as inhabited nature, suburban growth, and interactive landscapes, and their post-1975 work continued to expand upon these concerns.

Mark Klett, influenced by the exhibition, began photographing landscape in his own work and lead the Rephotographic Survey Project (RSP) which aimed to re-photograph the nineteenth-century Survey

Plate 6 Robert Adams, *Along Interstate 25, North of Denver, 1973*. (San Francisco Museum of Modern Art. Purchased through a gift of the Judy Kay Memorial Fund.)

images so that 'each image should be challenged and not regarded as a final statement ...' as 'a continued dialectic ... to reexperience the landscape itself' (Klett et al., 1984: 3), to show the constructed nature of the original images, and to remind us 'how survey photographs, as artifacts of a moment, have come to represent (or misrepresent) a place with historical authority' (Klett, in Bruce, 1990: 80). The photographs often represent a West in which little has changed, or where the change is in unexpected ways, such as the reclaiming by nature of the mines photographed by O'Sullivan in Virginia City, Nevada. The RSP was not an environmental project aimed at recording loss or the ravages of technology, although that might be part of its effect, but a broader cultural survey providing 'the multiple points of view which will ultimately enlarge the present understanding' (Klett et al., 1984: 2). Bringing together photography, history, and natural sciences, one can see the influence of revisionist thinking *before* New Western History, drawing upon the work of cultural geographers like Jackson and Meinig and in dialogue with the dominant tradition derived from painting and photography. The RSP wanted 'an unusual dialectic about a changing landscape, a discourse that may be combined through time' without solidifying into a 'definitive statement' and portraying instead 'time in motion . . . continuous change' (ibid.: 37). Echoing Gilpin's Rio Grande project, the RSP sought 'interaction . . . an exchange and interchange, an engaging and a blending, an agreement and an affirmation' (Dingus, in Klett et al., 1984: 37) wherein the human and the natural are seen as interconnected and dialogical rather than distant and divorced. Ultimately, the RSP was 'aligned to other disciplines simultaneously involved with examining the region's past, present and future' (ibid.: 40) in the representation of a complex West both real and imagined, past and present, legend and fact, science and art, humanity and nature interwoven, unfinished and problematical.

New Western Photography

In the wake of the RSP and the New Topographics, the sacred territories of Ansel Adams and Edward Weston had been unsettled, the epic West had been questioned, its myths contested and its fixed images fragmented and re-examined. From this emerged a diverse New Western photography, acknowledging the towering presence of Adams and the nineteenth-century Survey photographers, but in dialogue with their work rather than chained to its definitions of American Western space. Mark Klett (born 1952) has termed this his 'debt and burden' (Klett, 1990), while Len Jenshel (born 1949), acknowledging nineteenth-century photographers, felt his work could 'reeducate, and reshape one's thinking and attitudes about places and things – even history.' Jenshel's images are full of 'the detritus or evidence of the human race' through which he examines how people are 'fitting in with [their] environment' and using the land in a variety of ways, including tourism and advertising ('the classic car-in-the-Southwest shot', as he terms it) (Jenshel, 1992: 5–6). However, Jenshel, like others, still acknowledges the 'grandeur', 'the romance and myth', while striving to represent the intersection of multiple Wests, incorporating the 'stage set' theatricality of the place as well as its environmental destruction and its isolate beauty. In his *Route 127 near Death Valley National Monument, California, 1990* (See Plate 7) two worlds blur together in a new mixture of debris (picnic lunch), dashboard, windshield, and the highway, sky, and landscape beyond. His use of reflection, a technique used in Klett's work too,

Plate 7 Len Jenshel, *Route 127 Near Death Valley National Monument, California, 1990.*
(San Francisco Museum of Modern Art. Gift of the artist.)

allows the inside and outside, human and natural, to be merged and connected within the image, collapsing Ansel Adams's distance into an uneasy and problematic space so the viewer is implicated in the process of making meaning and responding to a West no longer, 'out there', framed and orderly, but somehow closer, jostling for attention along with all the other elements of everyday life.

At the heart of Mark Klett's work since the RSP is the concern 'to go beyond the idea of the West as an exotic place out there' and represent instead 'a place where millions of people live' (Klett, 1992: 10). Mirroring the nineteenth century photographers, his collection *Revealing Territory* (1992) uses inscriptions on the prints, exact dating, and titles, and has the diaristic quality of their work. Like O'Sullivan, Klett's West is contradictory, full of uneasy, ironic, humorous collisions in a diverse, ever-changing landscape. Klett values the work of cultural geographers like J. B. Jackson who wrote:

> Whether we like it or not we cannot really see our country merely as a succession of views to be judged in esthetic terms. We have to see it in terms of social and human process, an unending creation in which all of us are taking part. (quoted in Jussim and Lindquist-Cock, 1985: 106)

Patricia Nelson Limerick, worked with Klett on *Revealing Territory* (1992) and a photographic study of the ghost town Rhyolite (1992). These collaborations acknowledge Klett's work as part of the revisioning of the West and further suggest a recognition from Limerick that photography was crucial to a 'creative unsettling' (1992: 107) going on on a number of fronts.

> The West . . . is not a region where Americans escaped history, not a region of inconsequential, quaint, and distant frontier adventure, and not a region permitted by Providence to escape failure. It is instead the region where we can most profitably study the interplay of ambition and outcome, the *collision between simple expectation and complex reality*, and the fallout from optimistic efforts to master both nature and human nature. (Limerick and Klett, 1992: 34 – my emphases)

In Klett's work, the West is lived ideological space. For example, in *A View of the Grand Canyon in Homage to William Bell*, 1988 (see Plate 8) the epic grandeur of the canyon is interrupted by the shadow of the photographer and his sunglasses reminding us, like the raw edges of

Plate 8 Mark Klett, *A View of the Grand Canyon in Homage to William Bell, East of Toroweap, 1988*. (Courtesy of the artist.)

the print, that this is a postmodern representation. Klett works to 'lessen the distance', rejecting monuments framed to exclude humanity, in favour of being a 'participant and not just an observer of the land' (Klett, 1992: 164). Klett, like other new photographers, acknowledged his 'debt and burden' to Ansel Adams whose West was 'best experienced in the photographs themselves' (Klett, 1990: 72), but rejected his metanarrative in favour of micronarratives – complex, contradictory, alive – not a sealed themepark or a preserved epic wilderness. This new photography creates a dialogical space of many voices, places, contests, and visions – often actively political like Misrach, but always engaged in a search for 'new wilderness values' (Klett, 1990: 88) represented in images of the New West as ambiguous, mobile, inhabited space (see Plate 9).

Plate 9 Mark Klett, *Checking the Road Map: Crossing into Arizona, Monument Valley, 1982.* (Courtesy of the artist.)

The West on Film

'The story of the Western is the story of America' (Newman, 1990: xv), representing mythic distortions, dramatic struggles over identity and national meaning, ethnicity, sexuality, and attitudes to the land itself.

Akin to some paintings and photography, the western popularized simple oppositions: civilization and savagery, East and West, individual and community, wilderness and settlement, raising differences only to contain them, bringing them together to create drama and resolving them to create closure and a sense of assuredness. The western's attention was upon epic progress, like the Turner thesis's imagery of inevitability, individual heroism, and achievement, and generally avoided more complex portrayals of contest or resistance.

As Ray has commented, although western myths form 'American culture's Imaginary', the genre may both employ 'traditional paradigms' while simultaneously presenting 'marginal, dissident moments (formal or thematic)' (Ray, 1985: 363, 361) which create more complex questions for the audience. Thus, even the most traditional western can contain within it strands and elements that offer something more than the finale's resolution and containment of problematic forces. Hence, 'Hollywood's prevailing ideology' can be challenged by 'moments of excess', that is, when a thematic or formal moment seems disproportionate or overstated within the context of the entire film (ibid.: 18–19). In the post Second World War western in particular, many of the values that had been promoted and validated in the traditional western were re-examined in the light of immediate historical experience with issues like individualism, conquest, violence, and racism readdressed. Hence *Red River* (Howard Hawks, 1948) becomes a prototype of the 'pessimistic western' where the 'effect completely contradicted its intent' (ibid.: 170–1), linking it with Anthony Mann's *The Far Country* (1955) and *The Searchers* (1956) whose traditional patterns of reconciliation and resolution are unsettled from within.

I will examine two westerns which contain some of these traits of 'excess' and, as a result, demonstrate the healthy questioning of the mythic Imaginary. Rather like the photography examined in this chapter, film can be dialogical, bringing together mixes of images and ideas that may act upon the viewer in complex, unsettling ways. Thus even mainstream Hollywood films engaged in revisionism before the New Western historians gave it academic credence, a point made in essays by Tatum and Robinson with regard to literary texts which 'address, even as they seemingly "legitimate the values and priorities of bourgeois society"' (Robinson, 1998: 186). Robinson calls this tendency 'a self-subversive reflex, to undermine what it appears so clearly to approve ... a kind of textual unconscious' (Robinson, F. G., 1993: 2).

Film, like photography, cannot be excluded from the revisionism of the New West, for rather than demonizing popular culture a fuller 'history' of the West must 'begin considering how at times in even the most retrograde popular texts critical thinking about ideals, drives, contradictions, and prospects can and does occur' (Tatum, in Robinson, 1998: 164). Thus, *Shane* (George Stevens, 1952), in one respect a formulaic western about wilderness and civilization, the isolate gunfighter redeeming the community for progress while he is left to wander, is simultaneously a film examining homosociality and the tensions across genders, between Shane, Joe, and Marian. It probes the dynamic nature of community *before* it resorts to the familiar and inevitable celebration of traditional family, community, and settlement. Texts like this create an 'ongoing cultural conversation on central, painfully vexing questions of power and authority' (Robinson, 1993: 2), a dialogue moving two ways, challenging and affirming myth, while allowing the audience to look upon significant 'cultural embarrassments' (ibid.) without fully resolving them in the text.

Two John Ford Westerns

Ford's westerns, like *The Searchers* (1956) and *The Man Who Shot Liberty Valance* (1962), are seen as archetypal in their use of myths and oppositions, but one can trace dialogical, revisionist elements in their textual inconsistencies and contradictions. In *The Searchers* Ethan Edwards (John Wayne) emerges from the landscape to intrude into the lives of his brother, his wife, and their family. Combining elements of all previous western heroes (ex-Confederate soldier, Indian fighter, outlaw and Texas Ranger) Ethan has gaps in his past since the Civil War, a bagful of gold, the desire of his brother's wife, Martha, and an abiding racism (see Slotkin, 1993). These alert us to the conflicts and contradictions in the film and the West itself. On the brutal death of the family at the hands of Chief Scar, Ethan begins his mission of revenge *and* redemption. His mission, carried out with the zeal of a Puritan martyr, is an effort to restore ideal law and order to the community's life by restoring the captive daughter Debbie intact to a 'new' family, and simultaneously displacing his own feelings of guilt about his love for Martha. The confrontation with Scar, visually framed in the film as the two men stand opposite each other almost nose to nose, represents the 'scars' in both but also the similarities between them. The 'savage' need for revenge exists in them both and as a consequence the audience finds it increasingly problematic to see Scar as 'Other,' sharing, as he does, many similarities with Ethan. As Slotkin writes, the importance of this is to announce

> the absurd illogic of the categories by which we define 'us' and 'them', and it suggests that the hidden logic of these categories is to tempt us into a cycle of victimization and revenge from which it is possible that no one will escape alive and untainted. (Slotkin 1993: 469)

Ethan and Scar are survivors who understand each other's language (in every sense), fighting for their own particular sense of community and law without compromise. Ethan's categories are simple and binary, based on race, sex, and blood kinship where miscegenation equals racial betrayal. Hence, his initial desire to kill Debbie when she has been Scar's 'wife' or the terrifying look on his face as he sees the white captives whose femininity, for Ethan, has been 'polluted'. Yet the film questions Ethan's racism and, therefore, the binaries that structure his view of the world. For example, when we see Debbie at Scar's camp not traumatized like the captives at the fort, but content and adjusted, such apparent inconsistencies raise important critical questions: 'inter-racial marriage can produce the well-balanced Martin [a mixed-blood] and apparently well-integrated Debby [*sic*]; [but for Ethan] . . . miscegenation can be imagined only as rape and its results as madness, violence and death' (Pye, in Cameron and Pye, 1996: 234). However, the film cannot sustain such visions of 'contented assimiliation' (ibid.: 235) since issues of racial mixing, whether through intermarriage or social community, were still taboo in the 1950s. Although the film has few problems with the idea of Martin (part Cherokee) marrying Laurie (Scandanavian American), it cannot linger too long on the possibility of a different mixing of the races, and the film resorts to a resolution plot that allows Debbie to be rescued and restored to the communal law and order. However, it is significant that it is Martin who kills Scar and Ethan who saves Debbie, for it 'completes the demystification of Ethan's heroism by showing that hate-madness is not the only possible basis of heroism' (Slotkin, 1993: 470). Ethan does not kill Debbie, rejecting hate in favour of tolerance and love, but the film's final shot excludes Ethan and his repressed hatred from the community he has restored coherence to and banishes him to wander back into the landscape from where he came in the film's mirroring opening sequence. Thus Ford resorts to a tradition, seen in countless westerns, of the exiled hero and the forming settlement, but in the course of the film, he has, at least, opened up contradictions and inconsistencies that continue to be important in any reconsideration of the West (and America) today. As Pye argues, 'Ford internalised the "language" of the Western and, however unconsciously, its accumulated resonances' (ibid.: 235) and that generic tradition provided a frame for *The Searchers*, within which exists 'a dialogue both in and with the "language" he inherited' (ibid.). Within this dialogue the film examines deeper, more complex themes (racism, sexuality, and miscegenation) not comfortably resolved in the narrative itself.

In *The Man That Shot Liberty Valance* released in 1962 during turbulent civil rights and anti-war protests, traditional generic forms of reconciliation provided its apparent focus. The film reconciles, through James Stewart and John Wayne, the opposing influences on the West of civilization and wilderness, the law of the gun and civil law, and competing definitions of masculinity. The film's abandoning of Monument Valley's sweeping landscapes for a noticeably claustrophobic, town-based drama signal a development of the ambiguities discussed in *The Searchers*. It is a film ruminating on loss, change, containment, and myth, where the Old West is dead, seen only in flashback, allowing Ford to juxtapose and compare the two worlds, old and new. In the opening scenes of the film, Ransom Stoddard (Stewart) returns for Tom Doniphon's (Wayne) funeral and Hallie, his wife, comments in a melancholy voice, 'The place has sure changed, churches, high schools, shops'; but there is no sense of community in Shinbone for it seems lifeless and static, a point emphasized by Ford's use of black and white. Doniphon is the Old, mythic West, strong but inarticulate, unable to settle, unaccustomed to changing times, whose individualist virtues are perverted into the villain Liberty Valance. 'Out here', he says, 'a man settles his own problems', but Stoddard reminds him, 'you're saying just exactly what Liberty Valance said'. Doniphon's efforts to adapt are symbolized by his half-built house on the edge of town where the desert cactus still grows wild. His aim is to complete the house for his future bride, Hallie, but neither will come to pass, for he is a man outside of this process of history, and like the desert cactus, destined only to be contained by the New West fast approaching. As the story unfolds around Doniphon's dead body in the funeral parlour, we are reminded of this link as the potted cactus is placed upon his coffin. Both are now displaced, contained and controlled by the conditions of Stoddard's West, the man whose opening statement in the film concerns 'mending a few political fences.'

Stoddard represents the modern West, a man who governs, knows the law, articulates his ideas with clarity but cannot use a gun or cope with the lawlessness that is his inheritance. It is Doniphon who kills Valance, but a 'legend', a version of 'history', is formed around the belief that Stoddard has united the law and the use of the gun in order to tame the town and make it safe for its future. Thus, Doniphon becomes the absent presence of the West, the lawless 'tamer' that makes it possible for Stoddard's law and democratic government to follow, but who dies anonymously. The two visions of the West embodied in Stoddard and Doniphon, which might have been resolved in other westerns with a gunfight or with the latter disappearing into the mythic landscape like Shane, are shown as 'bound in a relationship of reciprocal implication – as relative terms in the generic pattern, they can have no independent life' (Pye, in Cameron and Pye, 1996: 121). Pye is right to suggest that 'the old West and the present are incompatible: [it] . . . dies immediately the tensions on which it is centred are resolved' (ibid.), but might add that the modern West is precisely the 'relational' mix of Ranse and Tom, emphasized by the linking presence of Hallie, who is married to Stoddard but longs for Doniphon. She earlier reminds Tom, 'you don't own me' and yet in the 'present', she appears to be little more than another product of Stoddard's West, sophisticated, affluent, literate, but unhappy. The Old West exists within the New, the imagined alongside the real, but for John Ford its repression has produced a lifeless 'garden' out of the 'wilderness' rather than a healthy and purposeful vision of the future. The film is a complex, sombre mixture – 'wry, ambiguous, ironic. The hero does not win. The winner is not heroic' (Anderson, 1981: 178).

At a key moment, the film cuts between Doniphon's burning house with its overwhelming sense of a dying Old West, and the State convention where a different West is being born. What remains is only a parody of the Old West, with speeches by General Cassius Starbuckle in support of Buck Langhorne introduced by 'Home on the Range,' a rodeo rider, and lassoo tricks. The Old West has already become a kitsch simulation, an act of advertising played out for entertainment value where a sense of loss is powerful and poignant. As the film ends in the New West, Stoddard and Hallie discuss their pride in turning the wilderness into a garden, but the visual messages are far more potent as the two sit slightly apart, eyes downcast, dressed in their mourning clothes. Doniphon's funeral has not taken place, they leave before it happens, suggesting the film is about another, more significant death, the death of the Old, mythic West and the pervasive sense of loss that comes with it. As the camera focuses on Hallie we are reminded of the difference between her in the present day and her younger, vibrant self, indicating that marriage, settling down, and literacy (Ranse teaches her to read) have subtracted from her life, not added to it: 'As Hallie has become literate she has lost her voice' and with it her 'mobility, energy and agency' (Tasker, 1998: 53). 'When the legend becomes the fact, print the legend', the film tells us, but in many ways what the film is really concerned with is the relationship *between* 'fact' and 'legend', between Hallie, Tom, and Ranse, signifying the complex mix of desire, hope, and disappointment that characterizes the West.

Ford's westerns begin to interrogate many of the issues later brought to prominence and codified by New Western History, but under the cover of traditional generic forms. However, other films, both before and after these, engage in still more complex representations of the West.

Two Modern Westerns

Bad Day At Black Rock (John Sturges, 1954) predates *The Searchers* and represents a very specific postwar moment, 1945, in the Californian New West. It follows a familiar generic pattern with the intrusion into a rudimentary community by a stranger, here John McCready (Spencer Tracy), who arrives by train (like Stoddard), out of the desert (like Ethan Edwards). The film echoes other westerns using the train as a harbinger of change (*High Noon*, *Liberty Valance*, *Unforgiven*) and the outsider, McCready, the one-armed man, testing the community and exposing its bigotry and backwardness. Although a mid-twentieth century setting, this is a classic western town awaiting the arrival of the gunfighter or the town-tamer, but as the train guard says, Black Rock is 'woebegone and far away', a pure white, patriarchal space, run by Reno Smith (Robert Ryan), a mythic Western Everyman, with the aid of sidekicks reminiscent of earlier westerns. The train brings with it the twentieth-century reality of an encroaching, multicultural world and its only passenger probes the repressed past concerning the killing of a Japanese American, Kamoko, and the communal concealment of his brutal murder. The murder turns out to be another western battle over land possession, water, and power, and Kamoko its victim, having worked the harsh desert land and discovered water where others had thought none existed. Smith's vision of 'our West', as he calls it, is unchanging, where all the old rules apply:

> Someone's always looking for something in this part of the West. To the historian it's the Old West, to the book writer it's the Wild West, to the businessman it's the undeveloped West, they say we're all poor and backward and I guess we are, we don't even have enough water. But to us, this place is our West and I wish they'd leave us alone.

Smith's Cold War mentality rejects difference, clings to the static past, and retreats defensively into a nativist ideology rejecting any creative imagining of a plural New West. All strangers are seen as a threat to the town's ideological space: the Japanese-American, the one-armed outsider from the city (marked off by the dark business suit), and the woman. Like classic westerns, the film virtually excludes women, with only a brief role for one who is deceived and used by Smith before he kills her to cover up his own crimes. The film, comments not only on postwar American xenophobia, but also on the dangers of a West as closed, suspicious of otherness, and holding onto a definition of itself rooted in a Turnerian past of defiant individualism.

Bad Day At Black Rock uses as a central structuring motif the idea of the return of the repressed, of the past (the community's guilt over murdering Kamoko) haunting the present. Prefiguring New Western History, the film recalls forgotten, literally buried pasts and hidden stories, in order to present a counter-history showing the West as 'an ongoing competition for legitmacy ... [a] contest for property and profit ... for cultural domination' (Limerick, 1987: 27). McCready acts as the agent of the past and the future, forcing the community, like a psychotherapist, to revisit its actions and retell its history:

> You'd like me to die quickly ... without wasting too much of your time, or quietly, so I won't embarrass you too much ... so your memory of the occasion won't be too unpleasant ... It's gonna take an awful lot of whiskey to wash out your guts ... *why don't you tell me what happened?* (my emphasis)

McCready, part detective, part psychiatrist, part New Western historian, wants Black Rock to confront its secret history, articulate it, and accept its guilt in order to move on. The racial hatred against

Kamoko, whose son has saved McCready's life and died in Italy fighting for the Allies, diminishes the West – as Ethan Edwards's did – and the purpose of the film's cathartic structure is to bring the town into a broader vision of the New West as tolerant, liberal, multicultural, and open. It is significant that the youngest of the accomplices to the murder, Pete, does 'tell' and 'wash out [his] guts', as if to mark the possibility of purgation and a new start for Black Rock. As McCready leaves the town, its future in the balance, he hands over the medal he had brought for Kamoko to the mortician/doctor, as a 'start', since the town might die or be reborn in the light of its new acceptance of its dark past – 'some places do, others don't', he comments as he departs.

Another 'ghost', of a different sort, is the figure of Jack Burns in a second modern western released later than *Bad Day At Black Rock* and *The Searchers*, but in the same year as *The Man Who Shot Liberty Valance*, *Lonely Are the Brave* (David Miller, 1962). Burns, called a ghost by the sheriff chasing him after his prison breakout, recalls the Old West, like the return of the repressed, a contemporary Ethan Edwards, bringing back all the questions and uncertainties into the apparently settled social order of the modern West. Burns is an anachronism, riding a horse in a time of jeeps and trucks, struggling to come to terms with the fences he finds across his path and the borders that divide up his world. He is a man out of time, defining himself the 'natural man', individual, violent but bonded to the land and his friends by powerful loyalties. His 'nature' is rooted in the past, in a mythic West of hard-riding freedom, with no family, no community, brother to Shane, to Ethan Edwards, and to Eastwood's Man With No Name, finding his only solace in the wild landscape itself. Yet this mythic space is diminishing, as this early eco-western shows, with shots of highways, motel signs, truck-stops, and wrecking yards intruding into the desert. Burns's only escape is across the border into Mexico, figured as a place of ecological harmony, freedom, and lawlessness, but his route is perilous and at times has the feel of Sisyphus struggling against the existential weight of the change that he would rather ignore. A reiterative pattern of images signifying fragmentation, division, and opposition mark this sense and emerge early in the film when Burns crosses the highway and is caught in the traffic and yelled at by a sportscar driver 'What do you think you're doing?' Immediately, a split screen shot of the driver looking back at Burns, and of the horse rearing up in the middle of the road constructs a visual equation that is followed throughout the film, opposing the old and the new and emphasizing the division between them. The next sequence shows Burns riding through a junkyard of cars, and out past a Model T Ford rusting by the side of the tracks. To Burns's eyes this is regressive, chaotic, and unnatural, but the film emphasizes that he is incongruous, barely coping with change. His friend's wife Gerry says at one point, 'if you keep that up you're going to end up on a Dude Ranch', underscoring Burns's role as simulacrum, an image of an Old West that she says 'probably never existed'. Burns defines his West as the love of 'open country' and the hatred of fences, where 'the more fences there are the more he hates them ... they've got those fences that say this side's jail and that side is the street, here is Arizona, that's Nevada, this is us that's Mexico ...' His utopian vision of a world without borders is not an unfamiliar one, but it is not practical in a complex world of political identities and boundaries of power and influence. It is Gerry that reminds Burns of the changing social conditions: 'Out there is the real world, and it's got real borders and real fences and real laws and trouble and either you go by the rules or you lose, you lose everything ... I don't understand men anymore'. Gerry identifies the ideology of the Old West as masculine and mythic needing to be tempered by her experience of the real world of coping. It is men, for Gerry, that have perpetuted the utopianisn that will eventually kill them because it fails to include responsibility to others, to family, and to community. Gerry articulates a feminist cultural politics emerging in the 1960s that revalues women's roles and recognizes their differing perceptions of community in the West. It is Gerry's vision that Paul will ultimately endorse when he opts to stay in prison rather than join Burns on the run. Burns, however, will die bemused on the highway in the pouring rain and darkness, cradled in the arms of the truck driver. As he dies, he looks up at the crowd watching him and the shot has powerful significance: on one hand it represents Burns as spectacle (as Gerry's 'dude'), the object of fascination for the modern westerners, and secondly, it shows Burns's point of view, looking up with bewilderment at them, unable to comprehend his own situation and the destruction of his vision of the West. Again and again, he looks but cannot grasp or understand what he sees. Off camera, his horse is shot and the pain of recognition is echoed in his own dying eyes. Like Edward Abbey's novel upon which the film is based (see Chapter 1), there is a strong sense of ambiguity about the kind of West we are being shown and about the 'hero' Jack Burns. The friend he goes to jail to free, Paul, a writer imprisoned for helping 'wetbacks' across the border, prefers to remain there knowing that freedom in the New West is more than the open road and the endless horizon, more than the mythic individualism of the 'brave (but futile) cowboy', but is connected to his wife Gerry's vision. The filmic dialogues of *Lonely Are the Brave* are deliberately ambiguous, tinged with sadness at Burns's death and its inevitability within the context of the New West as a modern, techno-logical space, while representing Burns as a fading Marlboro Man, clinging onto a dream of a time that never really existed. Paul (the writer-activist) and his family of Gerry (the painter), son Seth, and their home on the edge of the desert, present an alternative West to the mobile individualism of Burns, perhaps a necessary vision of a more politicized, communal West able to build a different world in which 'lighting out for the Territory' and ignoring borders is no longer an option.

Out of the 1970s

Many westerns adopted more overt alternative or counter-cultural positions where a number of the themes we have discussed emerged as central concerns of the films rather than exisiting within the dialo-gical texture of the film: *The Wild Bunch* (1969), *Butch Cassidy and the Sundance Kid* (1969), *Soldier Blue* and *Little Big Man* (1970), *The Last Picture Show* (1971), *Pat Garrett and Billy the Kid* (1973), *Rancho Deluxe* (1974), *Heartland* (1979). Issues of race and gender alongside further considerations of myth often produced films which 'either repeated some version of the myth or claimed to reveal at last the "true" history that lay behind the myth, a "reality" that, more often than not, turned out to be another mythical invention' (Cawelti, 1996: 9). Cawelti called for a less fixed response to the West to 'show both the power of myth and its dangers, revealing not just the ambiguity ... but the way in which myth and history are engaged in a problematical dialectic' (ibid.). A spur for this step came at the end of the 1970s with an important watershed.

In 1979 John Wayne died and the following year Ronald Reagan was elected President, bringing with him the Hollywood persona of the cowboy hero and the honest, hard-working westerner into the heart of American politics. Reagan filled the White House with the western art of Moran, Catlin, Remington, and Hill, and was often pictured in western clothing at his ranch in California, trading on these mythic images as magic touchstones for his Presidential quest of returning America to past glories and the core values he imagined rooted in the frontier. Revisionism appeared to have had no impact upon Reagan, whose 'Morning in America' advertising campaign endorsed small town, church-going, family-centred values, like the town-builders of *My Darling Clementine* or the dreams of Ransom Stoddard. Reagan's imagined 'West-as-America' was a retrieval of myths defined by end-less reworkings of heroic westerns where simplistic battles were won and stereotyped enemies overcome in the name of right and justice. As Slotkin (1993) argues, Reagan's political agenda and his 'supply-side' economic policy was reminiscent of Turner's frontier thesis, based on a belief in 'bonanza' profits derived from new capital that would 'trickle down' to the rest of the community as long as government enabled the flow of money and intervened as little as possible in the process. As Garry Wills writes:

Supply side was cowboy economics – you get your free lunch by roping and throwing meat on the hoof, lassooing it with the Laffer curve. Any cowboy can do that on his own, so long as he is not obstructed by timid city folk in green eyeshades. (Wills, 1988: 364)

Reagan's desire was for a mythical frontier world of order, hierarchy, and industrious responsibility, and in 1982, welcoming home the space shuttle, spoke of 'the conquest of new frontiers for the betterment of our homes and families' as 'a crucial part of our national character'. By the time of his second inaugural address he was even more effusive:

The men of the Alamo call out encouragement to each other; a settler pushes west and sings his song, and the song echoes out forever and fills the unknowing air. It is the American sound. It is hopeful, bighearted, idealistic – daring, decent and fair. That's our heritage, that's our song. We sing it still. For all our problems, we are together as of old. (quoted in Grossman, 1994: 83)

While Reagan was elected on this appeal to such 'eternal' American traits, a new epic western film was released that took a very different approach to the interpretation of the westward movement. *Heaven's Gate* (Michael Cimino, 1980), however, failed to recoup the money invested in it, eventually putting its studio, United Artists, out of business. The film has been roundly criticized as flawed, incoherent, and lacking in points of identification between narrative and audience, yet I would suggest that *Heaven's Gate* revises American history and ideology, the western genre, and reflects upon dominant, contemporary American values by challenging assumptions about all three at the very time Reagan was reinvesting in their eternal value.

Many of the instabilities and contradictions about race, gender, class, the acquisition of land, and how history was recorded that earlier westerns had touched upon, resolved, or pushed to the margins of the film, are central to *Heaven's Gate*. Traditional genre expectations about taming the land, individual heroism, establishing community, and developing a national character are all displaced in *Heaven's Gate* into a non-linear, symbolic film that rethinks issues that have become inscribed in the American mythic consciousness. It begins in 1870, not in the West but in privileged Harvard, immediately unsettling the audience's genre memory with images closer to the Old World (the scenes were filmed at Oxford University) than the rugged archetypes of the frontier. In this world of dreaming spires, tradition, and order, the Reverend Doctor (Joseph Cotten) speaks of 'high ideals' and the 'education of the nation' as the 'mandate of imperative duty' for these rich, privileged, white, male Americans setting out beyond the university's ivy-clad walls. With the crusading idealism of Manifest Destiny, he speaks of 'the contact of the cultivated mind with the uncultivated', of civilization with the wilderness, but in his reply William C. Irvine (John Hurt) offers arrogance and complacency: 'we must speak according to our ability', maintaining the rules of social 'gravity' and 'disclaim all intention of making a change in what we esteem on the whole well arranged'. In the scenes that follow, this 'well arranged' world is defined by masculinist, mock-violent territorial games around the Harvard yard tree; objectified, passive, onlooking women; and competitive nationalism (the 'Battle Hymn of the Republic' is audible throughout), connected to strong, ruthless individual action. Cimino's ideological web of meanings about character, nation, class, and gender provide an introduction to the events of the film and become focused around the winner of the territorial game at Harvard – James Averill (Kris Kristofferson) who is next seen arriving in Casper, Wyoming in 1890. This is not a typical western town from Hollywood films, but a semi-industrialized, crowded, chaotic place with a different kind of 'contact' than that spoken of twenty years before by the Reverend Doctor. Here, the 'uncultivated' are immigrants in a West still forming through contacts, migrations, and exchanges along train lines and roads (a constant motif in the film), and signified by the hubbub of voices and noise. Averill's looks of confusion and dismay register the audience's own surprise at this scene and are foregrounded by two statements: Averill's 'Maybe I'm overdue for a new life myself' and an immigrant woman whose husband has just been beaten: 'You are all evil here. You call this a free country?' Of course, it is not 'free' in any sense of the word for her, for everything has a price in the economics of this frontier, including, as we quickly discover, the lives of the immigrants who are defined as 'thieves and anarchists' and placed on a 'black list' by the wealthy Stockgrowers Association. Averill, who has the means to maintain the possibility of a 'new life', asks 'What's going on here?' of the station master, and repeats it again in a later scene with Irvine, as if to reinforce his growing sense of unease at the West he has come to. In a later scene Averill says, 'In principle, everything can be done', but opportunity is only for the rich and powerful class from which he comes bolstered by greed, violence, class war, and genocide.

Cimino's ambiguous text rejects conventions of classical Hollywood in favour of 'big impressionist blocks' that work rhythmically, requiring the audience to 'participate imaginatively in its construction, to use our own judgment in making connections back and forth' (Wood, 1986: 303). Each block in the film 'constitutes a separate and forceful "history lesson": about privilege ... poverty ... compromise, about being unprepared, about power, about community, ... collective action ... betrayal ... about the destruction of a possible alternative America by the one that is so much with us' (ibid.). Individual characters are less important than the collective in the film, but when they do emerge, they are contradictory and problematic, like Nate Champion (Christopher Walken), a hired killer of the immigrants: 'You look like one of us', says an immigrant; 'I'll decide what I am', replies Champion, believing he is in control of his identity and his life. Unlike Averill, he is not of the privileged class and so must rely on his skill and 'labour' to survive in the West making him closer to the fate of those he is hired to kill. He is Averill's 'class double', sharing the same lover, Ella (Isabelle Huppert), trying on Averill's hat in the mirror, looking enviously at Averill's Harvard photograph, and papering his humble cabin in newsprint because he believes 'it civilizes the wilderness'. Ultimately, Nate has to die once his 'labour' is no longer of use to Canton, and likewise his dream of agency in the West is swept aside like the immigrants themselves. This is not a land of promise or opportunity, but of brutality and class power where change is signified as an inevitable process of accumulation and destruction.

However, Cimino does also convey a possible alternative American community in the roller-skating scene where men, women, and children join in a joyous mixing, at turns haphazard and unstable, but always energized and democratic. It contrasts with the Harvard scene's formal, ordered dancing and hierarchical rules. However, filmed in sepia tones, it is problematic for the audience, presenting Ella as part of the community (as a prostitute she is an outsider), as if Cimino's enclosed, utopian moment encapsulates Ella's dream of a perfect community: diverse, tolerant of difference, where all can succeed. As the scene ends Ella stands in an empty hall reflecting on the impossibility of the moment, as if it has already passed and is now captured only in her imagined West, like the tones of old, faded photographs. Community is a vision in many films of the West – such as Ford's *My Darling Clementine* (1946) and *The Searchers* – and yet is undone here my the dreaminess and by the horrors of the world beyond the hall (called Heaven's Gate) where Ella, Nate, and the immigrants will all die.

Cimino's film offers no reconciliatory pattern healing oppositions that structure so many westerns, and even the ambiguities exposed in westerns like *The Searchers* or *Shane* are nothing compared to Cimino's insistence upon challenging his audience right to the very end of the film. The lack of resolution is the point. As the film's violent climax ends with a sense of surreal futility, only Averill can survive, not as a lonely gunfighter who has at least saved the community before he returns to his mythic life, but as a wealthy Easterner whose life is to be played out in a series of meaningless social rituals cushioned always by inordinate wealth and security. The final images of the film's epilogue are of Averill, silent, restless, and becalmed with a passive woman on a luxurious boat at Rhode Island. One is left with no single, clear story at all, but contesting stories, like the many voices that echo through the soundtrack of the film reflected in the perplexing rearrangements of Hollywood conventions. Ella Watson cannot be neatly slotted into the stereotyped whore of many westerns, for she is a fusion of opposites: economically independent, longing for marriage but with two lovers, earth mother and prostitute, French with a British name, and so on. She indicates Cimino's incipient but tragic vision of the real possibility of the West as a space of inclusion:

A possible alternative America [echoing the radicalism of the 1960s and 1970s] destroyed before it could properly exist . . . a democracy in which Otherness is accepted and valued, in which women become the equals of men, in which sexual arrangements have at least the potential to become nonpossessive and noncoercive, and in which the family is subordinated to the collective community. (Wood, 1986: 314, 316)

Heaven's Gate questions class and gender roles, problematizes the primacy of individual action, and reinvents the genre by involving the audience in issues of meaning and politics. Few film-makers have taken up this challenge, but rethinking and revision are evident in the developments in other arenas of Western critical studies, such as history, literature, and photography. The Reagan era had begun in the same year that this radical and extraordinary film attempted to challenge so many of the values that would form its heart. It would be for others to take up and expand on Cimino's bold beginning.

Two Post-Cimino Westerns: *Unforgiven* and *The Ballad of Little Jo*

Clint Eastwood's *Unforgiven* (1992) was hailed as a revisionist western questioning gender roles, race, violence, and the 'legend-making' elements associated with the West. Here, the West is a place of struggle over power, authority, and meaning, locked into a dynamic climate of change and tension, and in this respect it does add to the genre in some interesting ways. At the heart of the film is a familiar idea about settlement and order, with the town of Big Whiskey attempting to prove its own rudimentary civilization through the power of its sheriff Little Bill (Gene Hackman) curbing violence, licensing prostitution and, like Doniphon in *The Man Who Shot Liberty Valance*, trying to build himself a house. The incomplete and unstable nature of the house symbolizes his fragile grip on the town and on his own violent instincts. The balancing point gives rise to the tensions that the film explores. The railroad signifies change, the possibility of difference and otherness because beyond the town is the diverse, modern West already seen in *Heaven's Gate* and both threaten Little Bill's white, male dictatorship.

Like Little Bill, William Munny (Clint Eastwood) is a man in tension, wrestling with settlement, farming and domesticity but clearly failing. The film breaks genre expectations placing the old, masculinist West under question with Little Bill struggling to repress his violent self and authorize a system of order in the town and Munny unable to maintain domestic order, preferring the simpler life of a 'killer'. Munny escapes his children and the surveillance of his dead wife, whose moral code is a source of his repression and failure, for one last masculine adventure. Both men exist in worlds without women and can only truly express themselves through violent assertion, achieving power over others as a substitute for relationships and sexuality. As Tompkins writes, the Western is 'about men's fear of losing their mastery, and hence their identity' (Tompkins, 1992: 45) to the encroachments of a modernizing world outside, which includes domesticity, technology, and the gathering forces of otherness.

Whereas *Heaven's Gate* had placed Ella at the heart of the action, an independent business woman (though still a prostitute), and shown immigrant women as active, engaged working people, *Unforgiven* is still limited in its representations of women. The film has a significant dead woman, Munny's wife, a Native American wife to Ned (Morgan Freeman), and the prostitutes who give motivation to Munny's return to killing. After the initial violence Strawberry Alice says 'Just because we let them smelly fools ride us like horses don't mean we gotta let 'em brand us like horses', stating their resistance to subordination, while acknowledging the reality of their economic situation. In this respect the film is fairly traditional, where 'Westerns either push women out of the picture completely or assign them roles in which they exist only to serve the needs of men' making 'women ... the motive for male activity' (Tompkins, 1992: 39–40, 41). Tasker comments that women in westerns have a peculiar position of 'marginal centrality' (1998: 51), functioning as defining oppositions to men and yet having a vital role in the constructions of narrative. This is precisely Tompkins's point when she argues that 'women's discourse, or some sign of it, is a necessary and enabling condition of most Western novels and films', and yet within these narratives, women's 'lives are devalued ... [with] no attention to women's experience' (Tompkins, 1992: 41–2).

One film that attempted to examine women in the West from a different perspective was *The Ballad of Little Jo* (Maggie Greenwald, 1993), released in the wake of *Unforgiven* as a 'realistic' portrayal based on a 'true life' of a woman who pretended to be a man to survive on the frontier. It's part of a group of films that sought to revise the West through the eyes of women such as *Thelma and Louise* (1991), *Bad Girls* (1995), and *The Quick and the Dead* (1995). In *The Ballad of Little Jo*, directed by a woman, unlike the other films, Greenwald explores the double standards of 'marginal centrality' in the West where women are required as mothers, sexual partners, medics, and housekeepers, and yet can have no role beyond these boundaries. Dressed as a man, Josephine Monaghan (Suzy Amis) becomes 'Little Jo', in order to escape the sexual violence and prejudice of patriarchy, and is permitted access to the world of men, as shepherd, farmer, and voter in the incipient town of Ruby City. Jo and her Chinese lover 'Tinman' Wong (David Chung), both outsiders in the patriarchal, racist culture of the West, are connected in a scene after they make love for the first time by examining each other's scars, the visible marks of their otherness written on their very bodies. In the enclosed, pastoral world of Jo's homestead, they enjoy an equalitarian utopia where race and gender do not matter and where Tinman can move comfortably between the roles of lover and cook without fear of social prejudice because all social surveillance is far away. The threat of 'civilization's' values and judgements are, however, ever-present in the film and it is clear that they can only remain in this utopia because they are outside history – like the roller-skating scene in *Heaven's Gate*. Greenwald's fleeting utopian moment rejects old binaries, man/woman, occidental/oriental, master/servant, to embrace the cultural politics of difference where new identities and relations are formed and contested. Towards the end of the film, Jo, about to sell out to the Cattle Company, looks out through the window at the owner's wife fresh from the East, seeing a vision of a world she can no longer be a part of nor wishes to be. Her choice is to reject it, remain with her lover in the West and to 'live as we are' for 'many years' in the utopia she has created. Tinman says at this point, 'I want peace for the last years of my life. You found it living as a man. I found it living with you', confirming the film's utopianism and the recognition that there is 'peace' in Jo's existence. Jo's agency, her choices, and her power to construct a world where she can live if only as a cross-dressed 'free white man' is a border territory, between genders, classes, and races, between silence and expression (she disguises her voice, hides her emotions throughout the film), occupying her own utopian space on the edge of the town and across the river (the film refers to these geographies constantly). Although far from ideal, Jo's life focuses on issues relevant to the contemporary West, especially the need for 'peace' and tolerance in the spaces between conventional lines defining identity. Unlike Adobe Flats, where Kamoko is murdered in *Bad Day at Black Rock*, Little Jo's space is an unsettled refuge for ethnic and gender harmony, an uncertain and tentative vision of New West community reflecting upon the contemporary problems of racial disharmony and tension in the USA of the 1980s as much as it does of the 1890s.

A Postmodern Western: *Lone Star*

Lone Star (John Sayles, 1996) takes up the challenge of *Heaven's Gate* while fully aware of the tradition of the classic Western out of which it comes. Sayles's first experience of films were 'westerns with John Wayne' (Asinof, 1999: 1) and *Lone Star* refers to a number of classic westerns. For example, the film is based upon the idea of a 'legend', Buddy Deeds, being investigated and unravelled – a direct reference to *The Man Who Shot Liberty Valance* (1962). *Lone Star* also refers ironically to the events of the Alamo as a mythic-historic marker of Texas-Mexico political and social relations, requiring its viewers to 'remember the Alamo' in new ways. However, one cannot help but remember John Wayne's film *The Alamo* (1960) as an example of how the West has been constructed by imagined myth where the white Texans achieve sacrificial victory over the duplicitous and cowardly Mexicans. In his 'manifesto' for the film, Wayne wrote it was about 'a pattern of freedom and liberty ... the priceless legacy they left us' (quoted in Frayling, 1981: 220) and compared his views to those of Davy Crockett, played by Wayne, delivering a speech full of the rhetoric of the traditional West:

> When I came down to Texas, I was looking for something, I didn't know what ... It's like I was empty. Well, I'm not empty any more ... I feel useful in this old world – to hit a lick for what's wrong, or to say a word for what's right, even though you get walloped for saying that word. (quoted in Wills, 1997: 206)

Crockett is 'right' only in a world divided into binary oppositions of good/bad, right/wrong, empty/full, and white/brown, where to be 'American' meant rejecting any possibility of the intermixing of the races like Wayne's character Ethan Edwards in *The Searchers*. Sayles revisits these tensions and deconstructs them to represent a West where myths are complicated by the negotiations and relations of a new history not defined as a grand narrative about heroic events and last stands, but about the interconnected lives of a multicultural border community, Frontera, and their tentative movements into the future.

Lone Star is structured around the discovery of the buried corpse of sheriff Charlie Wade (Kris Kristofferson) and the investigation led by the current sheriff, Sam Deeds (Chris Cooper), whose father had become the sheriff after the 'disappearance' of Wade. The investigation delves into a whole, secret history of the border southwest in which the film is set. The community of 'Frontera' (frontier) is 'a pretty lively mix' of ethnic groups trying to live together on the border and coming to terms with 'a good number of disagreements over the years'. Rather like the wider West, Sayles's film argues, dominant stories have emerged that now have to be contested and reconsidered. The older, white, male generation resent change and display a racist dislike of the erosion of white dominance on the border: 'They call everything else in the country after Martin Luther King and we can't have one measely courthouse [named after Buddy Deeds] . . . it's bad enough that all the street names are in Spanish'. When Sam reminds them that 'they were here first', he replies 'well then let's call it after Big Chief Shit-in-the-Bucket' as they were there even before the Mexicans. This is the complex history of the West's cultural landscape:

> A lot of what this movie is about is history and what we do with it. Do we use it to hit each other? Is it something that drags us down? Is it something that makes us feel good? You can have six different people look at the Alamo and they have six different stories about what actually happened and what its significance was. The same goes for your personal history. At what point do you say about your parents that was them, this is me amd I take responsibility for myself from this day on. That's also what this movie is about. (Sayles, 1996: 1)

In a central scene in the film, a staff/parents meeting discusses how history is taught in the school and it brings into sharp focus Sayles's point about 'versions' of stories. One white woman accuses Pilar (Elizabeth Pena) of breaking away from the official, 'textbook' history: 'the way she's teaching it she's got everything switched around . . . her version is not . . . what we set as the standard', and a white man adds that 'the men that founded this State have the right to tell the story the way it happened, not the way you wanted it to happen'. As Mexican voices attempt to put their views across as 'historical perspective', a further voice shouts 'you call it history, I call it propaganda and they might have their own story of the Alamo on the other side but we're not on the other side'. Pilar's defence of her teaching is central to the position of the film itself: 'I've only been trying to get across part of the complexity of our situation down here, cultures coming together in both negative and positive ways'. But this is a community where such 'complexity' is seen by many as a rejection of fundamental, national myths about Manifest Destiny and about the loss of power and status. Pilar's revisionism indicates Sayles's representation of women as having significant roles in the community, shaping opinion and involved in business and decision-making. Her mother, Mercedes, is a successful, independent business woman despite having entered the USA illegally, who is later seen aiding border-crossers to make a new start in America.

In the film's main plot, Sam Deeds is engaged in a revision of his own father – something of a local hero – whose life has been 'worked up into a whole big thing' but could be 'built on a crime' (Wade's murder). Self-consciously echoing *The Man Who Shot Liberty Valance* we are told that Buddy Deeds 'had the finest sense of justice of any man I ever knew' and that he was a 'goddamned legend'. However, rather than 'print' that legend, Sayles's film investigates it to reveal the web of relations that constitute the secret history of the Deeds family and the border community of Frontera. From a Mexican perspective, one man tells Sam, 'a bird flying South, you think he sees this line? You think half way across that line they're thinking different? Why should a man?', while an Anglo bar tender tells Sam his theory of civilization:

> We are in a state of crisis, the lines of demarcation are getting fuzzier and to run a successful civilization, you have got to have your lines of demarcation between right and wrong, between this-un and that-un, your Daddy understood that ... people don't want their salt and sugar in the same jar ... your the last white sheriff this town's gonna see ... this is it right here Sam, this bar is the last stand, se abla American goddammit.

The irony of this monologue is revealed ultimately when Sam discovers his father has had a relationship with Mercedes Cruz, and conceived a child, Pilar, with whom Sam now has a relationship. The fuzzy lines of the border run right through Sam and Pilar's own life to the point that their incest becomes a metaphor for the mixing taking place throughout the region. However, Sayles's metaphor is a productive revision of the oldest taboo of miscegenation across races, and suggests a new hybrid American identity, a mixing of bloods, not in war, violence, and 'disagreement', but in hope and renewed possibility.

In the final scene of the film, played out in an adandoned drive-in cinema, the site of their first love, Pilar and Sam look up at the blank screen and she asks, 'When does the movie begin?' Of course, Sayles's 'movie' is a revision of the old myths projected endlessly onto this screen in the past, and Pilar, who finds out about their incest in this scene, calls for a clean break, a new beginning: 'all that other stuff, all that history, to Hell with it, right? Forget the Alamo.' The film seeks both a rejection of cinematic stereotypes and mythologies, and offers a positive vision of a 'mixedblood' (Owens, 1998), hybrid, relational New West where legends can live alongside the realities and the dreams of the present day.

Conclusion

In Sayles's new history, having to know about the past is vital but only as a way forward rather than as something to dwell upon, and as part of a multifaceted spatial appreciation of living in the West with its many stories and many peoples. In this respect, Sayles's film is hybrid in the sense defined by Homi Bhabha:

> Hybridity to me is the 'third space' which enables other positions to emerge. This third space displaces the histories that constitute it, and sets up new structures of authority, new political initiatives, which are inadequately understood through received wisdom ... The process of cultural hybridity gives rise to something different, something new and unrecognisable, a new area of negotiation of meaning and representation. (in Rutherford, 1990: 211)

In the postcolonial environment of the border, Sayles ends with a sense of optimistic newness, of Sam and Pilar as hybrids on 'the cutting edge of translation and negotiation, the *in-between space*' (Bhabha, 1994: 39) about to begin a life in the New West by displacing the old histories and prejudices and commencing 'something different, something new'. This act of displacement based on a recognition of myth and a creative rethinking of the future can be seen in much of the visual works discussed in this chapter. They revise and re-represent the West, critique and celebrate its multiple identities, and refuse to become locked into a single, monological position. In many cases predating New Western History, they have consistently engaged in dialogical relationships with the traditions of the past, with mythic visions, tourist development, romantic fixings of place, popular culture, and the day-to-day experience of living in the changing environments of the West. This is a diverse body of work that acknowledges the influence of John Ford and Ansel Adams, of the Marlboro Man and the Lone Ranger, of Ralph Lauren's fashioned West and the awe-inspiring vistas of the Grand Canyon, of developing urbanism and the continued existence of isolate places in the West. It is in the dialogical mix and in the tensions that these texts capture that the New West is articulated as conflictive, interactive, heteroglossic space and, therefore, part of a more complex version of history than that projected in Ansel Adams or Frederick Jackson Turner.

CHAPTER 3

Alternative Histories/Other Wests

As earlier chapters have shown, the New West – as real and imagined space – speaks through many voices, constructing multilayered, multi-accented cultural texts existing simultaneously in the complex region it names. William Deverall has expressed a similar thought about the West freed from the dominant, single metanarrative and now concerned with

> a bundle of visions ... [a] collection of new stories (exactly that rendering of West into Wests) ... the histories of people, living and dead, the raw stuff of social and political history. Too many of these men, women, and children remain historically mute and invisible ... The West is conceptually massive ... at once place and many places, process and many processes ... When gathered as a collection of Wests, the loose package of western landscape, ideas, and people becomes all the more meaningful, all the more significant. (in Milner, 1996: 32, 34)

American Western history should not be seen as monumental nor epic, nor static and fixated on some sense of a lost unity and pristine past, but mobile and relational. As Eagleton writes, 'tradition *is* [or should be] the practice of ceaselessly excavating, safeguarding, violating, discarding and reinscribing the past. There is no tradition other than this, no set of ideal landmarks that then suffer modification' (Eagleton, 1992: 59). However, as we have seen, the representation of the West has often rejected difference in its search for authority and power and inscribed a narrow version of history. Postcolonial and postmodern critique has, however, reinscribed the 'speech of the other' to intervene into linear historicism and allow the subaltern's different histories not to be subsumed into some master-narrative, but to become a significant part of a new history. In the American West, the 'speech of the other' has become increasingly important as a source of revision, presenting perspectives which rupture the smooth flows of metanarratival history, that is history from the centre, told in the language of the dominant power.

Foucault's notion of 'new history' (see Introduction) influenced postcolonial thought by seeing spaces as sites of relations and networks of meaning providing complex histories to be analyzed and excavated. Foucault offers another way of looking at space as heterogeneous, multiple, and textured, telling many histories, whereas conventional historicism prefers to substitute system, order, fixity, and pattern to establish a closure, a totalizing 'story' of cause and effect, reason and purpose. Turner's totalizing narrative of frontier in the West, is once again an example of this approach. The 'postcolonial' nature of New Western representation traces Foucault's 'effective history' or 'genealogy,' disturbing what was previously considered static and natural and fragmenting what was presented as unified and logical, like the mythic, epic West of Turner proceeding as glaciation. Opposed to the formality and the enclosure of 'monumental history', Foucault's genealogy asserted 'subjugated knowledges' (Foucault, 1980: 81), voices from below, against the 'centralising powers' (ibid.) defining 'knowledge' by a process of exclusion and privilege. The emergence of these kinds of voices has been a significant feature of the representation of the New West.

The legacy of conquest 'shapes the present' West, according to Limerick, 'never fully escaping its consequences' (1987: 18, 26), for everywhere are the traces of enforced settlement, land possession, and ethnic conflict. With the acquisition of Southwestern lands at the Treaty of Guadelupe-Hidalgo (1848) and the Indian wars culminating at Wounded Knee in 1890, America defined itself through white hegemony in the West and in so doing installed its version of history as the norm. Many peoples, red, bronze, black, yellow, and white, have been caught up in the consequences – some have gained and many have lost out to the processes of empire, but often their stories have simply been erased from mainstream history, submerged in a torrent of nation-building rhetoric and righteous claims for 'necessary' assimilation. Rudolfo Anaya quotes the proverb, 'until lions have their own historians, histories of the hunt will glorify the hunter', and argues, 'we must be the lions' (Anaya, 1995: 433). Anaya's 'lions' are non-whites engaged in the counter-hegemonic retrieval and production of previously hidden stories, and those whites, influenced by this process, whose own stories reassess their involvement in the creation of the modern West. These practices represent a genealogy of the sort set out above, a means of excavating the West, understanding the multiple constructions out of which it has been formed and seeking to imagine a future outside the frames established by restrictive mythic definitions. This chapter will examine how Native Americans, Chicano/as, and Anglos have contributed to this genealogy of the New West through their explorations of cultural difference and fusion. It is precisely in this dynamic and ambiguous process that we can locate the New West.

In 1936 radical writer Haniel Long, living in New Mexico, made a free translation of the story of Cabeza De Vaca, a Spanish nobleman shipwrecked on the coast of America whose wanderings took him across the South and into the West where he lived among the Indians for eight years. In 1994 Chicano critic Juan Bruce-Novoa claimed Cabeza De Vaca as the 'mestizo voice speaking for the first time' as a 'hybrid New World Man' (in Lauter, 1994: 129). These intersecting readings of the original story of 1542 by Anglo and Chicano writers are representative of the emerging climate of cultural interchange in the New West, from the inter-war years of Long's work to the postmodern ethnocriticism of Novoa's. The focus is De Vaca's 'alterability' (Bruce-Novoa, in Herrera-Sobek, 1993: 16) as he modified his European identity in contact with the landscape and peoples of the New World. His 'migration,' symbolic of 'neither native or foreigner, but a mixture of the two' (ibid.: 17), defined an 'American reality [as] essentially a shifting, changing one' (ibid.: 19). For Long, De Vaca stood for a rediscovery of humanity through interrelations with others – 'we were more than we had thought we were'; through empathy – 'I saw my grandfather through the eyes of his slaves'; and through 'encounter' – 'the steady currents of adaptation and sympathy' (ibid.: 33, 35, 42). In the key chapter of the original text, De Vaca wrote of an encounter between 'we,' the 'Christians' (Europeans), and the 'Indians' as if he saw himself as a new group existing within both the others but acting as the translator/intermediary and hence crossing the border between the traditional poles. De Vaca embodies the West as a space of hybrid encounter, becoming a border-crosser capable of seeing both sides and moving between them in the construction of a new identity. These 'alterabilities' are relevant to continuing issues of identity in the New West where borders, real and metaphorical, structure and determine lives, but also present possibilities for the kind of new subjectivity prefigured in Long and Bruce-Novoa's examination of De Vaca. Remember, Pratt defines a 'contact zone' as a 'space of colonial encounters' in which 'subjects are constituted in and by their relations to each other ... in terms of co-presence, interaction, interlocking understandings and practices' (Pratt, 1995: 6–7). Acknowledging the issues of power and oppression, Pratt argues for 'mutual appropriation' between groups on contact, like De Vaca with the Indians and Christians, and the degrees of 'reciprocity' created in the two-way process (ibid.: 80). This type of contact has been specifically defined by Kolodny in her call for a new thinking about the West rejecting the Turnerian linear frontier in favour of seeing the region as a contact zone of interpenetration (see Introduction). In this spirit, the West has been a continual space for such dynamic, often problematic and violent, negotiations, appropriations, and encounters between different groups. By the late twentieth century De Vaca's symbolic contact can be read as symptomatic of the cultural dynamics of the region of the New West – unstable, fragmentary, and yet capable of reinvention and reformulation as hybrid space.

In a postmodern West where the one-dimensional notion of the frontier has been replaced by a more complex sense of multiple borders, multiculturalism, and diversity, the idea of hybridity has a particular contemporary resonance. Just as Bruce-Novoa saw De Vaca as 'silence in search of a name' (Bruce-Novoa, in Herrera-Sobek, 1993: 17) aligned with the struggle of Chicanos to express their history alongside the established version of the West, one can examine the New West as a series of such struggles over meaning, identity, and power. As Gloria Anzaldúa has written, 'Dominant paradigms, predefined concepts that exist as unquestionable, unchallengable, are transmitted to us through the culture' and, therefore, there needs to be a resistance to such traditions and a productive alternative put in place (Anzaldúa, 1987: 16). Once the grip of the official, normalized, white, patriarchal metanarrative is loosened by attacks from all sides, alternative voices can be heard, new stories and histories enter into a more sophisticated, if unstable, dialogue redefining the West as 'New'.

Such interventions in the 'colonial,' nation-building grand narrative of Manifest Destiny and the frontier thesis can, however, be linked to a wider argument over colonialism and diasporic cultures emerging in the postwar era. Postcolonial critic Frantz Fanon, for example, wrote in 1961 that the dominant culture 'turns to the past ... and distorts, disfigures and destroys it ... devaluing pre-colonial history' (Fanon, 1980: 169) reducing 'native' culture to barbarism and irrelevance. Fanon, like many other postcolonial critics, felt 'the past [should be] given back its value' (ibid.: 170) through the writings of new 'native

intellectuals' engaged in reconstructing a previously erased history. The
civil rights movement in America developed these ideas as a direct
assault on the assumptions and exclusions that had formed a particular
history of the nation, and sought to assert alternative histories and
voices, or genealogies, to counter such long-held and unquestioned
views. Native Americans and Chicano/as formed nationalist movements in the 1960s – the American Indian Movement and the Chicano
Youth Liberation Conference – aimed at raising these issues and
asserting their histories and traditions. Rudolfo Anaya, a leading figure
in the Chicano renaissance, wrote that 'the ceremony of naming, or self-
definition ... restores pride and infuses renewed energy' and was the
task of the artist (Anaya, 1995: 369). For him, this meant the revival of
history, myth, and spiritualism linked to 'Native America' as a 'collective history ... the umbilical cord that led to Indian Mesoamerica'
(ibid.: 374) predating the white conquests of the West. The Aztlán
movement claimed a mythical, symbolic homeland for the Chicanos
that refused to accept the imposition of the border and saw a more
continous history and a 'new consciousness,' which for Anaya, at least,
might lead to a more universal acceptance of difference, to a 'world
without borders' (ibid.: 382).

This radical cultural assertion had been witnessed in the struggles of
African Americans in the 1960s where James Baldwin, Malcolm X, and
others saw the need for 'black consciousness'. Toni Morrison would
later argue that her work was 'a kind of literary archeology ... to
reconstruct the world' out of the remains of previously written, but
incomplete, texts (Morrison, 1987: 111–12). For Morrison it is about
'trying to fill in the blanks ... to part the veil that was so frequently
drawn, to implement the stories that I heard' (ibid.: 113) involving a
creative process of fictional-biographical retrieval or 'rememory', as
she terms it. This process applies to 'any marginalized category ...
seldom invited to participate in the discourse even when we were its
topic' (ibid.: 110–11), and so is equally important to the history of the
West where the 'marginalized' were the women, homosexuals, Native
Americans, Mexican Americans, and other ethnic groups whose voices
were not included in the dominant narratives. Where history has
failed, as Fanon would claim, imagination for Morrison reinvents
hidden histories and places them back into the cultural mix giving
the marginalized a voice and contributing to a fuller sense of history
itself.

Within Morrison's work is an important feminist voice that seeks to intervene in the version of history told by men and to rethink it through the experiences of women. This strand of radical revision, emerging from the women's movement in the 1960s–70s, can be seen in the work of many prominent Western revisionists such as Tempest Williams, Kolodny, Limerick, Didion, and in particular through the work of Gloria Anzaldúa and Sandra Cisneros examined in this section. From different perspectives, such writers associate the myths and histories of the West with those in power – men – and interpret a fixing of identity as of benefit to those who support the status quo. Thus their work attacks the dominant discourse by challenging assumptions, 'norms' and conventions that maintain and bolster the official version of history. Anzaldúa calls it 'an absolute despot duality' that divides the world into simple binaries and forces us all, male or female, to choose one or the other 'claim[ing] that human nature is limited and cannot evolve into something better' (Anzaldúa, 1987: 19). Anzaldúa's lesbian Chicana perspective allows her to see beyond this simple split, to live in the borderland in-between, having to see both and forge something else besides. It is this radical position that informs the borderlands as psychocultural space, a way of seeing in '*los intersticios*, the spaces between the different worlds she inhabits' (ibid.: 20).

Postcolonial theory, the impact of the civil rights movement and feminism can be seen in the gradual shift towards the inclusion of marginalized voices in New West cultural representation. As Saldivar argues (1997), 'our America' is not singular but multiple, with beliefs evolving and shifting in contact and conflict with one another. It is hybrid 'in-between' space of the kind termed 'contact zone' by Pratt, defined at length in Kolodny (1992), and described by Native American critic Louis Owens as 'dialogically agitated space' where 'discourse is multidirectional and hybridized' (1992: 58). This, I would argue, is the multicultural space of the New West, a complex mixing of cultures in phases of tradition, agitation, negotiation, and hybridity.

'Modern Indians'

Like Fanon and Morrison, many Native Americans felt that their histories were being stifled and that it was vital for the health of the community that they be voiced anew. Native artist Jimmie Durham has said that 'I was just trying to continue a conversation with the world that the world never wanted and still doesn't want' (Durham, 1993: 13), and for Leslie Marmon Silko storytelling is a 'web of differing versions, disputes ... outright contradictions which created a space of "vast dialogues", a map of meanings for the people, for the community – history, tradition, morality, geography, hunting tips and so on' (Silko, 1996: 32, 43). This deep source could not be ignored since:

> The myth, the web of memories and ideas that create an identity, is a part of oneself ... intimately linked with the surrounding terrain, to the landscape that has often played a significant role in a story or in the outcome of a conflict. (ibid.: 43)

A buried, forbidden knowledge emerges in 'a new kind of historical fiction' – like that written by many marginal groups – whose aim, in part, is to ensure people 'can no longer be severed from [their] context in history' (Rich, 1987: 148–9). Adrienne Rich refers to women trapped in the dominant discourse of patriarchal history – the 'version of events told by the conqueror, the dominator' (ibid.: 141) – but apply generally to all those seeking to break the 'silences of history,' and 'to see patterns, connections, which the false assimilation of liberal humanism obscures. To draw strength: Memory is a nutriment, and seeds stored for centuries can still germinate' (ibid.: 146). This is apparent in Native American writers like Louise Erdich, N. Scott Momaday, James Welch, and Linda Hogan, and Mexican American writers like Rudolfo Anaya, Ana Castillo, Oscar Acosta, and others examined in this chapter, who in different ways, strive to tell significant stories, marginalized by the powerful, official versions of history that have dominated the West.

Their alternative histories represent counter-memories to those myths discussed earlier, starting 'with the local, the immediate, and the personal' and shunning the metanarrative of the West in favour of 'the particular and the specific', looking

> to the past for the hidden histories excluded from dominant narratives ... But unlike myths that seek to detach events and actions from the fabric of any larger history, counter-memory forces revision of existing histories by supplying new perspectives about the past ... embodies aspects of myth and aspects of history, but it retains an enduring suspicion of both categories ... (Lipsitz, 1990: 213)

The 1960s civil rights movement and counter-culture made visible 'those inner colonized of the First World -"minorities", marginals, women', exercising 'the right to speak in a new collective voice' and to question the 'hierarchical positions of Self and Other, Centre and Margin' (Jameson, 1984: 181, 188). Alongside cultural resurgence, the 'Declaration of Indian Purpose' (1961) signified the growing activism of groups like the National Indian Youth Council and the American Indian Movement, calling for better education and general economic improvements, self-determination, the protection of tribal lands, and continued federal aid. Increasingly direct actions, such as 'fish-ins' protesting against the loss of land rights, the occupation of Alcatraz in 1969 to reclaim land, and the confrontations at Wounded Knee in 1973 and Oglala in 1975, show the growing resistance and anger among Native Americans.

The apparently invisible people, contained on reservations, dismissed from the history books and stereotyped by the 'cinematic colonization' of Hollywood (Churchill, 1998: 167), became increasingly visible and engaged in the 'recovering or rearticulation of an identity, a process dependent upon a rediscovered sense of place as well as community ... a *re-membering* or putting together of identity' (Owens, 1992: 5 – emphasis in original). Native American ideological resistance, or 'Red Power', became a feature of the New West, surfacing even in Ken Kesey's countercultural novel *One Flew Over the Cuckoo's Nest* (1961), where Chief Bromden, a silent Indian, symbolizes this reassertion of power as he becomes more aware of the importance of his own history and memory as a source of inner strength, regains his voice and becomes proactive within the asylum, ultimately escaping to Canada. As Edward Said has written, echoing Fanon:

> To achieve recognition is to chart and then to occupy the place in imperial cultural forms reserved for subordination, to occupy it self-consciously, fighting for it on the very same territory once ruled by a consciousness that assumed the subordination of a designated inferior Other. (Said, 1993: 253)

Native Americans sought to 'reclaim, rename, and reinhabit the land' (ibid.: 273) both literally and metaphorically through the process of reinscription of 'Indian voices' into the New West. Gerald Vizenor argues that such writers are 'postindian warriors' who have come through the 'Indian' phase of being spoken for and 'invented' by others, and now 'encounter their enemies with the same courage in literature as their ancestors once evinced on horses ... [to] create their stories with a new sense of survivance ... and counter the manifest manners of domination' (1994: 4). Recalling postmodernism's 'micro-narratives', the traditions of trickster storytelling from Native American oral culture, and Bakhtinian carnival, Vizenor creates 'postindian' stories that reject the margins, reassert pluralism, and intervene in and construct the discourse of the New West, while simultaneously strengthening tribal identities. Vizenor writes of 'tragic wisdom' born out of tribal power, as 'a pronative voice of liberation and survivance, a condition in native stories and literature that denies victimization' (ibid.: 6). It is precisely this sense of empowerment that he celebrates, while being fully aware that the Native American way is the oral tradition and that writing is inevitably associated with the dominant culture: its written treaties broken, its translations that mislead, its scripts that stereotype, and its histories that erase.

Leslie Marmon Silko's work combines feminist revisionism and 'postindian' restorying with New West issues such as loss, imperialism, hegemony, technology, education, and the land. Silko's novel *Ceremony* (1977) has a mixed-blood war veteran, Tayo, at its centre who, like Chief Bromden, is 'invisible', silent, and trapped in a 'fog'. He returns to a postwar New Mexico where, unlike in the Marines, the 'feeling they belonged to America' is replaced by discrimination as a second-class citizen (ibid.: 43). Tayo's New West is Gallup and 'the dirty walls of the bars along Highway 66' where Indians 'had forgotten the sun in the sky' (ibid.: 107), and where white tourism, poverty, and homelessness were the norm. There is a significant tension here between the new, urban Indians cut off from tribal cultures and the perpetuation of the ceremonials and rituals of the medicine men. The medicine man Betonie's ceremony, which will eventually heal Tayo, acknowledges this New West: 'bundles of newspapers . . . telephone books . . . Coke bottles . . . layers of old calendars' were all 'part of the pattern' (ibid.: 120). As Betonie says, 'All these things have stories in them' and, as Silko writes, stories 'are all we have' (ibid.: 121–2). Although Tayo's traditional quest for healing through the land reinforces specific ideas of Native Americans as 'naturally' connected to the wilderness (see Comer, 1999), he does find in his 'convergence' a new vision fusing the old and new. Significantly, the ceremony cannot be static for 'ceremonies have always been changing' since the arrival of the whites, and 'only this growth keeps the ceremonies strong [because] . . . things which don't shift and grow are dead things. They are things the witchery people want' (ibid.: 126). Witchery is the force of destruction (beyond red and white) that must be resisted by the reinvention of meaningful ceremonies. For Betonie, 'Nothing is simple' and rituals must reflect this complexity and not resort to a binary split of white versus red, or old versus new, for like Tayo's mixed-blood, these are definitions of a New West of hybrid identities existing within a global culture, where 'human beings were one clan again', united by the atomic bomb, 'the point of convergence where the fate of all living things, and even the earth, had been laid' (ibid.: 246). Sitting among the rocks mined for uranium at Los Alamos and the Trinity site, Tayo sees in the stars the New West as part of this global pattern of convergence with 'no boundaries, only transitions through all distances and time' where worlds mix like the 'big diesel trucks rumbling down Highway 66 past Laguna' and the pale sun on the 'leaves of the big cottonwood tree ['los alamos' in Spanish] ... [making] them bright gold' (ibid.: 246, 255). In this subtle imagery, the Mother Road meets Mother Earth, travelling and migration routes merge with natural and organic roots to suggest the beginnings of a different, 'never ... easy' vision of the future for the West (ibid.: 259).

In Vizenor's fiction and theory Native resistance takes a postmodern turn, fascinated by the 'crossblood' and the trickster as more extreme mobile figures linked together as metaphors that 'seek to balance contradictions and shatter static certainties' while mediating between worlds (Owens, 1992: 225). Vizenor is interested in all forms of deconstruction and so his works 'break out of all restrictions ... out of the mixture in their blood ... out of invented cultures and repression' as a new expression of a 'spiritual quest' related to the transgressive 'comic spirit' and its capacity to 'break out of the measures that people make' (Vizenor, in Weaver, 1997: 141). Quoting Bakhtin, Owens claims Vizenor's carnival laughter 'destroyed the homogenizing power of myth' with the power to 'uncrown' and bring closer a world often kept at a controlling distance (ibid.: 226). His 'crossblood' is a 'transitive contradancer between communal tribal cultures and those material and urban pretensions that counter conservative traditions' (in ibid.: 228) waging a war against the 'terminal creeds' of American myth. These are the beliefs that impose and fix definitions and meanings on the Native American world and discourage the multiplicity that Vizenor argues will liberate us all. In particular, Vizenor wants to liberate 'Indianness' from its invented simulations and one-dimensional portrayals, whether originating in the white world or the Indian. Both are capable of limiting Native people, presenting only a 'narrative of tribal doom' instead of a contradictory but dialogical world of crossblood-trickster-ism with its double-edged sense of possibility and danger. What counts is 'trickster hermeneutics, the stories of liberation and survivance with-out the dominance of closure. Tribal consciousness is wonder, chance, coincidence, not the revisions of a pedate paradise' (Vizenor, 1994: 14). His vision *flies* forward through the 'shimmer of the imagination' not backwards to a lost past *footed* ('pedate') in simulations of manifest manners and the 'ruins of tribal representations' (ibid.: 8).

Native American representations struggle with these double issues of defining how to live within a changing New West which is at least two cultures. Movement and travel between places, for work, education and family ties and the increasing urban Indian population have given rise to ever more complex renditions of identity as 'mixed-blood' or 'cross-blood'. As poet Wendy Rose has written, 'halfbreedness is a condition of history, a result of experience, of dislocations and reunions, and of choices made for better or for worse' (Rose, 1994: xvi) and her poetry captures this sense of mobility and intercultural exchange: 'I have balanced my bones/between the petroglyph/and the mobile home' (ibid.: 42). Traditional expression and new road culture coexist in Rose's non-essentialized reading of identity. For her, to exist in the New West as woman and Hopi Indian is to construct one's identity from relations derived from movements and contacts with land, people and ideas: 'I must build myself ... I am not merely a conduit, but a participant' (quoted in Anderson, 1999: 21). Like Tayo, or Vizenor's tricksters, Rose's journey reflects the migratory nature of Native cul-tures, crossing and recrossing the West in contact with various peoples from which new cultures form. This hybrid process is evidenced in Native writing, such as Paula Gunn Allen's sense of her life as 'con-fluence', 'a journey-in-between, a road ... connected in some way to The Road [with] ... many directions ... many planes ... where I am going, where I am from' (ibid.: 32). As noted earlier, Gunn Allen sees the West itself as 'confluential' space where peoples 'do not fuse into one, nor do they remain entirely separate ... each retains its separate and unique identity while engaging in a variety of modes of interchange' (in Wrobel and Steiner, 1997: 345). She echos Bakhtin's definition of 'dialogic encounter' which 'does not result in merging or mixing', for each element 'retains its own unity and *open* totality, but ... are mutually enriched' (Bakhtin, 1990b: 7). The product of such encounters, for Gunn Allen, is a 'new country', a 'neverending tale' (in Wrobel and

Steiner, 1997: 346, 353) which places the Native American at its heart, separate but interconnected and participating with other groups: whites, Chicanos, and blacks, all forming at the cultural crossroads of the West.

In Sherman Alexie's first novel, *Reservation Blues* (1995), the cross-roads is the starting point for the work, a space where the troubled bluesman Robert Johnson wanders onto the Spokane Indian Reservation, literally bringing together worlds: black/red, past/present, real and imagined. For Alexie too, movement and change are characteristics of the modern Indians presented as complicated human beings living between the reservation and the city, participating in both, and struggling with their identities: 'I wrote my name in Magic Marker on my shoes, my first name on the left toe and my last name on the right toe, with *my true name in between*' (Alexie, 1994: 194 – my emphasis). Recalling the film of David Seals's *Powwow Highway* (Jonathan Wacks, 1988), journeying between sites becomes a key motif with Philbert 're-Indianized' by sacred sites in the Black Hills and Buddy's angry cynicism tempered by the ancestral discoveries of his friend. In what is, ultimately, an over-romantic vision, the film does at least portray Native Americans as protagonists, and raises issues of modern reservation life and the interrelations with the outside world. Alexie's work shows an 'in between' world which is often an angry, painful place to be, as in Silko's or James Welch's fiction, with the problems of poverty, racism, addiction, and unemployment limiting opportunities to discover Gunn Allen's 'new country'. Instead, it can be a 'cable television reservation' where 'we hid our faces behind masks that suggested other histories' and held onto imagination as the 'only weapon on the reservation' (ibid.: 149, 198, 150). As one Alexie character says:

> How can we imagine a new language when the language of the enemy keeps our dismembered tongues tied to his belt? How can we imagine a new alphabet when the old jumps off billboards down onto our stomachs? . . . How do we imagine a new life when a pocketful of quarters weighs our possibilities down? (ibid.: 152)

There is no easy route back to ceremony or to the land that heals, in Alexie's work, for 'there is a moment when an Indian realizes he cannot turn back toward tradition and that he has no map to guide him toward the future' (ibid.: 134). Even community cannot provide solace since 'the only thing he shared with anybody was a bottle and broken dreams' (ibid.: 74). And yet alongside the despair, Alexie's writing is full of humour and survivance – as he writes, 'Indians have a way of surviving. But it's almost like Indians can easily survive the big stuff. Mass murder, loss of language and land rights. It's the small things that hurt the most. The white waitress that wouldn't take an order, Tonto, the Washington Redskins' (ibid.: 49). Part of the 'in between' is this to and fro from pain to laughter, from despair to imaginative storytelling and lively, honest exchange: Bakhtin's 'dialogic encounter' on fast forward. It's no surprise that one of Alexie's epigraphs is from Lou Reed, 'There's a little bit of magic in everything and then some loss to even things out.' The reference to rock music links Alexie to a wider American 'language' which is, in itself, a hybrid mix of musics from many cultures. One of the reasons for so many references to music in his work is precisely to tap into a code that exists 'in between' distinct social worlds and can address the differing audiences through a common language. In *Reservation Blues*, music 'just might be the most important thing there is' (ibid.: 29), the 'powerful medicine' through which his modern Indians 'find a voice' in another version of Betonie's new ceremony that has the capacity to hybridize the old with the new, the black (Johnson's blues) with the issues of the rez (i.e. the reservation), storytelling with rock lyrics. It is the blues that 'always make us remember' but when '[t]hose blues lit up a new road, . . . the Spokanes pulled out the old maps. Those blues churned up generations of anger and pain: car wrecks, suicides, murders. Those blues were ancient, aboriginal, indigenous' (Alexie, 1996: 22, 174). Alexie's cross-cultural connections of oppression through the blues suggest the importance of remembering, just as Toni Morrison and others have, but in his work it is the 'old maps' that people cling to, unwilling to expose 'something hidden behind the words' (ibid.).

Victor, a key character in *The Lone Ranger and Tonto* and *Reservation Blues*, claims that Johnson 'understood what it meant to be an Indian on the edge of the twenty-first century, even if he was black at the beginning of the twentieth' (Alexie, 1994: 35). Yet tribes 'buried all of their pain and anger deep inside, and it festered' turning into self-destructive violence and abuse (ibid.: 175) like that manifested in the alcoholism and destitution of many of Alexie's characters. Alexie's work resonates with ambivalence, a sense of the New West as a 'dangerous crossroads' where 'collisions occur . . . decisions must be made . . . [but providing] a unique perspective, a vantage point where one can see in more than one direction' (Lipsitz, 1994: 7–8, 12). Alexie connects Natives and African Americans through the tormented figure of Robert Johnson whose blues created 'a whole, new common language [which] grew up around that negation, that affirmation' – a 'poetic opposition to playing by the rules' (Marcus, 1995: 148–9). The music of Coyote Springs, a hybrid mix of styles beginning with cover versions but becoming increasingly 'Native', articulates Alexie's dialogical culture of negation/affirmation and symbolizes identity as mobile, about becoming not being. As the novel unfolds through music, so do the identities of its characters – leading in different directions, positive, negative, and points between.

Here cultures collide, overlap, and interweave like dream and reality in the mind of his central character, Thomas Builds-the-Fire, who 'tried to be as traditional as the twentieth century allowed' (1996: 49), with the novel full of movement in spatial, temporal, and psychic terms, constantly collapsing expectations, exploding cliches and challenging readers' atitudes. Alexie's mobile identities of the 'in-between' parallel the New West as a complex border territory in which cultures 'translate' one another, as in music, where this process 'renews the past, refiguring it as a contingent "in-between" space, that innovates and interrupts the performance of the present' (Bhabha, 1994: 7). Thus in Alexie's work there is no Silko-like return to ceremony, for on the 'rez' where identity is a 'goofy ... mixed drink,' '[i]f you don't like the things you remember, then all you have to do is change the memories' (1994: 27, 34), and the 'past-present' coexists in the dynamic, tension-filled environments of his fiction.

Although Alexie does not follow the same path as either Vizenor or Silko, his work portrays an Indian West which is not reduced to stereotypes or locked into a nostalgic longing for the past, but embodies a complex, ambiguous existence – negative and affirmative – in transition. Projecting the contemporary, lived experience of the reservation, stories still circulate, alongside the realities of poverty and alcoholism, basketball games, and police violence. Rather than mysticism or postmodern tricksterism, Alexie's work maps a territory in which both are as likely to coexist as the contemporary reality of casinos *and* sweatlodges, sacred sites *and* landfill. Thus, at the end of *Reservation Blues*, as Thomas leaves the rez for the city, Alexie describes it in part mythic, part postmodern terms: 'Those horses were following, leading Indians toward the city, while other Indians were traditional dancing in the Longhouse after the feast, while drunk Indians stood outside the

Trading Post' (1996: 306). The reservation communities have their despair and joy, but Alexie always places them within the wider West, with his characters constantly journeying to and from the 'rez', to bars, towns, and cities beyond its lands. In this way, he dramatizes relations between cultures in terms of difference, conflict and empathy which widens both the audience and influence of his work. The youthful themes also connect Alexie with an audience that would see Silko and Vizenor as writers with little to say to their generation. Significantly, Alexie's works are now being made into films, *Smoke Signals* (Chris Eyre,1998) and *Reservation Blues* (forthcoming), which will further widen the impact of his vision. Lacking the momentous, often apocalyptic, mood of other Native writers, Alexie asserts at the end of *Reservation Blues* that there is a 'new song' turning 'mourning' to 'celebration' and it is a song of survival, remembering the 'dead Indians' but singing for the living and for the unsung 'songs . . . waiting for them in the city' (ibid.: 306).

The emphases in these works are all different, but there are common concerns with exploring 'mixed bloods' or 'in-betweens' as signifiers of participation in multiple cultural sites. In this way Native Americans have always engaged with the West as dialogical, hybrid space constituted by enormous diversity both now and in the past, resembling a kind of cultural 'mestizaje' defined as

> the confluence of different races, in the senses of descending from an original hybrid begetting, of continually procreating mestizo offspring, and of being, in the present incarnation, multiracial . . . And a consequence of essential hybridity is subjective ambiguity . . . For the body that is the product of diverse roots is more than the sum of those roots: there is *something additional in being hybrid* . . . (Arteaga, 1997: 11 – my emphasis)

This kind of exchange recalls Bakhtin who viewed language dynamics as a 'zone of contact,' a phrase later used by Mary-Louise Pratt to redescribe the relations of colonial encounter. This 'zone' defines the ways in which different discourses interact spatially 'in interanimating relationships with new contexts' (Bakhtin, 1990b: 346) and helps explain the hybrid process in the West. Hence, in the 'zone of contact' – in the borderlands and across frontiers of various kinds – amid struggles over 'ideological points of view', new contexts and therefore new 'languages' form at the moment of 'encounter' (ibid.: 358).

Hybridity, for Bakhtin, was 'an antithetical movement of coalescence and antagonism . . . that both brings together, fuses, but also maintains separation' (ibid.: 22), echoing Gunn Allen's sense of 'confluence' or Alexie's negative/affirmative. For Bakhtin too, attempts to restrict language to a single voice and to create an authoritative discourse that seeks to speak for all – Vizenor's 'terminal creeds' – will be challenged from within by the other voices of the hybrid formulation who demand to be heard.

Chicano/a Identities in the New West

Through the works of Native American writers one sees the emergence of postmodern notions of identity and place, but in the work of Chicano/as they have been even more pronounced. The borderlands of the West are a confluent space of multiple voices, the product of colonization, migration, and adaptation, interrogating the dominant discourses of power with gestures of fusing and of countering – always the double-action of hydridity.

> Hybridization as creolization involves fusion, the creation of a new form, which can then be set against the old form, of which it is partly made up . . . [it] produces no stable new form but [a] restless, uneasy, interstitial hybridity: a radical heterogeneity, discontinuity, the permanent revolution of forms. (Young, 1995: 25)

In contemporary borderlands culture with its contesting elements there is this strong sense of overlapping, mixing forms, of a space not just defined as a simple text, but an intertext, where meanings and interpretations are connected and interrelated, cross-referred, divergent, and inconclusive. What hybridity cannot do is to resolve the differences and tensions between groups or ideologies, but instead establishes a problematic in which 'other "denied" knowledges enter upon the dominant discourse and estrange the basis of its authority' (Bhabha, 1994: 114). The emergent histories of marginal groups serve to articulate and rearticulate hidden pasts and excluded voices in the 'production of "partial" knowledges and positionalities' (ibid.: 119) that provide a heterogeneous, multiplicitous remapping of American culture and identity relevant to the New West as a region. The significance of these actual and symbolic borderlands can be seen most clearly in the work of Chicanas like Gloria Anzaldúa and Sandra Cisneros.

'... a thin edge of barb wire': Gloria Anzaldúa and Sandra Cisneros

Gloria Anzaldúa's Western borderlands are a real geo-political reality signifying oppression, colonial conquest, and a legacy of violence, but out of her life spent between two worlds and juggling its various histories, she creates a wider cultural dimension in which the border-lands are psychological, sexual, and spiritual as well. This is postmodern space 'of contradictions,' 'at the juncture of cultures' and 'not a com-fortable place to be,' and simultaneously a place full of possibility where 'languages cross-pollinate and are re-vitalized; they die and are born' (Anzaldúa, 1987: Preface). These borderlands, unfixed and fluid, permit 'one's shifting and multiple identity and integrity ... to swim in a new element' (ibid.), a hybrid space, for the 'new mestiza' (mixed blood), where multiplicity defines the creation of a new subjectivity. Echoing the postcolonial writings of Salman Rushdie, Anzaldúa endorses a postmodern identity in which, 'The broken mirror may actually be as valuable as the one which is supposedly unflawed' (Rushdie, 1992: 11). She writes, 'I am a wind-swayed bridge, a crossroads inhabited by whirlwinds ... Think of me as Shiva, a many-armed and legged body with one foot on brown soil, one on white, one in straight society, one in the gay world, the man's world, the women's ... Who, me confused? Ambivalent? Not so. Only your labels split me' (in Moraga and Anzaldúa, 1983: 205). Living in the New West, with its many contesting voices, is parallel to Anzaldúa's crossroads (Alexie's metaphor too, remember), multidirectional, puzzling but also strangely liberating.

The Treaty of Guadelupe-Hidalgo (1848) that ended the Mexican-American War (1846–8) divided up the Southwest along the line of the new border, creating the borderlands as a focus for political questioning and for issues of cultural identity, since the arbitrary line had severed many who identified themselves with the south as opposed to the north of which they were now potential citizens. Excluded groups, silenced by the processes of history, sought to have some role in the renewal of ideas of identity, including the new Mexican-Americans or Chicana/os who lived in the liminal space of the border. For them, the West was defined by Manifest Destiny and American expansionism and their sense of identity had to be carved out of the two cultures in which they found themselves. Hence the mestizaje (mixing Spanish and Indian) present in Mexican culture was extended to the new cultural mix of the borderlands where migrations back and forth across the border made identities unstable and unfixed. Anzaldúa makes this unfixing of identity the starting point for a new consciousness – 'accounting with all three cultures – white, Mexican, Indian' (Anzaldúa, 1987: 22) – a mobile way of being that rejects old modes of thinking rooted in patriarchal, colonial mythologies and attempts to imagine 'a new culture' at the 'interface' of multiple cultures (ibid.: 37). It is the Coatlicue state, disruptive, protean, ambivalent, simultaneously birth and death, 'duality ... a synthesis of duality ... a third perspective' (ibid.: 46) which, for Anzaldúa, one has to learn to live with rather than the old, fixed notions of identity. For a woman, in particular, this sense of unfixing was a means of redefining identity beyond the norms of the dominant discourse and asserting a new subjectivity based on a plural sense of self.

This suggests a tentative beginning in the West of a 'new cultural politics of difference' which

> affirms the perennial quest for precious ideals of individuality and democracy by digging deep in the depths of human particularities and social specificities in order to construct new kinds of connections, affinities and communities across empire, nation, region, gender, age and sexual orientation. (West, 1993: 29)

Anzaldúa's version of this 'new politics' breaks down the 'paradigms' that fix and define identity so that 'new connections' can span the old divisions, both real and theoretical, in her quest for a healing of rifts and the movement towards a new mestiza consciousness. The parallels to the Native American writers considered earlier are apparent here, especially through the critique of cultural myths, stereotypes, and the drive for new affinities.

Anzaldúa's intent to 'deconstruct, construct' extends to her form which mixes poetry, personal history, myth, folk story, religion, and politics into a a new 'corrido' (a traditional border ballad) rewritten by a new mestiza, articulating the contradictory space of the borderlands. The space is one of 'convergence', transition, and fusion: 'The convergence has created a shock culture, a border culture, a third country' (Anzaldúa, 1987: 11), which is of both and yet distinct in itself. It is 'una herida abierta [open wound] where the Third World grates against the first and bleeds. And before a scab forms it hemorrhages again, the lifeblood of two worlds merging to form a third country – a border culture' (ibid.: 3). Gómez-Peña, in his postmodern analysis of a hybrid 'new world border' wrote 'I live smack in the fissure between two worlds, in the infected wound ... there cohabit two histories, languages, cosmologies ...' (in Simonsson and Walker, 1988: 127). Yet out of this 'infection' comes a similar mood to that explored in Anzaldúa's work, for as Gómez-Peña writes, the 'two traditions converge in my border experience and they fuse together ... I am a child of crisis and cultural syncretism ... creating and decreating myths ... [producing] alternative cartographies, a ferocious critique of both countries, and, lastly a proposal for new creative languages' (ibid.: 129–30). The ambivalent, shifting perspective, crossing borders of place and identity, gives Gómez-Peña, like Anzaldúa, 'models of a new hybrid culture, full of uncertainty and vitality' (ibid.: 130) which extend beyond the actual border itself, into a vision of a postmodern, multiple West – 'a future dialogue ... capable of transcending the profound historical resentments that exist between communities' (ibid.: 133).

Anzaldúa's experimental form and Gómez-Peña's radical texts clearly represent a wider sense of 'borders' than those of the New West but nonetheless their analysis provides a significant language through which it can be rethought:

> I see a mosaic pattern (Aztec-like) emerging, a weaving pattern, thin here, thick there ... Numerous overlays of paint, rough surfaces, smooth surfaces ... I see the barely contained color threatening to spill over the boundaries of the object it represents and into other 'objects' and over the borders of the frame ... a hybridization ... an assemblage, a montage, a beaded work with several leitmotifs and with a central core, now appearing, now disappearing in a crazy dance. (Anzaldúa, 1987: 66)

Anzaldúa's spatial metaphors suggest the fluid, transformative, multiple identities of the New West in which the old binary, dualistic thinking can no longer suffice: North/South, Anglo/Hispanic, Anglo/Indian, male/female and so on. For Anzaldúa, there must be a 'third element' formed in the intersection of the old binaries, but whose strength is derived from the 'continual creative motion that keeps breaking down the unitary aspect of each new paradigm' (ibid.: 80). Gómez-Peña imagines a 'third alternative' with 'a more complex system of overlapping, interlocking, and overlaid maps ... [where] "others" are those who resist fusion, mestizaje, and cross-cultural diaolgue' (Gómez-Peña, 1996: 7). Significantly, Anzaldúa and Gómez-Peña echo William Kittredge's new Anglo perspective (see later): 'Our paradigms and stories fail, and we have to reinvent our understandings, and our reasons for doing things.' Anglo 'mythology doesn't work anymore' and so the only route is 'to find a new story to inhabit ... after re-imagining our myths' (Kittredge, 1996: 158 and 1987: 67, 64). Anzaldúa writes of the 'interface', drawing upon its meanings in sewing, as 'a piece of material between two pieces ... to provide support and stability ... Between the masks we've internalized, one on top of the other, are our interfaces', and claims that contemporary writing should 'rip out the stitches, expose the multi-layered "inner-faces" ... acquire the agency of making our own *caras* ... transform the ... apertures, ... *abismos* that we are forced to speak from. Only then can we make a home out of the cracks' (Anzaldúa, 1990: xv–xvi, xxv). In the New West, for its many voices and cultures, 'to make a home out of the cracks' is to reconstruct and create a 'new mythos ... a change in the way we perceive reality, the way we see ourselves, and the ways we behave' (Anzaldúa, 1987: 80) – to live on the 'interface' between the masks.

As all these voices remind us, living on this interface is not an easy place to be, but increasingly it is the experience of the New West with its odd mixtures, differences, and contrasts. Anzaldúa wrote that living in the mixed 'third country' was like walking a tightrope, 'an acrobat in equipoise, expert at the Balancing Act', in a place where 'my own affinities and my people with theirs can live together and transform the planet' (ibid.: 209). Sandra Cisneros represents a further exploration of these speculations on new identities forged in the New West, and in 1990 spoke of her own position in very similar terms to those used by Anzaldúa: 'There's always this balancing act, we've got to define what we think is fine for ourselves instead of what our culture says' (Aranda, 1990: 66). For Cisneros, the balance is a 'schizophrenia' (ibid.) to be worked out in the everyday lives of women whose lives are split along complex borderlines of class, gender, and sexuality by 'culture' both north and south of the border. In this way, Cisneros applies aspects of Anzaldúa's theory to her imaginative case studies of women living hybrid lives both in and beyond the West. Cisneros was born in Chicago and lives in San Antonio, and her work is concerned with New West characters struggling within postmodern contact zones that mix traditions, like Gómez-Peña and Coco Fusco (1995) – Indian, Catholic, American – and issues such as sexuality, gender-role expectations, independence, in a variety of ways. Her fiction crosses between

American popular culture and Mexican traditions, 'telenovelas' and the Alamo, ponders the Marlboro Man and Barbie, the Virgin of Guadelupe and dim sum, and like Anzaldúa, Cisneros's work embodies this 'schizophrenia' through its formal and linguistic structures mirroring the 'borders' the characters engage with. To borrow a line from Gómez-Peña, Cisneros's characters are 'en route to other selves/& other geographies' (Gómez-Peña, 1996: 2). For example, Cisneros hybridizes language shifting between and across Spanish and English, and in 'Bien Pretty' describes a character, Lupe, moving from northern California to central Texas, spanning the West with her 'past pared down to what would fit inside a van': 'A futon. A stainless steel wok. My grandmother's *molcajete* ... My Tae Kwon Do uniform ... My crystal and copal. A portable boom box' (Cisneros, 1992: 141). In San Antonio, near the border, she meets Flavio whose unconscious 'Mexicanness' is contrasted with her intellectual, artistic grasp of what she feels is her 'Pan-Hispanic' identity. As he comments, 'I don't have to dress in a sarape and sombrero to be Mexican ... "I know who I am" ...'(ibid.: 151). As she falls in love with Flavio – or with what he appears to represent to her – he leaves her, without a second thought, to return to his family in Mexico. Cisneros underlines the limits of a singular identity and especially one based upon notions of 'authentic' romantic essentialism, such as 'Mexicanness' or 'Hispanicism', and presents a New West female identity which is hybrid, shifting, and multiple. Texas becomes the space of biculturalism, as in Anzaldúa, where North and South are in contact and where archetypes are questioned and false ideals, like the god-like Flavio, examples of the 'ghosts' Cisneros knows, have to be recognized and lived with. Women, for so long, defined only by the world of machismo and the expectations of family and religion, step outside the borders that hem them in to discover new, complex, resistant identities. The old definitions, like the old traditions, cannot, however, be left behind, but echoing Anzaldúa, they must be accepted in the 'balancing act', or as Cisneros says, 'The big ghosts still live inside you, and what happens with writing ... you make your peace with those ghosts. You recognize they live there' (Aranda, 1990: 67). To accept is not to give in to the dominant discourse rooted in these old ways, but to rescript them in the new language of 'transfrontera feminist politics' (Saldivar-Hull, 1999: 255).

In the story 'Woman Hollering Creek', Cisneros rescripts Chicana folklore for a contemporary culture via Cleofilas, an oppressed woman, who moves north across her father's 'threshold', over the 'border' to America and a married life of violence and containment. Through 'telenovelas' (soap operas) Cleofilas sees another life of 'passion', but it is contrasted with the reality of her domestic torment, bound to a husband – 'this keeper, this lord, this master' and living between Dolores and Soledad (suffering and solitude) who have little connection with their past – not even knowing the origins of the creek's name (Cisneros, 1992: 49). It is the landscape of the multi-named arroyo that signifies another world; Woman Hollering Creek, 'a thing with a voice all its own,' reminds her of the stories of La Llorona calling out for her lost children. The ambiguous cry may be for a lost life – what Anzaldúa terms 'the lost parts of herself' (Anzaldúa, 1987: 38) – or for the possibility of resistance to its limits and borders – her cry 'predict[s] something is to happen' (ibid.: 36). Cleofilas will, ultimately, only escape her husband to return to her father's house, but the hope resides in her unborn child. The pregnant Cleofilas crosses the creek with an independent woman, Felice (happiness), who hollers 'like Tarzan', speaks 'Spanish pocked with English' and notices that 'nothing around here is named after a woman ... Unless she's the Virgin' (Cisneros, 1992: 55). Felice's hybrid, independent character breaks the traditions that bind Cleofilas to patriarchy and persuades her to find a voice of her own at the end of the story as she felt 'gurgling out of her own throat, a long ribbon of laughter, like water' (ibid.: 56). Cleofilas's liberation begins with speech, like the creek itself, whose 'water' will nourish her unborn child who embodies an emerging hybrid mestiza consciousness, still forming in the womb, but alive in the borderlands. The creek also signifies the fluidity and multiplicity of the new identity, as it both flows with water and has many names and meanings discussed throughout the story. In Cleofilas's crossing and recrossing the border, Cisneros builds a spatial image of potential transition in the New West that maps a resistance to stereotypes and to patriarchal boundaries through the hybrid independence of redefined gender identity. Cleofilas represents the folk story revised because unlike La Llorona she escapes with her child, and bridges the border between traditionally fixed geographical and psychological territories. Cisneros's fictions continue to explore the borderlands as a site for contact and contest in which Anzaldúa's theoretical struggles can be played out and negotiated in women's everyday lives, which, as always in the New West, is a potent mix of imagination, dream, and reality.

Anzaldúa and Cisneros are just two examples of Chicanas like Ana Castillo, Helena Viramontes, and Cherrie Moraga who have contributed to a feminist revision of identities and constructed what Castillo terms 'Xicanisma': 'an ever present consciousness of our interdependency specifically rooted in our culture and history' (Castillo, 1995: 226). Chicanos (male) have engaged in similar questionings as we have seen in the work of Gómez-Peña, but the struggle began with the Chicano movement in the 1960s that found literary voice in the poem 'I Am Joaquin' (1969) written by Corky Gonzáles. It spoke of being 'lost in a world of confusion . . . the whirl of gringo society . . . in a country that has wiped out/all my history/stifled all my pride . . .' (in Muñoz, 1989: 61–2). The poem was filmed by Luis Valdez, who later directed *La Bamba* (1987) which used the Chicano rocker Ritchie Valens as the focus for an examination of similar border themes. A long-term activist in the Chicano movement, Valdez helped write *El Plan Espiritual de Aztlán* in 1969 ('We are a bronze people with a bronze culture'), and his theatre group El Teatro Campesino articulated many of the concerns over identity and power.

La Bamba, however, is a good example of the 'dangerous crossroads' discussed earlier for it uses popular film as a 'new public sphere that uses the circuits of commodity production and circulation to envision and activate new social relations' (Lipsitz, 1994: 12). It portrays complex issues of struggle and identity through the Valenzuela family living in a postwar West undergoing change – symbolized through the contrast of Ritchie's assimilationism and his brother Bob's Chicano/Aztec/bandido/macho tendencies. Playing consciously with stereotypes, Valdez dramatizes a complex, unstable set of identities, revealing racism and prejudice, as well as the vitality of tradition and the importance of family. In the opening sequence Valdez juxtaposes sign systems from North and South: leather-jacketed Bob on a Harley marked with an Aztec warrior's head and feathered Indian body, his arm tattooed with a cross, a snake crossing the highway and the pumping 'R & B' soundtrack. These unresolved tensions over Chicano identity and its place within the West resonate through the film. Bob's macho persona echos Cisneros's 'authentic' neo-Mayan gods like Flavio, but Valdez refuses to make Bob one-dimensional, for he is vulnerable too and wise because he is still connected to the subjugated knowledges of the South. Ritchie knows only the North, cannot speak Spanish, has never been to Mexico, and will change his name from Valenzuela to Valens. Ritchie is an identity in crisis, drawn to the USA mainstream represented by Donna – the ideal, blonde, suburban dream girl – 'She's way above your class', we are told – whose father is the white racist, suburban guardian who refers to Ritchie's 'Goddam jungle music.' In the Tijuana scenes, Ritchie is exposed to Bob's alternative knowledge of a different culture, hearing 'La Bamba' in a brothel and visiting the 'curandero' (shaman), like in Anaya's influential novel *Bless Me Ultima*. Ritchie wakes up (literally and metaphorically) to Mexico, eats snake, a symbol of transformation, and asks Bob, 'What is all this?', to which he gets the reply, 'Mexico'. Overall, the film counters stereotypes, unsettles 'easy' definitions of Chicano identity as one-dimensional, and represents instead an emerging New West in which the ideal identity would appear to be a hybrid mix of the film's doubles, Ritchie and Bob. Locked into their separate worlds, they are both tormented, but together as the film's final slow motion shots suggest, they are something better. Valdez once wrote:

> They say this is a melting pot ... Horrible term! You melt people down, God! It shouldn't be that way. Our country should be a place where the individual is sacred. We have so many different sorts of people. Every man has his own heart. Who gives you the right to cut out a man's heart and put it in a melting pot? There are beautiful things in our lives. We have had them in our past and we will have them again. We will create our own 'flowers and songs' ... (In Steiner, 1970: 337)

It is towards this that the film ultimately points.

As we have seen, Chicanos have had to work out the realities of living this hybrid existence, and some like Luis Alberto Urrea in *Across the Wire* (1993) explored the dark lives of border crossers around Tijuana-San Diego, and wrote of himself as 'a son of the border [with] a barbed-wire fence bisecting my heart' (1998: 11). He compares the multiple identities of the 'son of the border' with the words that make up American-English: 'a quilt work of words, and continents and actions and tribes and even enemies dance all over your mouth when you speak' (ibid.: 15), as if to prove Bakhtin's linguistic-social theory of heteroglossia. Every act of speech or writing is a mixing of many languages, of layers and references drawn from many places. For Urrea, a white-skinned mestizo, 'I know how much color and beauty we Others really bring to the American mix' (ibid.: 16) and every utterance is a reminder of the hybrid mix of the West. His book, *Nobody's Son*, is a genealogical excavation of words, names, and cultures, stripping away notions of essence to reveal fundamental hybridity running, like the border, through everyone. From the Visigoths, to Spain, to Mexico via Ireland, England, and Hungary, Urrea traces his parents back so as to attempt to define himself because 'so many of us live in a nightmare of silence' (ibid.: 58). Urrea's sense of identity is the 'middle region, nobody's children, marching under a starless flag. I am Other. I am you ... We're all heading the same way ... together or separately' (ibid.). Urrea's work relates to another younger Chicano, Rubén Martinez, whose more apocalyptic vision of the West sees tensions, economic differences, and ethnic divisions becoming insurmountable. For him, 'the ideal of existential unity crumbles' but the hope is that 'the many selves can find some kind of form together without annihilating one another' (Martinez, 1992: 2). His multiple postmodern Western identity, born out of the fears and possibilities of the region, recalls Anzaldúa's 'third element' with its 'tolerance for contradictions ... for ambiguity ... juggl[ing] cultures ... turn[ing] ambivalence into something else ... greater than the sum of its severed parts' (Anzaldúa, 1987: 79–80), is defined as 'a search for a one that is much more than two ... I must be much more than two. I must be North and South in the North and in the South ...' (ibid.: 2–3).

Autobiography and Memoir: 'a new western emotional history'?

In 1996, Richard Maxwell Brown noticed that from the 1970s onward Anglos were producing a 'new emotional history of the West' (in Milner, 1996: 56) which sought to 'engrave a lesson of courage without illusions ... [demonstrating] the grassroots western heritage of courage without the disabling illusions that have misled so many into failed and fruitless lives across the western dreamscape' (ibid.: 60). White American memoirs, like those of William Kittredge, Ivan Doig, Wallace Stegner, Teresa Jordan, Mary Clearman Blew, Gretel Ehrlich, and Terry Tempest Williams, parallel the ethnic writing I have already discussed in their concern for identity, place, and rethinking histories. When official history ignores or erases you from its records, as so often was the case with ethnic westerners, the tradition of life-stories or 'testimonials' took on enormous significance. As I have shown, these textual spaces articulate an alternative history or counter-memory to the legitimized version: they 'talk back' to the mainstream.

These Anglo texts voice aspects of white experience that counter the normalized, mythic view of the West as a place of Manifest Destiny, success, and wonder. In many of these works, the illusions are exposed through hidden histories providing a memory of place often silenced in conventional accounts. Just as New Western History examined diverse sources through which to revise accepted history, so too did these western memoirs. The 'white history' of the West had to be revised precisely because it had been viewed for so long as the only history of the West that mattered. Even the revisionists implied that the white process of settlement was conquest and that this was dominated by the European pioneer at the expense of other settlers. It was if as the balance could only come from outside traditional history – the voices of other Anglo-Americans now had to be heard alongside the already emerging voices of ethnic Americans.

These Anglo autobiographies reconstruct the past both because the official history has been incomplete and has excluded the personal stories and the diversity of experiences, but also because it perpetuates certain myths of power and dominance in need of critique. The process of 'rememory' and archaeology that Toni Morrison has written of (see earlier), and the need to dialogue with the past that we have examined in Native American and Chicano/a writing, is also part of the Anglo desire to reconstruct histories of inclusion. Rather than the metanarrative of conquest, settlement, and nation-building, these white memoirs concentrate on different stories, on an equivalent to Foucault's genealogy, 'a differential knowledge incapable of unanimity ... local popular knowledges ... disqualified knowledges ...' (Foucault, 1980: 82). In their own voices, these Anglo stories are personal and local, aiming to widen the discourse of the West, to revise the old myths and to place their versions alongside the multiplicity of voices emerging as the New West. This 'restorying' is central to the representation of the New West, as we have already seen in the earlier part of this chapter with writers like Silko who wrote 'through the stories we hear who we are' and '[t]hus remembering and retelling were a communal process ... within the web of differing versions' (Silko, 1996: 30–1, 32).

In Anglo-American William Kittredge's work a similar concern for stories/histories exists, but coming from a ranching family, his work maps a different territory. Born into a set of expectations and myths about the West derived from the notions of frontier and Manifest Destiny, much of his most powerful work is an interrogation of his own family's place within this particular script. He writes 'we were enclosed in stories and often couldn't see out ... driven to repetitively act out certain stories in hopes the enactments might defend us, save us, protect us' (Kittredge, 1996: 45, 47). In *Owning It All*, Kittredge wrote '[p]ossibility is the oldest American story. Head west for freedom and the chance of inventing a spanking new life for yourself' (1987: 6) and yet his writing recognizes the limitations and responsibilities that follow in the wake of this mythic sensibility.

> We shaped our piece of the West according to the model provided by our mythology, and instead of a great good place such order had given us enormous power over nature, and a blank perfection of fields. (ibid.: 62)

For Kittredge, Western history is constructed by the stories told about it, repeated, embellished, and bound into a series of myths or discourses that legitimate actions and ideologies. He writes that stories 'are ways of enclosing otherness and claiming ownership' (ibid.: 10). The historian Keith Jenkins writes that

> the world/the past comes to us always already as stories and that we cannot get out of these stories (narratives) to check if they correspond to the real world/past, because these 'always already' narratives constitute 'reality'. (Jenkins, 1991: 9)

Kittredge suggests that what has to be undertaken is a new writing to usurp or exist alongside the previous stories in order for westerners to remix and reinvent themselves (Kittredge, 1996: 5). He explains the reason for this very clearly:

> We figure and find stories, which can be thought of as maps or paradigms in which we see our purposes defined; then the world drifts and our maps don't work any more, or paradigms and stories fail, and we have to reinvent our understandings, and our reasons for doing things. (ibid.: 158)

Certain dominant stories, of Manifest Destiny, the 'Frontier', masculine assertion, and the Nation formed in the West, no longer provide maps of meaning, but instead offer myths and dead-ends that enclose and cut one off from the vibrant possibilities of reimagination and reinvention. For Kittredge the West should always signify possibility rather than closure, but the old stories mask ideologies and therefore distort and disfigure this vision; 'at heart it is racist, sexist, imperialist mythology of conquest; a rationale for violence – against other people and against nature' (Kittredge, 1987: 63). The task has to be 'to find a new story to inhabit' (ibid.: 64).

Kittredge's memoir *Hole in the Sky* (1992) refers self-consciously to other Western memoirs and fiction, A. B. Guthrie's *The Big Sky* (1947) and Ivan Doig's *This House of Sky* (1978) – 'books ... about infinity and shelter, prospect and refuge, individualism and community' (Kittredge, 1987: 166) in which a 'kind of emotional ownership' is conveyed (ibid.: 167). However, the certainty and comforts implied in these descriptions of the books is not Kittredge's autobiographical territory, since for him, the West is fragmented like his own life symbolized by the hole in the sky. The memoir charts the Kittredge family history in America, self-consciously reviewing their contribution to the very stories he knows have to be rewritten by his and future generations. Exploring the mistreatment of the Native Americans, for example, Kittredge comments: 'In Warner Valley we lived surrounded by ghosts, but we forgot' (1993: 19) and 'We knew a history filled with omissions, which can be thought of as lies' (ibid.: 23). Kittredge's project is, firstly, to give voice to the 'ghosts' of his own forgotten past, and secondly to use these as a method to counter the omissions and the lies. In a crucial passage he writes, 'I find myself searching for history out of books and dim rememberances, trying to fit it together in strings which reach from generation to generation, trying to loop myself into lines of significance' (ibid.: 27). The desire to construct an identity despite the realization that the dominant story in his family is 'work and property and ownership' remains strong. But the voice of Kittredge's hindsight tells the dark truth: 'We were heedless people in a new country; we came and went in a couple of generations. But we plowed a lot of ground while we were there' (ibid.). Recognizing a tragic wisdom akin to Silko's or Vizenor's, Kittredge focuses upon rescripting the New West through his own admission of guilt and abuse of the land as 'a perfect little imperialist' whose family 'irrevocably alter[ed] the ecology of everything, including our own lives' (ibid.: 71, 91). For Kittredge, this was possession, like 'inscribing their names onto the land' (ibid.: 232), but his new aim is to rewrite this relationship as a different version, more attuned to the ecology in which human and nature coexist in a dialogical process aimed at the future.

Our old pilgrims believed in stories in which the West was a promise, a place where decent people could escape the wreckage of failed lives and start over. Come along, the dream whispers, and you can have another chance. We still listen to promises in the wind. This time, we think, we'll get it right ... We must define a story which encourages us to make use of the place where we live without killing it, and we must understand that the living world cannot be replicated. There will never be another setup like the one in which we have thrived. Ruin it and we will have lost ourselves, and that is craziness. (ibid.: 234–5)

Referring to *Hole in the Sky*, Kittredge said that he thought it was, ultimately, 'an ecology book; it's a story about taking care of ourselves and taking care of the world and how to conduct ourselves in what I conceive to be proper ways' (Kittredge, in Morris, 1994: 173).

This recent growth in white Western memoirs, or personal histories of the West, have become the literary site wherein various stories – myth and anti-myth – are examined. At the very intersection of personal and public, this group of writings, fiction and autobiography and the grey area in between, form a new body of white Western representation whose effect is to rememory the West. In Ivan Doig's memoir *This House of Sky*, the metanarrative of the West is described as 'the pattern of remembered instants so uneven, so gapped and rutted and plunging and soaring' simply because his worldview came from parents like 'tribal gods, as old and unarguable and almighty as thunder' (1978: 10). Part of the task as a writer is to fill in the gaps and ruts with the other stories excluded from the overarching and authorized narrative. Teresa Jordan terms these gaps 'unconformities' in her *Riding the White Horse Home* (1994) which, like Kittredge's book, looks back at life in the West in an effort to understand the forces that constructed her identity. In doing so, Jordan explains the difference between official knowledge, like that of the geologist with his 'field maps' who 'reads the landscape like a book,' and the 'the missing record' with all its 'unconformities':

I think of unconformity as something similar to the white space or break on the page writers sometimes use to leap from one idea to another. Or perhaps an unconformity is like all that hazy history that lies between the legends we have of our ancestors and the realities of our own particular lives. (Jordan, 1994: 9–10)

The gap Jordan identifies, the 'break' between 'legends' and 'realities,' is a liminal territory explored in many of these Anglo memoirs, for it is here that the New West is formed and contested. Jordan's task is 'to excavate the unconformities that connect my heritage with who I am now' (ibid.: 15), not just to understand herself, but to see how those same forces 'shaped the rural West' as well (ibid.: 16). This quest for 'knowing' (ibid.) all the 'hazy history' is a call for a genealogy of the West which retrieves lost histories and voices to put alongside the well recorded and mythic ones. She rejects, like many of these Anglo memoirists, the old definitions of the frontier, to forge ahead and never look back, in favour of reflection, analysis, and a perpetual rethinking of the past as a form of therapy, 'a way to keep my people with me and also let them go. I have a way to hold on to the land' (ibid.: 17). The sensibility of loss here is very close to that of Native Americans also reconstructing relations between past, present, and future. Jordan's white settler-ranching family have been driven from their lands by economics, by corporate agribusiness, the latest strands of imperial power in the West, and her work refuses to let their lives be forgotten. It is particularly the women, so often silenced in the histories of the West, who emerge as strong, determined, and resourceful in Jordan's work, as in her contemporary oral history *Cowgirls* (1982). She declares, '[t]hese women make me write' (Jordan, 1994: 18) and through them and their alternative histories Jordan is empowered: 'Once I understood these stories and the power they held over me, I was free to search out other narratives or write my own' (ibid.: 195).

As with many New West writers examined in this chapter, the past has to be re-entered not as a closure but as a bridge to some new space where new identities might be constructed and new communities forged. In this way these diverse voices constitute a new history or Foucauldian 'genealogy' of the West '*bringing forth differences* relative to continuities ... [to] stir[ring] things up ... *wearing out* ... the classificatory divisions ... [while it] jostles and corrodes the conceptual apparatus' (de Certeau, 1988: 79, 98). Like Michel Foucault's 'effective history' as opposed to 'traditional history', it is about discontinuity and interruption depriving 'the self of the reassuring stability of life and nature' and offering instead the desire to 'uproot ... traditional foundations and relentlessly disrupt ... pretended continuity' (Foucault, 1993: 153, 154). Under this philosophy of history, the notion of a regulated, destined, and coherent passage from the past to the present, such as that inscribed for American Western history by the likes of Frederick Jackson Turner, is unsettled and usurped by 'a profusion of entangled events' (ibid.) and the subaltern voices of the 'subjugated' who assert difference and counter the claims of a traditional, linear, and often mythic history.

Conclusion

To live in the New West is increasingly to live in multiple spaces or worlds of difference and to 'inhabit more than one of these "worlds" at the very same time' (Maria Lugones, in Soja, 1996: 130). These examples of 'alternative histories' show how different groups, from a variety of positions, attempt to live in the postmodern West and juggle their various identities. Their experiments with identity, born out of real experiences in the West, their re-examination of history and their 'restorying' of the region all contribute to a broad and necessary revision process that refuses to settle around old myths of possession or gender, or old divisions between groups, customs, and values, but seeks instead a genuine and complex revision akin to the radical 'cyborg' position described by Donna Haraway:

> lived social and bodily realities in which people are not afraid of their joint kinship with animals and machines, not afraid of permanently partial identities and contradictory standpoints. The political struggle is to see from both perspectives at once because each reveals both dominations and possibilities unimaginable from the other vantage point. Single vision produces worse illusions than double vision or many-headed monsters. (Haraway, 1991: 154)

Standing at the crossroads with Anzaldúa, Alexie, or Kittredge, we see a complex New 'cyborg' West in which groups interrelate and negotiate uneasily about their futures. The inequalities of power and authority are evident and still effect the nature of these relations, but increasingly the West acknowledges its multiple cultures as a source of strength and renewal. This is a 'nomad' West of change, mobility, and diffusion where the old ideal of 'settlement', of putting down roots in a single place, may no longer hold true for those whose lives are more transient, fluid, and fragmentary. Travelling for work, education, vacations, is central to most people's lives, particularly in the West where vast distances and ever-changing economies have always made this a region of movement.

CHAPTER 4

New West Postmodernism
and Urbanism

In Sam Shepard's play *True West* (1981) two brothers argue over the
nature of what the West means: Austin, the clean-cut screenwriter
claims he knows the truth because 'I drive on the freeway every day. I
swallow the smog. I watch the news in color. I shop in the Safeway.
I'm the only one who's in touch.' For him, 'There's no such thing as
the West anymore! It's a dead issue! It's dried up ...', while his petty-
criminal brother Lee, who has lived in the Mojave, not the suburbs,
loves *Lonely Are the Brave* and presents a contrasting view in the 'road
and horse' chase movie script he tries to write in the play (Shepard,
1981: 39). Shepard deconstructs these simple oppositions, reverses the
characters' roles and has them fighting on stage at the end amid debris
the effect of which 'should be like a desert junkyard at high noon'
with coyotes howling 'in a vast desert landscape' (ibid.: 54, 63). Here
there is no single truth, only people living in the landscape and
creating their own New West, not as a 'dead issue', but as a complex,
postmodern construction, real and mythic, city suburbs, small towns,
and desert.

The American West has always been, by the very nature of its
mythic representations, a type of hyperreality, a simulation reproducing
images conforming to some already defined, but possibly non-existent,
sense of Westness – as Eden or Golden Land or Lee's cowboy freedom-
highway in Shepard's play. Solnit writes that 'mediations taught people
how to see this place ... and, by implication at least, what not to see'
(Solnit, 1998: 30) and visions of the contemporary and future West have
drawn upon postmodern notions of simulacrum and hyperreality to
explain the look and structure of the urban New West. William Gibson
termed cyberspace a 'consensual hallucination', something close to the
effects of the myths of the West on the American psyche, while
Baudrillard wrote, 'I was here in my imagination long before I actually
came here' (Baudrillard, 1988: 72).

Baudrillard's postmodern West is mediated simulacra, blurring the differences between the real and the imagined. The familiarity of the landscapes, whether cities or deserts, mountains or small towns, are the result of representation, of endless replays of movies, advertising, and television projecting a 'screenscape' of the West, and yet they are also material places where people live and work. Baudrillard is fascinated by how all these elements 'are mingled in the vision' (Baudrillard, 1988: 70) creating a unique landscape capable of containing ancient hieroglyphs, natural vivid light, and 'the most total superficiality' (ibid.) 'at the same time' (ibid.: 63, 70). This simultaneity once again defines a sense of the New West as a 'stunning fusion' (ibid.: 126) of real and imagined spaces.

Similarly, for Eco the West is a bizarre mix of simulations, of 'cities that imitate a city' (Eco, in Docherty, 1993: 200), like Las Vegas, with its parallels to Disneyland; of rebuilt 'ghost towns', of Tombstone with its shoot-outs, of Knot's Berry Farm of Buena Park, Los Angeles. The latter simulates an Old West town, demanding interaction at the level of consumption, creating a 'hallucination' which serves to 'level the various historical periods and erase the distinction between historical reality and fantasy' creating 'the confusion between copy and original' (ibid.: 201–2). Unlike Hollywood's forms of illusion with its audience separated and distinct, in the theme parks that fascinate Eco, Baudrillard, Soja, and others, the lines are blurred and things are 'more real than reality', a 'total theatre' (ibid.: 203) that has today spilled out of the enclaves of the theme parks and into everyday life. Thus Western cities and landscapes form what Soja calls 'second wave hyperreality' because you no longer choose to visit them as leisure, they visit you through the fabric of everyday experience: in material and physical spaces – shopping malls, streets, parks, workplaces – but also in the 'other spaces' of postmodern life – the Internet, TV, fashion systems – and the spaces of the imagination. In the remapping of the postmodern West the distinctions of old and new, of myth and reality, of imagination and fact are uncertain, blended, fused – substituting reality with signs and doubles of the real. We can re-live the Old West as tourists at theme parks or 'heritage' experiences, shop in cyberspace at the New West Mall, 'dedicated to the pioneer spirit of the Old West ... [where] people prosper on their own terms ... find the deals that will make a difference in your life, just like in days of yesteryear' (http://www.newwestmall.com/), become 'one with nature' at a New Age community in Santa Fe or Bell Rock, Arizona, or become Pharoah-for-a-day at the Luxor in Las Vegas.

This hyperreality is a particular version of the postmodern which characterizes many aspects of the New West. A wider definition of the postmodern includes the questioning of inclusive metanarratives (like 'old' Western History), uncertain and fluid senses of identity, dynamic and relational networks of community and governance, diverse and heterogeneous cultural forms, and a mixed economy of signs. When we examine the New West, its multiplicities stare back as a kaleidoscope of fragmented doubts, uncertainties and anxieties *as well as* its potentialities as a site for political possibilities, redefinitions, and new forms of identity and community. The nature of the postmodern experience is associated with this double-edged riskiness, and with the simultaneity of responses which form the constant attempts to come to terms with 'this bewilderment of the contemporary' (Gregory, 1994: 139). Jencks once referred to postmodernism in architecture as 'double-coding': 'the combination of Modern techniques with something else (usually traditional building) ...' (quoted in Tallack, 1991: 133). The New West fuses old and new creating something different, shifting between the old 'cowboy economy' based on natural resources and the 'cosmopolitan florescence' of a 'postindustrial, services sector' (Riebsame et al., 1997: 12) within an increasingly hybridized cultural space.

The postmodern has often been defined through discussions of 'highly visible topoi' (Gregory, 1994: 139) located in the West: Jameson's Bonaventure Hotel in Los Angeles, Baudrillard's Mojave Desert, Eco and Zukin's Disneyland and Venturi's Las Vegas. These spaces have been 'read' as postmodern and used to describe the effects and challenges of postmodernity while alerting us to new ways of seeing the contemporary, asserting the importance of spatial rather than temporal considerations. Thus the cultural geography of the New West – urban and rural, human and natural – with 'its ability to compel consensus' diminished (Sarup, 1993: 145), has become the epitome of the postmodern experience. Without absolute, singular definition, mixing media imagery, myth, and an increasingly simulated sense of the 'real' with a diverse, hybrid, cultural identity and a collage-like multiple geography, the New West emerged in the postwar world at the very time postmodernism, in its various guises, became critically active in response to similar changes: 'to developments in contemporary capitalism ... which was going through an expansionist cycle and producing new commodities, abundance, and a more affluent lifestyle' (Best and Kellner, 1991: 15).

In particular, this version of the West as 'new' was associated with the rapid growth of the Sunbelt cities (San Diego, Houston, Pheonix, Albuquerque, etc.), the continued expansion of established urban areas (Los Angeles, Denver, Dallas), tourist and entertainment centres (Las Vegas, Reno, Santa Fe, Grand Canyon, National Parks), and the regeneration of smaller communities (Vail, Jackson Hole, Moab, Park City). It is the postmodern mix of these cultures and their real and imagined spaces that this chapter examines.

The Urban West

'What Raymond Chandler Knew and Western Historians Forgot', according to the title of Limerick's essay, was that cities were at the very heart of the West (in Meldrum, 1993). For Chandler, cities were full of class and economic differences and the landscapes within them reflected this variety. In *Farewell, My Lovely* (1940), the detective Marlowe passes through diverse Western urban landscapes: at Purissima Canyon he discovers 'some realtor's dream had turned into a hangover', while at the Grayle mansion he enters a proto-simulated theme park with 'a flying Cupid ... crouching griffins ... stone water-lillies ... and a big bull-frog sitting on one of the leaves [and everything] built to look like a ruin', while on the LA Strip he sees 'handsome modernistic buildings in which the Hollywood flesh-peddlers never stop talking money' (1971: 56, 108, 127). In the New West today, 80 per cent of people are classified as urban, dwelling and working in cities as diverse as Chandler's LA, and yet the imagined West is still primarily represented as rural, wild, and open. The relationships surrounding this interlocking of rural and urban, wealth and land, imaginary and real, are at the very heart of life in the region and recur in many of its core texts. *Chinatown* (Roman Polanski, 1974), for example, portrays the expansion of LA into its surrounding agricultural lands as a ruthless speculation driven by megalomaniacal men like Noah Cross, his ambivalent name symbolic of apocalypse and saviour, who simultaneously destroys and creates the very New West later generations will inherit.

The boom in the western states began in Chandler's 1930s and 1940s with the influx of federal aid through the New Deal's efforts to integrate the West into the national economy and encourage self-suffiency, and continued at a pace between 1940 and 1965. Populations increased, especially in the Pacific and Rocky Mountain states, and the continuous preparations for the Second World War, Korea, and then Vietnam guaranteed military and civilian economic upswings in the region. The most noticeable growth was in the metropolitan areas of California – San Jose, Orange County, San Diego, but increasingly other cities like Las Vegas, Phoenix, and Albuquerque developed like the so-called Sunbelt cities of Atlanta, Miami, Tampa, and Orlando in the South. Attracting both new industries and new populations, such as retirement communities and those fleeing the older cities of the so-called Frost and Rust Belts, these Sunbelt cities shared some similarities, but the West had a different ethnic mix, traditions, and geography, and its cities attracted diverse populations from the USA and beyond. The development of technology, from air conditioning to computers, efficient low-cost air travel to superhighways, enabled the rapid growth of cities in the West and, subsequently, new forms of urban space. For example, as Findlay (1992) argues, the West invented the industrial park (Stanford, 1958), the active retirement community (Sun City, Arizona), and the theme park (Disneyland, 1955), and these became central to the expansion of the region and to the lure of the West to outsiders. Combining good climate, geography, cheaper land and lower taxes, the West attracted big companies: Motorola and General Electric to Phoenix, Shell Oil to Houston, Boeing and later Microsoft to Seattle. Alongside the established military presence in the West, these companies' employees responded to the dual promise of business opportunity and quality of life, to what Fred Hofheinz, former mayor of Houston, called the 'frontiers of the new industrial America, where people can still reach the American dream' (quoted in Chudacoff, 1994: 415).

Populations grew with the cities, becoming increasingly diverse with people arriving from all over the USA and from beyond its shores with the ending of the quota system in the 1960s. The sprawl pattern of 'newer' western cities, like Pheonix, became a characteristic feature as their centres spread outward, annexing farmland and desert into city boundaries in order to house these growing populations, build new shopping malls, and service the expanding economies. Findlay argues these cities had 'a less rooted population' since so many had arrived in a relatively rapid time, and unlike Eastern cities, they had not grown in a conventional zonal manner around a 'distinct nucleus' (Findlay, 1992: 35). Instead, 'the particles increased in number too quickly to be held by the pull of the center', escaping its 'magnetic field' and forming 'orbits around new nuclei that competed against the attraction of the traditional center' (ibid.). Thus the West's new cities were mobile, sprawling, decentred and diverse postmodern spaces emphasized through the growth of the automobile as the main source of transport allowing flexibility of movement, but also the impression of an increasingly atomistic culture. The 'auto hegemony' (ibid.: 37) defined the West's new cities, but increasingly haunted them too with worries over pollution, crime ('car-jacking'), and the effects upon the downtown as central businesses failed while shopping and business spread with the affluent population to the suburbs. As 1980s recessions hit, downtowns became business centres without a population as the cities emptied at night, leaving only an economic underclass and the homeless. For Findlay, the new spatial order of the urban West was moderated by the presence of its controlled 'magic lands' where organization and pattern were imposed as assertions of rational design replacing the chaotic sprawl of the city. In its industrial and theme parks and retirement communities, the West created order from chaos and reasserted a new urban form, an alternative to downtown centralization, with the emphasis upon multicenteredness. The apparently unchecked sprawl of the explosive city was ameliorated by the 'familiar and understandable environment . . . [of] suburban enclaves' (ibid.) upholding 'the promise of amenities, prosperity, spaciousness, freedom, and autonomy' that had always characterized the attractions of the West. Here these were reinvented as new urban space, a 'chosen land', a 'mosaic of "voluntary regions" . . . (ibid.: 269) where mobile people made their homes far from where they were born, because they were economically able to do so. The effect of this desire to begin again has always been part of the western dream, and in the New West, has found renewed expression with the city 'not as a single place but as a series of environments catering to different needs or tastes' (ibid.) and its residents moving between its enclaves – strip, mall, industrial park, and entertainment complex. These mobile, affluent New Westerners constructed their city through these spaces, defining their mental maps of the city according to their own interest communities while simultaneously excluding themselves from others in that city. Hence, as Davis (1990) argues, a sprawling city like Los Angeles is divided along economic and racial lines with the suburban, mobile communities often literally gated in areas well away from the underclass. Planned communities, urban villages, alternative downtowns – the magic lands – defined the growth of the urban West and reshaped its spatiality in a bold and clear manner learnt, some would claim, from Disneyland's sense of order. The idea of the unreadable city, out of control and beyond human organization, was countered by these attempts to create orderly cities in the West through communities that had definite uses and relationships. They were 'either landscaped or walled off so that outside distractions could not intrude on the more orderly life within', restating the promise of the West in a new urban form which deliberately 'eliminated the complexities normally associated with urban settings', oversimplified 'the social realities,' and distilled 'visual and functional diversity to a few basic images and ideas' (Findlay, 1992: 297). Disneyland was conceived as the 'antidote to perceived urban malaise' (ibid.: 67), organizing and sanitizing space as a narrative, telling only good stories about the past and the future. The hope for developing New West cities and their satellite communities was to imitate the 'orderly sequence of messages' (ibid.: 69) projected in Disneyland, to 'manage nature' and 'imagineer' a city without pathologies. The city-within-a-city could be as familiar and pleasant as a small town envisaged by Norman Rockwell or Ronald Reagan, a vision closely related to the dream of frontier communities and new beginnings. Disney idealized urbanism, heightening its visual appeal, controlling space and privatizing its management – the very same lessons to be applied in New West cityscapes and their 'theme park' satellites.

   The tension between this desire for order and the inevitable expansion within the cities of the West has often led to a 'sprawling and poly-nucleated decentralization' (Soja, 1989: 208), as in Los Angeles, where its counties – especially Orange County – have grown to form peripheral areas or 'outer cities', with residential communities, shopping mega-malls, environments for leisure and entertainment, universities and military/industrial complexes. For Soja, this fragmenting LA metropolis represents postmodernity, 'stubbornly simultaneous', unwilling to be defined, deceptive and incomprehensible, heterogeneous and eerily familiar – a complex space needing careful exploration, 'turning everyday urban life inside-out and outside-in at the same time and in the same places' (Soja, 1996: 17). To examine such multiple spaces, LA and other Western cities require new ways of seeing, incorporating time, space, and social being so that economic and social spaces as well as imagined spaces of desire, contest, and otherness are recognized. For Soja, Western cities seen in this way are problematic, but not without hope, for they represent a 'thirdspace' – 'a constantly shifting and changing milieu of ideas, events, appearances, and meanings' (Soja, 1996: 2) where juxtaposition and co-presence – ethnic, racial, economic, gendered – may enable new hybrid identities and more democratic forms of relations to emerge over time.

However, such guarded optimism is countered by the more prevalent 'noir' vision of Western urbanism; as Joan Didion wrote, Los Angeles was 'a beautiful place that contains a . . . *putrescence*' (1985: 182), and it is this vision that Mike Davis develops in his 'post-liberal Los Angeles' epitomized by class and ethnic division, corporate carelessness and exploitation, and the polarization of urban space. For Davis and Didion, fragmentation is a symptom of individual, cultural, social, and economic breakdown and is difficult to reconcile fully with the more optimistic postmodern geography of Edward Soja. This 'noir' West found its form in the 1930s 'hard-boiled' fictions of James M. Cain, Raymond Chandler, and Dashiel Hammett, and the subsequent and inter-related period of classic 'film noir' (1940–55) in which the exiled European directors, like Billy Wilder, Edward Dmytryk, and Edgar Ulmer, brought a German Expressionist sensibility to the exploration of 'American' themes. Ending up in Hollywood, they explored the illusions of the West and the dream of a Promised Land tainted by greed, desire, and the complex urbanism of LA, employing distorted lighting and camera angles to decentre more conventional, idealized approaches and to assert new subjectivities emerging in this era. Women, for example, emerge in 'film noir' as capable of individual action, violence, and anti-traditional roles. Thus, Phyllis Dietrichson (Barbara Stanwyck) in *Double Indemnity* (Billy Wilder, 1944) epitomizes much of this new sensibility, appearing to be the blonde object of desire, while gradually revealed as a 'femme fatale', plotting the manipulation of the gullible Walter Neff (Fred MacMurray). She is the murdering wife, the wicked stepmother, the rich Californian who wants more. As a film of the New West, it goes further in its utilization of place to reinforce these issues of subjectivity and deceit situating the early scheming in 'one of those Californian-Spanish houses everyone was nuts about ten to fifteen years ago'. Neff arrives at the Los Feliz home in bright sunlight, driving past carefree children playing ball on the street, but as the camera pans across the LA cityscape, the idyllic dream of Californian wealth and freedom, one can see the earthquake scars across the road, reminders of the fragile faultlines of this domesticated and national utopia. The outer scenes will quickly be followed by scenes inside this ideal home, full of images of deceit, entrapment, and social unease: Neff's gendered assumption of authority, the maid's mistrust, Neff's walk through the living room symbolically 'stuffy', dusty, and barred by the light streaming in through the Venetian blinds, and Phyllis's knowing exploitation of her sexuality to trap Neff, even though she admits her 'face' isn't 'on straight'. This is a family narrative, so often the core of the Westward dream, about to be blown apart by the darker vision of an imminent postwar world of boom, expansion, and greed, where all the places of the city of dreams are transformed into spaces of deceit. Hence, the home, the Pacific All-Risk Insurance building where Neff works, and his apartment all become shadowy duplicitous spaces, but perhaps the darkest of all is the use of Jerry's suburban supermarket, which on one level epitomizes the New urban West's affluent sprawl, as the meeting place for the plotting of murder, double-dealing, and the destruction of patriarchal order. *Double Indemnity* ushers in a new era as a time of dangerous change, of an old world being turned upside down and its ideologies and social orders put under question: gender, work, family. It is unsurprising that the style and content of 'film noir' should recur throughout the next decades to analyze continued changes in the cultural politics of California and the West, most notably in *Chinatown* (1974) and *True Confessions* (1981). One notable example is Joan Didion, who co-wrote the script of *True Confessions* with husband John Gregory Dunne, and whose writings from the 1960s have interrogated the apparent ease of life in the West and exposed its illusions and uncertainties from a female perspective. Didion's West is primarily urban and her work has parallels with aspects of postmodernism, particularly in its multiple narratives, fragmenting subjectivities, detached surfaces, and its formal strategies. Her apparently cold style mirrors the indifference of the West she explores, where 'much of it was merely imagined or improvised', where individual memories are 'only the traces of someone else's memory' and 'the truth about the place is elusive' (Didion, 1985: 147, 148). In *Play It As It Lays* (1971) Maria Wyeth, a woman on the edge, symbolically raised at Silver Wells 'on the test range' in Nevada (Didion, 1973: 148), intersects with Western spaces (Los Angeles, Las Vegas, the Mojave) in her efforts to recover her self from breakdown. For example, she describes her sense of being in Las Vegas: 'Her mind was a blank tape, imprinted daily with snatches of things overheard, fragments of dealers' patter, the beginnings of jokes and odd lines of song lyrics' (Didion, 1973: 133). The interpenetration of identity and place is uppermost in Didion's work for places 'dominate the California imagination ... Deriving not only from the landscape but from the claiming of it, from the romance of emigration, the radical abandonment of established attachments' (Didion, 1994: 100). In the whirl of the city, Maria's sense of self is affected by the fragmented experience so that she was unsure 'where her body stopped and the air began [or] ... the difference between *Maria* and *other*' (ibid.: 134). Rather than give in to this sense, she longs for control and order, fearing the implications of allowing the 'other'-as-place into her life. Elsewhere, she feels herself connected to the Hoover Dam 'where great power grids converged', where water and desert collide, suggesting she is of the city with its artificial paradise, of the desert with its arid vacuity, and of the dam with its 'pressure and pull of the water' (ibid.) all at the same time. She cannot, of course, control such experiences – the experiences of the West and its multiple landscapes – and her only solution is a cold detachment from them all. Didion's postwar New West is typified by the desire to forget such places and the past, and to replace them with an endless present simulated by the movies or the LA freeway where time and space are conflated, and to substitute communication with fragments of dialogue, 'scripts,' and telephone messages (see Didion, 1992: 102). Maria's past, symbolized by Silver Wells, which has been blown away in a nuclear test and is, therefore, only a blank on the map, is a series of moments that she tries to hold on to in order to give some pattern to her life and to the world in which she finds herself empty and bereft of hope. For Didion, Maria's struggle and her location between Hollywood freeways and pools and Nevada casinos and deserts exemplifies the unstable postmodern West 'haunted by the Mojave ... devastated by the hot dry Santa Ana wind' liable to ignite at any time in a 'season of suicide and divorce and prickly dread' (Didion, 1985: 19). History is pushed aside in Didion's West because all that counts is the future: 'Here is the last stop for all those who come from somewhere else, for all those who drifted away from the cold and the past and the old ways' (ibid.: 20). These new migrants into the Sunbelt cities, echoing those in Nathanael West's *The Day of the Locust*, have gained their visions from the media, from the projected and simulated West that Didion argues is, at best, fragile and illusory. Employing the parallel of Hollywood itself, Nathanael West referred to California as the 'dream dump' – a place where all the remnants of people's dreams settle and mix. In Didion's fiction, Maria is a fragmented, ambiguous identity in a postwar West where women are objectified like the artificial landscapes in which they live, struggling to reconnect herself with something deeper, below the glossy surface of Hollywood, with something like 'the deep still water with the hidden intakes' 'below the dam's face' at the Hoover Dam (Didion, 1973: 134). Maria longs to be reborn out of her aborted life with its simulations and emptiness into something that has meaning. 'She wanted to stay in the dam, lie on the great pipe itself ...' (ibid.: 135), but can only just barely survive in a world where 'NOTHING APPLIES' (ibid.: 7). Finally, Didion's West is full of unease, caught in the glare of contemporary surfaces and yet marked by a sense of profound loss for an equivalent dream to that of the early settlers, who, risking everything, moved West with a faith in family, home, and the land.

Out of these landscapes of filmic or literary noir critics like Paul Virilio claim the urban West is a 'phantom landscape', with LA 'the city of living cinema where stage-sets and reality, tax-plans and scripts, the living and the living-dead, mix and merge deliriously' (Virilio, 1991: 27, 26). Here, as Eco and Baudrillard also noted, reality and 'reality-effect' blur, so that the city's sprawl and its endless stream of images become captivating and dislocative at the same time, suggesting a world which is at once both controlled and out of control. These are the end products of Didion's landscapes and the foreunners of Davis's politicized noir vision in *City of Quartz* (1990) and *The Ecology of Fear* (1998b), where the city is contained and privatized space determined by growing surveillance and 'militarization ... grimly visible at the street level' (Davis, 1990: 223).

The Western city dream has become the nightmare 'noir' of science fiction, of *Metropolis*, *Blade Runner* and *Escape from LA* that 'only extrapolate from actually existing trends' (ibid.). Whereas Findlay viewed the 'magic lands' as the assertion of urban order and Soja saw them as versions of postmodern diversity, Davis sees them entrenched and fortified to the extent that the city is divided like a war zone, between rich and poor, white and non-white, powerful and powerless. This is 'fortress LA', a 'scanscape' of surveillance, gated communities and total security – the world that William Gibson will explore fiction-ally in *Virtual Light* (see later). The magic lands turned inward and closed off have become the model not just for architecture and spatial use, but for attitudes, human responses, and future planning. Public spaces are privatized, incorporated into the autoculture of an elite with access to the new downtown corporate citadels, depedestrianized and raised up above the street like 'a Miesian skyscape raised to dementia' (ibid.: 229). For Davis, this ideological control cuts downtown off from its past and from the 'non-Anglo urbanity of its future' and builds instead 'spatial apartheid' as a 'seamless continuum of middle-class work, consumption and recreation' (ibid.: 229, 230–1). The Watts riots in 1965 and the LA riots of 1992 (Davis calls them 'a hybrid social revolt ... a postmodern bread riot' in Gooding-Williams, 1993: 142) mark resistance to the city in gestures of despair and destruction, and act as reminders that the cities of the West are increasingly complex places, divided along lines of race, class, and power. Davis admits to 'a nostalgized vision of what Southern California was like 30 years ago – the freedom of its cruising streets and the kinds of careless, libidinal adolescence that used to be possible' (Davis, 1992: 3) and so shares some of Didion's sense of melancholic loss of an earlier utopian dream. These old freedoms, long associated with the West Coast – cruising, surfing, the counterculture (but only for whites) – have been transformed into no-go areas for Chicanos and African-Americans, to intense gang loyalties in poor neighbourhoods, gangster rap and to the kind of explosive violence seen in 1992. Davis charts an economically determined West where individual freedoms are subsumed by the corporate grip of repression, exclusion, and surveillance, where space is divided hierarchically and the only resistance are sporadic gestures of despair in the face of relentless control, and the only freedom allowed is the freedom to consume. The enclosed, normalized spaces of the city aim to keep out undesirables, defined as those who don't conform, aren't 'normal', creating a city whose ideal is Disneyland wrapped up in what Soja calls a 'semiotic blanket' that acts to screen out the real tensions so that 'all that is seen is so fragmented and filled with whimsy and pastiche [that] the hard edges of the capitalist, racist and patriarchal landscape seem to disappear, melt into air' (Soja, 1989: 246).

Postindustrial Los Angeles's 'semiotic blanket' projects an ideal image of urban order to the growing number of tourists who wish to visit the city, but, claim Davis and Soja, echoing the European postmodern critics, an 'artificial Los Angeles' is emerging in the form of Universal Studios' City Walk, designed by Jon Jerde, who also designed Treasure Island in Las Vegas, providing a simulation, an 'idealized reality' as a cleaned up, reduced version of the city's Olvera Street, Hollywood and West Side packaged for tourist consumption. It represents a new urban planning dream, 'the city emptied of all lived

human experience ... eras[ing] any trace of our real joy, pain or labor'
(Davis, 1995: 8) in an effort to Disneyfy and control urban experience as
'a monumental exercise in sociological hygiene' (Davis, 1998b: 397).

However, even this vision can be contested: as Gottlieb asserts, 'Los
Angeles is not City Walk' and cannot stand for the New West as a
whole, for that has greater diversity and conflict, something closer to
the Pico Farmers' Market in Santa Monica with its global meeting
ground of ethnicities, products, languages, and cultural capital (in
Rothman, 1998b: 183–4). For more optimistic writers and critics, the
hope for the future lies with the increasingly hybrid forms and communities forming at the edges of the city and in its subcultures, who are
able, contrary to the impression conveyed by Davis, to resist and to
project alternatives to the normalized identities defined by the new
urban elites. The increase in the multiethnic population in the West,
discussed in Chapter 3, may gradually shift some of the power in cities
like Los Angeles away from the declining Anglo minority and encourage 'a politics of deterritorialization and reconnection ... resistances
and transgressions' (in Gooding-Williams, 1993: 192). The dynamics of
Western cities are such that there may come a time when the possibilities of hybrid intercultural democracy can flourish and reinvent, once
again, these urban spaces as examples of Soja's 'thirdspace', breaking
the cycle of utopian/dystopian visions that have characterized urban
representations. For example, in Guillermo Gómez-Peña's work, discussed in Chapter 3, cities (like cultures) become 'multicentric, hybrid'
borderlands where groups, communities, and ideologies are 'overlapping, interlocking, and overlaid' and eventually disappear into 'a place
in which no centers remain. It's all margins ... there are no "others", or
better said, the only true "others" are those who resist fusion, mestizaje,
and cross-cultural dialogue' (Gómez-Peña, 1996: i, 6–7). Gómez-Peña
reinvents the 'space between' traditional groupings as a 'Fourth World'
deliberately breaking down the usual First/Third World dichotomy in
favour of a more fluid space without fixed identities or nationalities and
within this a 'third alternative' of hybrid cultural exchange closer to the
kind of deterritorialization called for above.

However, the darker 'noir' vision still persists in Gómez-Peña's later
satiric future vision of America, *Friendly Cannibals* (1996), where the
pendulum of power has swung even further: 'It's like an upside-down
version of the Wild West', with the Anglos as 'marginal others' and
Latinos as the 'mainstream' (Gómez-Peña, 1996: 17). He writes, 'This

land that once was called "the land of opportunity" is now ridden with fear, violence, and guacamole. Mexican vampires are everywhere ...' (ibid.: 43). Mythic space is transformed to a 'land of hatred and fractured geographies' (ibid.: 46) echoing another apocalyptic vision of LA published in 1994, Bret Easton Ellis's *The Informers*, where the city is literally 'swarming with vampires' (Ellis, 1994: 149). In all these projected future cities of the West, one is struck by the sense of instability, inevitable change and contests between the creative and destructive energies of people and place which portray cities − for better and for worse − as the epitome of the West as contact zone, as a space of encounters where negotiations may happen and hybrid forms emerge.

The Other Urban West: 'Aspenization'

For many people experiencing the sprawling cities of the West with their escalating problems of crime and disharmony, there has been a new wave of reverse migration inland to smaller towns, in search of a second chance at a new beginning. Sometimes linked to 'white flight' away from urban blight, this has been significant in the growth and, indeed, regeneration of many smaller communities in the rural West as new technologies and communications systems permitted work and leisure to be conducted from further afield. Writing in 1986, Wallace Stegner claimed the cities of the West were 'overflowing the edges of their agar dishes and beginning to sicken on their own wastes', believing that smaller towns were 'more western' balancing mobility and stability in an effort to live with the sparseness of the landscape, representing 'the most quintessential West' (Stegner, 1987: 24, 25, 85). In 1993 the *New York Times* announced in a headline, 'Eastward Ho! Disenchanted Californians Turn to the Interior West', with 30,000 Californians moving to Colorado alone in 1993–4. John Sedgwick, writing for *GQ Magazine*, saw this influx, or 'Californification' as the 'loosing of postmodernism' into a land once 'so rugged, so permanent and so down-to-earth that residents had legitimately come to view it as reality itself' (1995: 243). This version of 'postmodernism' indicates the fear of new ideas, new capital and different values flooding into the West and disrupting and unsettling older systems and ways of life. Ironically, what Sedgwick fails to acknowledge is what Stegner recognized, that this kind of migration and change has always been a process consistent with the development of the West as a space of contact and mobility. The information superhighway and the freedom it gave to live away from the cities and still work effectively was a new extension of the old Route 66 dream of migration and a new start.

In *Explore!*, the Yellowstone Country Visitors' Guide, Livingston is described as 'one of the most exciting small towns in Montana':

> Nowhere in Montana does the Old West combine with the New West in such a fashion. This is a town where people in cowboy hats and boots are real cowboys. Here the pickup truck is the standard form of transportation. On the other hand, the town boasts the finest collection of art galleries for a town of its size to be found anywhere in the West. (*Explore!*, August, 1997: 13)

In the same publication are advertisements for 'The Cowboy Connection Old West Collectibles and Gallery' and 'Outlaw's Pizza and Casino', while nearby Robert Redford was at work on *The Horse Whisperer* and Dennis Quaid and Meg Ryan had just finished shooting a TV movie. Down the road in the Gallatin Valley Ted Turner and Jane Fonda, and Steven Seagal, own ranches; across in Colorado, fashion designer Ralph Lauren owns the 'Double RL Ranch', a 14,000 acre spread outside Telluride. The New West has an almost surreal ability to juggle the commercial realities of the age and the longed-for retention of older values – to be both Old and New, ranch-riding cowboy and art gallery-goer, outlaw and pizza vendor, media star and recluse. In the New West, the fusion is everything as sites compete for attention within the multilayeredness that characterizes the West.

This 'Aspenization', whereby old, small towns like Aspen, Colorado have been reinvented as postmodern tourist, residential, and enterprise centres, is an increasingly important aspect of the New West. Places like Vail, Aspen, and Telluride, Colorado, Moab, St George, Park City, Utah, Kalispell, Montana and Coeur d'Alene and Ketchum, Idaho, and Jackson Hole, Wyoming have developed considerably in the last twenty years as tourist, outdoor pursuits destinations, second-home outposts, and new economic communities. These towns often share common histories as mining boom towns that spiral in wealth and population only to decline even more rapidly when the ore runs out. Thus in March 1959 businessmen looked upon the landscape of Colorado and saw the potential for a ski resort development. One of them, Earl Eaton, had first seen the land on a failed uranium prospecting trip in 1954. The new uranium was tourism and Vail was opened in December 1962 aiming to develop the area as a ski resort with an eye on the 1976 Olympics. In 1960 California had promoted the Squaw Valley via the Winter Olympics and this led to the growth of Lake Tahoe as a tourist destination, and currently a similar tactic is being used over the Games in Salt Lake City, Utah in 2002. Moab, Utah, an ex-uranium mining town, where Edward Abbey lived and worked, has developed as a centre for tourism connected to the national parks and to mountain biking. Charles Wilkinson wrote that for all its change and for all Abbey's attacks on industrial tourism, Moab is a dynamic place, 'both blessed and beleaguered by its surrounding glory,' and a meeting place with all the 'essential stresses and dreams that characterize the interior West', whose summer population swells from 7,000 to 16,000 (in Riebsame et al., 1997: 22). At any time in Moab, one might rub shoulders with stuntmen working on a nearby film-shoot, slickrock mountain bikers, hikers, microbrewers, or tourists taking in the Canyonlands (opened 1964 as a national park), as well as those older residents who have lived through the changes and still farm the lands around the town.

This 'resortification' of the West has become another focus for intense debates about growth, population changes, water and other resources, land use, housing developments, and employment which go on all over the West in cities like Las Vegas and Los Angeles, as well as in the smaller, developing communities mentioned above. As Ringholz puts it, the attraction of small towns for people are that 'they wanted urban experiences in a rural environment' (Ringholz, 1996: 8) and that this in turn has meant concerns over the way these communities are managed. Tourism and outdoor sports have generated the new econo-mies of the West in many of the towns mentioned, with the New West becoming 'America's playground' supporting mountain biking, skiing, white water rafting, rock-climbing, hiking, four-wheel driving, and fishing, with the best places becoming 'pilgrimages to the meccas of a civil religion sweeping America' (in Riebsame et al., 1997: 125). *The Places Rated Almanac* that began to publish in the 1970s, and *Money Magazine* have often promoted as highly desirable these smaller western towns, rating them as 'boom towns', 'small art towns', and even 'dreamtowns.' As Limerick writes, the appeal of these communities is their youthfulness and their perceived retention of earlier, mythic qualities:

> In the outdoor sports of the New West, the dreams of the babyboo-
> mer childhood and the dreams of babyboomer middle age coincide.
> Performed in the landscape associated with televised western adven-
> ture, the vigorous outdoor exercise associated with the New West
> seemed to promise a postponement of aging and an extension of life
> itself. (Limerick, in Riebsame et al., 1997: 161)

The New West is the affluent 'babyboomer's dream come true' for it
appears to reverse the process of time, the very logic of the Universe,
transforming the Old West into the New, appealing to a desire for
immortality. In this sense, these New West towns present a remedy for
those in need of healing, just as the frontier once provided a chance to
begin again. The shift away from the Sunbelt cities to these smaller
towns with their perceived 'quality of life' is a perpetuation and
reinvention of the Edenic, utopian dream of the West remodelled in
the language of real estate and New Ageism, selling not fabulous riches
but good neighbourhoods, schools, and 'space to breathe'.

The example of Park City, Utah that Ringholz discusses shows a
declining mining town developing rapidly after 1963 into a ski resort and
tourist location whose population increase and demand for land and
facilities has caused serious planning problems. This process of change is
recorded in the photography of Lewis Baltz's collection *Park City* (1980)
which captures the town's half-built edges, its ground-level fragments,
and its new booster real estate mentality. In 1978 its Main Street was
listed in the National Register of Historic Places in an attempt to
preserve some of the old mining heritage, but rapid development has
taken place around this core. By 1992 Park City adopted a development
code to direct growth rather than to control it, aiming to maintain rural
areas and sensitive lands, preserve open spaces, and to allow a 'growth
tier system' to prioritize and structure the continued urbanization of the
area. Above Park City, Robert Redford in 1969 bought Timphaven, a
small local ski area, and established the Sundance Resort, further adding
to the reputation and desirability of the area, making the county in which
it stands, Summit County, the second fastest growing county in the US
during 1990–5 (Riebsame et al., 1997: 96). However, the inevitable
process of change has been accelerated by the 2002 Winter Olympics
which will further expand Park City and, one assumes, put pressure on
the already strained resources. This struggle between local planning and
pressure group activity has been echoed elsewhere, in places like

St George, Utah where its aptly named 'Citizens for Moderate Growth' have worked in an effort to maintain *and* regulate the inevitable expansion of this popular town whose slogan is 'Utah's All Season Resort City'. However, the town is typical of the New West's diversity, becoming Utah's version of Daytona Beach at spring break when students arrive in their thousands to celebrate the onset of summer, maintaining a large retirement community, and continuing as a centre for the Mormon Church. Close to Las Vegas and Zion National Park, St George's population rose from 5,000 in 1960 to over 30,000 in the 1990s.

Ringholz hopes for 'Comprehensive master plans built on consensus and designed by the citizens through neighbourhood visioning programs', alongside a 'rethinking of ranching, mining, timbering, and other extractive industries' (1996: 193). But for such hopes to be realized it will be increasingly important that the diverse elements of the New West population come together in cooperation rather than splinter into entrenched and extreme positions of opposition. At the more extreme end of this equation are those who seek out small Western towns as imagined retreats from the technological values of the postmodern world and identify these places as the bastions of a rugged individualism associated by Jackson Turner with both the frontier and some vital American spirit. In Noxon, home of the Militia of Montana, a group associated with the Oklahoma bomber Timothy McVeigh, Jonathan Raban sensed a 'version of the West ... half boy-scout play-acting, half deadly paranoia, with some queer Bible-reading thrown into the mixture ... like bad-blood descendants of the homesteaders' (Raban, 1996: 299). They resented government, desired self-sufficiency and self-defence, and saw property rights as a legacy of older settlers and Manifest Destiny. In the 'instruction manual' or 'bible' of McVeigh, Andrew Macdonald's *The Turner Diaries* (1978) (a reference to supposed 'white martyr' Earl Turner), there is a violent rejection of urban, multicultural America and the desire to destroy it and replace it with a Nazi 'Order'. In these survivalist fictions, the city is corrupt and in need of a kind of ethnic cleansing of 'nonwhites' and 'mongrels' before a new system can return America (and the world) to a 'purer' vision and path. Similarly, the 'Unabomber' Ted Kaczynski, an urban exile who lived in Lincoln, Montana, wrote 'The positive ideal that we propose is Nature ... a perfect counter-ideal to technology' (in Raban, 1996: 302–3), and must have seen at first hand the New West's tourism and outdoor pursuits industry flooding into his town. This peculiar blend of distorted Western self-reliance and the endurance of the New West is summed up by those who, following the capture of the Unabomber in April 1996, set about exploiting the commercial possibilities by printing T-shirts with the logo 'Lincoln, Home of the Unabomber – The Last Best Place to Hide'. As always, this is 'the unreliable West, where a sense of impending upheaval has always come with the territory' (ibid.: 320), a place of terrible extremes, judicious hopes, and staggering fears.

'Some bleary-eyed vision of freedom': Charles Bowden

Many New Western writers live and work in these smaller towns (see Chapter 3), reflecting upon the changes, ironies, and odd clashes that surface between the Old and New West. As Holthaus reports, 'there is no part of the West that is at ease. It is a regional teapot in which all the world's tempestuous conflicts, contradictions, and questions simmer and boil' (Holthaus, 1997: xiv). This is true of Tucson journalist-writer Charles Bowden's work with its characteristic unease about the New West. He wrote in 1994 of living 'where almost all of the literature ignores the simple fact that for one hundred years this region has been urban, rock-hard urban' (in Temple, 1994: 15), and yet people cling to a rural myth. For him, the West is a 'mix' of 'great natural beauty with its abundant human ugliness ... a place of false values ... fraud, sentimentality and flim-flam' (ibid.) and yet this is not reflected enough in its literature. Bowden prefers films like *Junior Bonner* or *Raising Arizona* for their representations of New Western life. A friend of Edward Abbey, Bowden has called him the man who 'invented the Southwest we live in' and 'made us look at it' with new eyes (in Hepworth and McNamee, 1996: 244), and his own work is similarly 'characterized by an effort to understand rather than an obsession with ignoring' (ibid.: 23). He believes in an unsentimental portrayal of the New West rather than a dishonest retention of old, dangerous myths that can become distorted into *The Turner Diaries* or Unabomber fantasies of pure Nature.

Blue Desert (1986), a book of essays and reflections, summarizes Bowden's attachment to the West and testifies to his development from Abbey's work:

> This is the place they hope to escape their pasts – the unemployment, the smoggy skies, dirty cities, crush of human numbers. This they cannot do. Instead, they reproduce the world they have fled. I am drawn to the frenzy of this act. (Bowden, 1986: 1)

Reading the book is like watching the West from a train window, 'fat with contradictions but sound[ing] one steady note: the land', a land emerging in 'conflicting scenes ... [that] jar against each other as the train thunders toward its destination' (ibid.). This contradictory urban, 'Aspenized' New West, is where Bowden dwells – the 'blue desert' – real and surreal, known and unknown, imagined and factual simultaneously. Rather than ignore the 'blue desert' and its contradictions, or reduce it to myth, as others have done, Bowden participates in it, maps its 'coordinates' (ibid.) as a schizoid culture with him a part of it:

> For my body may be sprawled in the desert tonight, but a part of me is always seduced by the bright lights of the casino. All over the region I see my handiwork: the ghost towns, the mine scars, the butchered grazing tracts, the dull cities, the highways full of traffic racing to get nowhere, the crap tables, the damned and maimed rivers. We have taken our main chance and the results only look good on the Dow Jones. (ibid.: 36)

This cultural schizophrenia, seen earlier in Kittredge's writings, is mirrored in Bowden's own life again and again – part guilt and part self-recognition – and it provides a convincing location for the living paradox that Abbey had earlier begun to recognize.

> I walk out the door and across the parking lot. The air hums with sound from the generators rumbling in all the campers, vans and mobile homes. The booze feels wonderfully warm in my gut and twilight slips down.
>
> A line of geese V's up the river and I crane my neck to enjoy the sight. In the windows of the campers I can see the glow of the television screens. (ibid.: 38)

Bowden's New West is irresistibly *both*: resisting the pull to the pristine idealism of the signifying geese of natural freedom while asserting *simultaneously* the attraction of the television screens in the RVs. The lack of resolution here seems both appealing and honest. The unwillingness to reject one version in favour of the other is to accept the inherent plurality and diversity of this Western landscape, with all its contradictions. As Bowden writes, there is a 'new religion ... that seeks to stop the clock and perhaps wind it backwards to a time when the land was relatively unpeopled and the beasts held sway' (ibid.: 37), but this is a nostalgic idealism, an adolescent longing for the pre-Oedipal imaginary West-as-Eden outside the real 'language' of the here and now.

Bowden's uncertainty about the environment is not hidden away, but neither is it the source of avoidance. It surfaces in the push-pull dialogue he has within himself and with the world outside him. The West cannot retreat to a 'vision of a golden past', 'some imaginary day before Christopher Columbus docked' as if it were 'a timeless benchmark of continuity' (ibid.: 46), because it has always been a land of change and diversity where people live both apart from and within the desert landscape. Yet throughout Bowden's essays there remains a warning that 'under the skin' of his technological culture and self there existed 'the desert [that] teaches other dreams' (ibid.: 137), but he knows he cannot retreat into these 'dreams' for he is the product of his time and his knowledge, and cannot ignore or reject that in favour of the dream of innocence: 'I hear the distant thunder of the twentieth century's rush into the desert ... [but] To object to this act is to cut one's own throat' (ibid.: 139). Bowden is ambivalent about arguments of environmentalists who believe human beings can change the way they live in the West, and is divided between the 'television screens' and the 'geese,' between Sunbelt cities and the desert. Bowden argues that 'we don't have the courage to back away, to stop, to restrain ourselves. I know I don't' (ibid.: 144). He accepts fatalistically that the cities will not survive but the desert will: 'So I visit the past to taste the deeper present and prospect the inevitable future' (ibid.: 145). We have, writes Bowden, exiled the desert from our lives only to visit it as tourists, and yet it remains like the Freudian repressed, and 'one day, this exiled world will return' (ibid.: 146). In Bowden's schema, however, 'all these things are just a footnote to one more day' (ibid.: 98) in which the human part is minimal and fleeting in the broader sweep of change and growth. In the words of Abraham Lincoln, 'who never saw the place', the West, according to Bowden, is best expressed by 'Laws change; people die; the land remains' (ibid.: 4).

Later Bowden work, like *Frog Mountain Blues* (1994b), has reflected concern about the land and the way it is used in the West, charting encroachment into the Santa Catalina Mountains in Arizona. The growing residential and recreational use at the Ventata Resort has eroded the mountains, 'But we cannot seem to stop and we always go back and take yet more.' Bowden calls this 'the constant story of the

West, the region that people pour into seeking some bleary eyed vision of freedom, ... all want to possess and then seem to maim with our endless appetites' (Bowden, 1994b: 6). His views have hardened against any possibility of 'multiple use' of the land for it must remain wild as an alternative to the city, and yet a schizophrenia remains, knowing he lives amid and benefits from an urban, technological culture bound to the land's exploitation: 'My life', he writes, 'has no tidy consistency' (ibid.: 143). In this, Bowden is one with the New West itself.

Learning from Las Vegas

When Bowden wrote that he was 'seduced by the bright lights of the casino', he was writing of Las Vegas, the New West city *par excellence*. Beginning as a 'roadtown' for wagons heading West and later a railroad town linking Salt Lake City and Los Angeles, it grew on the back of federally funded projects like the Hoover Dam and military bases, and ultimately as a tourist centre. From small town to postmodern metropolis, Las Vegas 'offers the West as it is traditionally not pictured, because picturing the West has always meant representing what it is *not*' (Betsky, in Phillips et al., 1996: 56). In Las Vegas all the clashing particles of the New West seem to collide and fuse in its excessive mix of forms and lifestyles. Hunter S. Thompson wrote that, 'Psychedelics are almost irrelevant in a town where you can wander into a casino any time of the day or night and witness the crucifixion of a gorilla – on a flaming neon cross that suddenly turns into a pinwheel, spinning the beast around in wild circles above the crowded gambling action' (Thompson, 1983: 175).

It is no surprise, therefore, that Robert Venturi, Denise Scott Brown, and Steven Izenour's book *Learning From Las Vegas* (1972) published the year after Thompson's, is regarded as 'both an exemplar of and inspiration for postmodern architecture' (Strinati, 1995: 229). Its appreciation of the 'Strip', auto-culture, neon signs, and the 'decorated shed' form of architecture can be parallelled with the cultural geography of J. B. Jackson (see Chapter 1) who reviewed the book in *The Harvard Independent*, and is mentioned in the original preface as one of the 'particular intellectual and artistic underpinnings of this project' (Venturi et al., 1996: xii). Jackson was 'willing to understand instead of react to the strip' (Hess, 1993: 122), seeing dangers and promise in its new urban forms, relishing its 'ambidexterity', and capacity to transform and innovate along the desert roadside. Venturi et al. felt Las Vegas called for a 'non-chip-on-the-shoulder view' about the vernacular landscape of the Strip which worked with 'existing conditions' to create a 'new but old direction' instead of attempting a 'revolutionary, utopian, puristic' rebuilding as Modernists would have done (Venturi et al., 1996: 3, 87). In Las Vegas, they found 'a way of learning from everything' (ibid.) while acknowledging the fragmented, commodified landscape of surfaces and signs, where the Strip was saturated in image and symbol – what Baudrillard would later call the ecstasy of communication. Any sense of a fixed, absolute, definable 'real' was dismissed in the surreal world of Las Vegas, an illuminated, autopic, desert city with its 'commercial persuasion of roadside eclecticism ... in the vast and complex setting of a new landscape of big spaces, high speeds, and complex programs' (ibid.: 8). In the postmodern New West's capital city, there are 'paradoxical subleties within a dangerous, sinuous maze' but one has to trust the 'signs for guidance' and become absorbed into their version of the real, since 'if you take the signs away, there is no place' (ibid.: 9, 18). Venturi et al. argue that Las Vegas 'is a complex order ... [but] not the easy, rigid order of ... the fashionable "total design" of the megastructure' (ibid.: 52), and so like postmodernism, they articulate a rejection of mythic order and metanarrative in favour of complexity and contradictions much closer to the New West as I have defined it in this book. Venturi wrote that he was all for 'messy vitality over obvious unity ... I like elements that are hybrid rather than "pure", compromising rather than "clean", distorted rather than "straightforward", ambiguous rather than "articulated" ... [for] Blatant simplification means bland architecture' (Venturi, 1966: 22). The Las Vegas Strip

> *includes*; it includes at all levels, from the mixture of seemingly incongruous land uses to the mixture of seemingly incongruous advertising media ... a variety of changing, juxtaposed orders, like the shifting configurations of a Victor Vasarely painting ... 'Chaos is very near; its nearness, but its avoidance, gives ... force.' (Venturi et al., 1996: 53)

Here was inclusivism, a 'both/and' attitude, aspiring to 'simultaneously recognize contradictory levels' (Venturi, 1966: 103) linking to the 'cacaphonic context' (ibid.: 139) of the contemporary West, where conventional binaries such as rural/urban, human/nature, high art/popular culture, centre/marginal were beginning to alter and even collapse. Just as Venturi et al. call for the possibility of irony and 'the architect as jester', as ways by which 'a pluralist society' with 'divergent values' may come together in 'temporary alliances' to create new communities appreciated by all sides, so too is the New West engaged in a similar process on a wider front. The democratic impetus in Venturi et al. opposes the modernist expert's claim on authority and truth in favour of postmodernism's inclusive, contradictory, multiple and excessive view. Without blindly following the consumerism of the Strip, they are learning from it and seeking to 're-evaluate' the ideologies that produce it, in a manner that connects their project with both postmodernism and the cultural productions of the New West. Views of Las Vegas have been contested, often quite starkly between the 'dark' and the 'light', with the city viewed as aberration or as new urban model, and to some extent this mirrors attitudes about the New West: 'Las Vegas becomes a liminal space, of between and betwixt, where anything can happen, the oriental oasis in the desert where usual identities from the rest of the U.S. can be sloughed off . . .' (Docker, 1994: 88). With still the promise of new identities, of 'sloughing off' the old in favour of the new, Las Vegas's allure has often been seen as this oxymoronic dark wonderland of danger and promise, as in *Leaving Las Vegas* (Mike Figgis, 1995) where two desperate characters find moments of love and happiness among a prurient and apocalyptic desert city.

Approaching the fastest growing city in the USA from the Mojave Desert, Judith Freeman writes that:

In the distance, tall monoliths appeared grotesque and wavery in the blazing sun, like something seen through thick glass – liquid shapes shimmering in the heat: a pyramid, King Arthur's castle, Treasure Island, a Mayan palace, giant Easter Island heads – the whole plastic panoply of cargo-cult history reinvented in the desert. (Freeman, 1996: 4)

This sense of Las Vegas conveys the multiple, simulated and diverse nature of this New West city which has erased different elements in its history: Native American settlement, Mormon settlement, ranching, New Deal money through the Hoover Dam project (1931–5), military bases, in favour of gambling and tourist entertainment. Its first resort hotel was El Rancho Las Vegas (1941), followed by The Last Frontier (1942) which boasted headboards like oxen yokes and cow horns in the rooms. Ten years before Disneyland's Frontierland, it simulated the Old West with a mini-theme park in its Last Frontier Village including jail, rustic chapel – the 'Little Church of the West' – and a stagecoach to transport customers to and from the hotel. Its slogan 'The Early West in Modern Splendor' emphasized the liminal position of the rustic hotel of western myth mixed with its new neon signs and roadtown values. By the mid-1950s, it was sold, partly demolished and resurrected as the 'New Frontier' with its 'Cloud Nine Lounge'. Like the wider West, and contrary to the often reproduced myths, mobility, change, and unsentimental destruction characterized the development of the city as it moved with the times and the market. Las Vegas represents, in excess, the growth of the New West as a series of overlapping, often contradictory, phases from which emerges a complex space – city and desert, settled and transient, fragile and booming all at the same time. It is a postmodern space of simultaneity resisting easy definition because of its multiple, contradictory nature and its dynamic and dangerous identity. Part postmodern simulation and part inhabited, dynamic community where 4,000 people arrive to live every month, these anomalies are embodied in its very appearance as a neon lit wonderland glowing out of the bleak beauty of the Mojave: 'a religion, a disease, a nightmare, a paradise for the misbegotten', according to Nick Tosches (in Tronnes, 1995: 15). In describing Las Vegas, like the New West itself, writers are drawn to oxymorons and startling oppositions that attempt to capture the differences inherent in the place, but ultimately suggest the significance of co-presence, of diversity occupying the same space simultaneously. John Gregory Dunne describes it in his novel *Vegas* (1974) as the oddest of mixtures: 'An idiot Disneyland of architectural parabolas, overloaded utility poles, celestial hamburger stands and gimcrackery fairy palaces' as well as 'a dump that was not even an official dump. Just a place in the desert to dump the leavings of a lifetime ... Tires, old radios, television sets with no picture tubes ...' (Dunne, 1974: 19, 21). Las Vegas cannot be read in a linear fashion, as if everything could be sorted into an order and a progression, but instead can be seen as multilayered and hybridized, with the real and imagined overlapping and fusing. As Tom Wolfe argued, 'the existing vocabulary of art history is helpless' faced with the architecture of the Las Vegas Strip (in Tronnes, 1995: 24), so one invents a new language, another way of apprehending this landscape which is part Disneyland, part Purgatorio, part Fantasy Island. Las Vegas is 'over-inscribed' space that 'speaks' but 'does not tell all' (Lefebvre, 1991: 142).

When Steve Wynn demolished the Dunes Hotel in 1993 in a spectacular reminder of Las Vegas's (and the West's) postmodern credentials, he reinvented the city as a resort destination, building bigger and more fantastic hotels further divorced from the older western themes and traditions. The city was, once again, reinvented with the backing of corporations as a pedestrian-centred strip of themed environments and moving sidewalks that altered the earlier autoscape discussed by Venturi et al. Now Las Vegas is a theme park city made up of 'Luxor' and 'Treasure Island', and in a truly postmodern act of simulation has built a hotel called 'New York, New York' – a city within the city in the desert – of twelve skyscraper towers, including the Empire State, Statue of Liberty, and the Brooklyn Bridge (see Plate 10). The West out-Easts the East, condenses New York into sixteen acres of Las Vegas real estate, sells ethnic foods inside the themed restaurants, and simulates the dirty sidewalks with ornate carpeting. Such flamboyance erases time and history, happily blends, from block to block, the pharoahs with Hollywood, gambling with drive-through wedding chapels, providing any myth you desire with little sense of origin or meaning. It has been termed 'the terminus of western history, the end of the trail' (Davis, in Rothman, 1998: 54), for it has no relationship with the past, only with its own fantastic future.

Behind the grandeur and the increasingly sophisticated simulations, 'there were other stories and other people' as Dunne puts it, stories that tell another side to Las Vegas as the iconic New West (Dunne, 1974: 25). It is the 'paradigm of anti-life' (ibid.), a site of ecological disaster with a massive consumption of water and energy, supported by an exploitative economic system running on a low-wage workforce. It is, claims Davis, 'a hyperbolic Los Angeles – the Land of Sunshine on fast-forward' (in Rothman, 1998b: 59) repeating many of the mistakes of LA and other 'Sunbelt clones' by ignoring water issues, fragmenting local government in favour of corporate planning, abandoning public space, embracing the automobile, and perpetuating social and racial inequality (ibid.: 60). Las Vegas in its post 1993 mode has cut itself off from the Western past – its history – and created a new landscape devoid of reference to the desert beyond its city boundaries. Its self-generated fantasy resists the reality of arid land as much as it ignores the nuclear dumps on its doorstep, becoming the new 'world capital of amnesia', to borrow a phrase from Solnit (1998: 30). For Davis, this is the 'scamscape' of Las Vegas – a word Soja used to describe the worst features of

Plate 10 Neil Campbell, *New York, New York – Las Vegas, Nevada, 1999.*

Plate 11 Neil Campbell, *Urban West – Las Vegas, Nevada, 1999.*

expanding, sprawling LA and its 'edge cities'. Davis believes that the 'hypergrowth and inflexible resource demand' of Las Vegas makes the 'need for an alternative settlement model ... doubly urgent' (in Roth-man, 1998b: 71); a model involving Green politics, new urban design, and thoughtful, innovative use of planning is the only hope for 'an alternative urbanism, sustainable and democratic' (ibid.) (Plate 11).

However, Davis's dark vision is not shared by all, since for some, Las Vegas, with all its faults, represents a model of the New West city full of 'gathering places, monuments, the hierarchy of public spaces, diverse activities, plural tastes ... accommodated in a strip framework' (Hess, 1993: 117); a structure of 'mini-cities' juxtaposing consumption, fantasy and tourism with residential and commercial expansion while appealing to the 'long-running myths of [US] culture: knightly chivalry, adventure amongst the heathen, the winning of the West, Victorian homesteads, utopian futures, fabulous riches ... times past and future, imagined and remembered ...' (Hess, 1993: 119). Although excessive and larger than life, Las Vegas, for some, represents a city 'designed by accretion' (ibid.) that refutes any single design principle or metanarrative, like Disney-land, but rather echoes the New West in its pluralist evolution, its constant reinvention, and its attachment to the road itself from which it grew. It is a fragile city with a 'hybrid nature' (Rugoff, 1995: 6) that has had to reconcile the car with the pedestrian, the desert with the asphalt, popular pleasure with growing environmental problems, and 'nightmare' with 'cartoon' (ibid.). Yet it 'manages to be both at once', evolving a 'schizophrenic identity' full of 'excess and hubris' which 'thrives in a state of cultural tension' suspended between poles of a 'karmic cesspool' and 'delirious frontier freedom' (ibid.: 6). Always at the edge of postmodernity, Las Vegas continues to juggle all these elements like 'a video screen of the national consciousness' (Hess, 1993: 123), or more accurately a multiplicity of screens where the participant is 'called upon to . . . see all . . . at once, in their radical and random difference . . . [discovering] a new mode of grasping what used to be called relationship: something for which the word *collage* is still only a very feeble name' (Jameson, 1991: 31). Like the New West as real and imagined space, Las Vegas is a city of simultaneity, a 'museum without walls' (Rugoff, 1995: 3) echoing Foucault's exploration of 'other spaces':

> a set of relations that delineates sites which are irreducible to one another and absolutely not superimposable on one another . . . a kind of effectively enacted utopia in which the real sites that can be found within the culture, are simultaneously represented, contested, and inverted . . . capable of juxtaposing in a single real place several spaces, several sites that are in themselves incompatible. (Foucault, 1986: 23, 24, 25)

In Baudrillard's *America* (1988), 'Death Valley and Las Vegas are inseparable; you have to accept everything at once, an unchanging timelessness and the wildest instantaneity' (1988: 67). It is this 'violent, electric juxtaposition' that defines the New West for Baudrillard; in 'the violence of its contrasts . . . the waltz of simulcra and images' that 'follow one another, even if it seems unintelligible . . . [until] you must come to see this whirl of things and events as an irresistible, fundamental datum' (ibid). The New West is always more than one thing, a blurred and interrelated hybrid territory, a postmodern 'interstitial culture' full of 'a spellbinding discontinuity, an all-enveloping intermittent radiation' of wonder and horror (ibid.: 10, 127). Indeed, 'The West is Las Vegas writ large . . . It assembled itself out of lines of flight . . . used technology to impose an order on this world . . . a swarming transformation of land into real estate . . . A speculative landscape, Las Vegas is the Avalon of the West' (in Phillips, 1996: 56).

The various urban Wests discussed here have always fascinated writers and film-makers speculating about the future, and given rise to theories and fictions of the imagined shape of the Future West. Because of the postmodern context of many of these discussions, the work of cyberpunk writers, in particular, has become a focus for these future visions. From *Blade Runner* through Pat Murphy's *The City, Not Long After* (1989), Steve Erickson's *Rubicon Beach* (1986), Kim Stanley Robinson's *Pacific Edge* (1990), Neal Stephenson's *Snow Crash*, (1992) and many others, Future West has continued to produce both dystopian and utopian landscapes, often articulating discourses already present in debates about the New West. These futuristic visions reflect back upon current concerns – urban sprawls, social fragmentation, identity crises, and eco-horror – as well as daring to imagine some new social order in which the West is not engulfed by an apocalyptic inevitability, but continues to find new ways to live and prosper. To highlight some of these visions, I wish to concentrate on the work of William Gibson, and in particular his novel *Virtual Light*.

Future West: William Gibson's *Virtual Light*

Echoing Soja's 'semiotic blanket', William Gibson is fascinated by the 'semiotic ghosts' that haunt the national consciousness of America and provide an 'architecture of broken dreams', of myths and images that endlessly circulate in cultural discourse (Gibson, 1993a: 41, 44). These 'semiotic ghosts' are like the myths of the Old West, always hovering in the American psyche as 'pulp utopias', 'an idealized city,' a 'dream logic that knew nothing of pollution, the finite bounds of fossil fuel' – a 'smug, happy, and utterly content' Dreamland (ibid.: 47). In his story 'The Gernsback Continuum', Gibson critiques the static dream-world of these semiotic ghosts as frighteningly cold, 'near Disneyland', and closely related to Hollywood, spaces with 'too much of the Dream' (ibid.: 49). The horror is of a culture which is 'perfect' as defined by these ghosts and myths, rather than a world in which there is a mixture with 'the human near-dystopia we live in' (ibid.: 50). Gibson employed similar ideas in an essay on Singapore which he saw as 'an entire country run by Jeffrey Katzenberg' (ex-Disney supremo) full of 'conformity', 'idealized paternalism', and with 'the same ennui that lies in wait in any theme park' (Gibson, 1993b: 1, 3, 4). In both examples, Gibson outlines social control manifested as utopia and ideal order. Mike Davis's vision of Los Angeles (and Las Vegas) is similarly one of surveillance, control, and containment, a newly ordered city of the future similar to that of Singapore. However, excavating behind the facades of control and the semiotic ghosts, Davis seeks to reveal the racial and economic tensions that structure the city. Gibson admires Davis's work, crediting it in his novel *Virtual Light* (1993c), and Davis has written that Gibson's 'extrapolative' science fiction operates as 'prefigurative social theory, as well as an anticipatory opposition politics to the cyber-fascism lurking over the next horizon' (1995: 4).

In *Virtual Light*, Gibson's Sprawl is the American West Coast, NoCal, run by global zaibatsu (multinational) culture as a world of 'mega-cities', 'mirrored ziggurats', gunships, climate control, and urban micropolitics, echoing films like *Blade Runner* and *Strange Days*. In this arena, hybridity has become a lived reality because the centre has become so distant that the only connection people have is with their own group, their allegiance, their splinter from the whole social order. Gibson's novel, like Thomas Pynchon's *The Crying of Lot 49*, is full of groups: urban survivors, sects, conspirators, gangsters – all engaged in the contest for power and influence in a nexus of ownership and control.

Gibson divides the sprawl-like world into two: LA and San Francisco, suggesting, as Davis does, that LA has reached a point where public space has been consumed and organized by corporate interests into marketable, privatized space. At the heart of the novel is a plan to reorganize San Francisco as a simulated 'organic' city grown as a controlled experiment in social engineering out of 'little tiny machines' (Gibson, 1993c: 273). 'Sunflower' is a way of regulating the city into the total story constructed by the corporations. The novel, therefore, unravels a secret history of the city, of its subcultures and their interrelations with the dominant culture. San Francisco, typified by the Bridge community in the novel, exemplifies a tenuous alliance of resistance forces against this disciplinary society with its order, surveillance, and spatial 'fascism'. On the Bridge a more anarchic spatial authority pertains – a 'porosity', defined as interpenetration with 'the scope to become the theatre of new, unforseen constellations' where 'the stamp of the definitive is avoided' and 'no situation appears intended forever, no figure asserts its "thus and not otherwise" ...' (Benjamin, 1997: 169 – see Gibson, 1993c: 85), or a Bakhtinian carnival

illuminated by Christmas bulbs, by recycled neon, by torchlight, it
possessed a queer medieval energy ... [like] a ruin of England's
Brighton Pier, as though viewed through some cracked kaleidoscope
of vernacular style. (Gibson, 1993c: 58)

Whereas Davis's 'summary' of California's 'lost childhood' and
human 'debris' is his landscape metaphor of the 'junkyard of dreams'
(Davis, 1990: 435), in Gibson's novel, there is still possibility in the
energy of the carnival Bridge community. Gibson's New West is a
postmodern 'world without end' where 'everything ran together, blurring, melting in the fog', creating a vision of a hybrid culture which
'occurred piecemeal, to no set plan', 'startlingly organic' and yet
simultaneously 'an accretion of dreams' (Gibson, 1993c: 1, 59, 58).
Gibson's language echoes Foucault's definition of heterotopia quoted
earlier and the Bridge's ramshackle, free-form democracy has all the
characteristics of a vision of the urban New West as potential hetero-
topic space, 'not like a mall' but a bricolage with 'one thing patched
onto the next ... no two pieces of it matched ... different material
anywhere you looked' and the people 'all ages, races, colors' (ibid.:
162–3). This is unmappable space, or what Gómez-Peña terms a
'moving cartography' (Gómez-Peña, 1992: 2), and cannot be reduced
to a single meaning or a predictable order over which control can be
imposed. The centripetal forces of Gibson's city are the power-brokers
of information who control the matrix into which others slot, but their
authority is being resisted by individuals (Rydell, Chevette, Skinner)
and groups (the Republic of Desire – hackers), whose aim is to interfere
with their monological control.

Gibson's Bridge has evolved through otherness, dispossession, out-
siderdom, with its inhabitants bringing with them 'all kinds of stories',
rejecting the 'wire fences' and 'towers' of the gated city and of
privatized (once public) space that 'keep[s] people from getting together
in the street' (Gibson, 1993c: 87–8). Gibson proposes resistance from
within these Western urban spaces; a carnival of souls '... milling
around, singing. Crazy ...' (ibid.: 88). At one point Gibson writes,
'Modernity was ending' but that around the Bridge grew something
else, 'the new thing's strange [postmodern] heart' (ibid.: 90). The
implied anarchy is an assertion of alternatives, of seeing the city as a
space of otherness, a carnivalesque challenge to the set boundaries of
acceptable, contained, and controlled behaviour and norms. The novel

gives voice to the Bridge's stories which are, argues de Certeau, both the 'frontier and the bridge' 'setting and transgressing limits', 'a passing through or over ... a third element ... an "in-between" – a "space between" ...' (de Certeau, 1988b: 123, 127–8). As de Certeau writes, the bridge is 'ambiguous' because it 'welds together' and 'opposes insularities' (ibid.: 128); it is

> a transgression of the limit, a disobedience of the law of the place, it represents a departure, an attack on a state, the ambition of a conquering power, or the flight of an exile; in any case, the 'betrayal' of an order. (ibid.)

In Skinner's city, on the Bridge, Gibson offers this kind of alterity – 'Refuge, weirdness ... home to however many and all their dreams', where 'there is no agenda ... whatever, no underlying structure', with 'nobody normal in sight and people doing things right out in public' (Gibson, 1993c: 122, 115, 127). The hiddenness that characterizes new privatized, gated communities, the walled cities described by Davis as 'Fortress LA,' is thrown open in this alternative community where 'public' space is still possible and 'cognitive dissidence' encouraged. Here all is recycled, re-used like an inversion of the city as eco-apocalypse (see Davis, 1998) or disposable commodity; here, an old component board becomes the walls of a new dwelling.

The Bridge is fragile and unstable, 'like a kid's fort' (Gibson, 1993c: 164), but it is human, living, and maintains a connection between place and identity, even sustaining it. The community is not dissimilar to the tattoos described later in the novel: 'They were all different ... and they sort of ran together ...' (ibid.: 199) – an elaborate collage of fragments, different and in tension, contesting for space, but creating in the mix, the hybrid form, some new pattern, ever-changing and fluid, but nonetheless a variable 'infidel heteroglossia' remapping urban space in the New West's possible future (Haraway, 1991: 181).

Conclusion: 'a real politics of inhabitation'?

Amid Baudrillard's cryptic journeys across and through his 'America', he comments that the USA, and he really means the West's cities, small towns, and deserts, is 'the primitive society of the future, a society of complexity, hybridity, and the greatest intermingling ... a fractal, interstitial culture, born of a rift with the Old World, a tactile, fragile, superficial culture' (1988: 7). Although Baudrillard's paradigmatic West is limited by its failure to encompass the marginalized underclass and ethnic diversity and by its constant overstatement, it contains within its vision seeds of truth about the West as an extrapolation of the near, global future. This may not be a totally negative vision of postmodernity, since like Gibson's it appears to contain the belief in human agency and resistance to the expansions of capitalism and commodification. Often postmodernism appears to offer only passivity but in the complex spaces of the postmodern West there may be opportunities for change to 'bridge' the gap between conventional oppositions, to reinvent community as hybrid and to rethink identity as multiple. From all the stories of the New West – from its cities, towns, deserts, mountains, and plains – alternative histories gather, not to be silenced, but to be listened to and used in the construction of a newer, more inclusive Western history in which people feel they have a role and a voice in its diverse landscapes and discursive fields.

Epilogue: The Rhizomatic West

The abortionists of unity are indeed angel makers. (Deleuze and Guattari, 1992: 6)

Journalist Timothy Egan wrote in 1998 that '[it] may be easier to lasso the wind than to find a sustaining story for the American West' (Egan, 1998: 10), or as I said in the introduction, using the words of Cormac McCarthy, the New West is 'immappable' because it comes with too many questions and 'blank spots' and in its dynamic, hybrid reinventions is beyond any finalized, fixed state. Efforts to define the West inevitably reduce its complexities and smooth out its contradictions by transforming cultural processes into natural ones, history into myth. To view the West otherwise is to see it as several spaces simultaneously, overlapping, in contact and exchange, as 'thirdspace'. In this sense, the New West is always relational, dialogic, engaged in or capable of reinvention – and, therefore, contradictory, irreducible, and hybrid. This book has examined how various cultures of the New West have articulated and represented this 'immappable', real-and-imagined space and the various forms of identity constructed there through struggle and contest. In this final section, I wish to speculate on a further alternative cartography which might be helpful in our understanding of the New West, derived from the work of the French critics Gilles Deleuze and Felix Guattari whose work is fascinated by 'deterritorialization' or uprooting and flight, and 'multiplicity' – all characteristics of the West. They describe 'a set of lines or dimensions which are irreducible to one another' and where 'what counts are not the terms or the elements, but what there is "between", the between, *a set of relations which are not separable from each other* ' (Deleuze and Parnet, 1987: vi, vii – my emphases). Immediately, the emphasis upon the 'between' echoes this book's concern with 'thirdspace', or the dialogical contact zone that exists when binaries are collapsed. For Deleuze and Guattari, America is a 'deterritorialized' space of mobility, of becoming-other with a 'sense of the frontiers as something to cross, to push back, to go beyond ... [where] becoming is geographical' (ibid.: 37). This suggests the complex web of relational cultures explored in this book and helps provide a flexible frame to comprehend its many diverse elements.

They develop some of these ideas in their concept of the *rhizome*, suggesting principles of connection, heterogeneity, and multiplicity, signifying 'diverse form', 'the best and the worst', 'a throng of dialects', 'connection and heterogeneity ... [with] any point ... connected to anything other ...' (Deleuze and Guattari, 1992: 7). As I argued in the introduction, the New West is less about 'roots' than about 'routes' since the search back to find origins and essences seems counterproductive in the migratory, hybrid cultures of the region. Indeed, Deleuze and Guattari argue that the idea of roots which 'plot a point and fix and order' should be challenged by that of rhizomes that grow outward, not down, in complex, multiple ways (ibid.: 5). They connect these ideas specifically with the 'rhizomatic West, with its Indians without ancestry, its ever-receding limit, its shifting and displaced frontiers' (ibid.: 19), and contrary to the Turner thesis's view that 'The United States lies like a huge page in the history of society' to be read 'line by line from east to west' in an orderly and coherent manner (in Milner, 1989: 6), they reject 'the book as an image of the world' as 'vapid', since 'the multiple must be made' in a 'book all the more total for being fragmented' (Deleuze and Guattari, 1992: 6). The rhizomatic West is the New West,

> reducible neither to the One nor the multiple ... It is composed not of units but of dimensions, or rather directions in motion. It has neither a beginning nor end, but always a middle (milieu) from which it grows and which it overspills ... [it] operates by variation, expansion, conquest, capture, offshoots ... a map that is detachable, connectable, reversible, modifiable, and has multiple entryways and exits and its own lines of flight ... (ibid.: 22)

In parallel with the idea of hybrid, dialogical 'thirdspace' as a means of understanding the New West's diverse communities, the rhizome has no beginning or end, 'it is always in the middle, between things, interbeing, *intermezzo*. ... alliance ... conjunction' and like 'American literature ... know[s] how to move between things ... do away with foundations, nullify endings and beginnings. The middle is by no means an average; on the contrary, it is where things pick up speed ... a stream ... that undermines its banks and picks up speed in the middle' (ibid.: 25). Only in these multiple metaphors can the New West be approximated but never fixed or defined, for it is a 'reversible, modifiable' map, 'agglomerating very diverse acts' (ibid.: 7), and therefore no single book can express it. Deleuze and Guattari claim that the 'ideal for a book would be to lay everything out on a plane ... on a single page, the same sheet: lived events, historical determinations, concepts, individuals, groups, social formations ... always in relation with each other' (ibid.: 9), for this would counter the obsession with linearity, cause and effect, and binary structures, opting instead for simultaneity as a method of reflecting upon history. How close this is to the opening of Larry Watson's novel *Montana 1948*, which is a New West plea for changing the way we think about history:

> Imagine instead a movie screen divided into boxes and panels, each with its own scene, *so that one moment can occur simultaneously with another*, so no action has to fly off in time, so nothing happens before or after, only during. That's the way these images coexist in my memory, like the Sioux picture calendars in which the whole year's events are painted on the same buffalo hide, or like a tapestry with every scene woven into the same cloth, *every moment on the same flat plane* ... (Watson, 1996: 12 – my emphasis)

Watson's post-1948 West demands a new history capable of seeing many things at once, working together 'on the same plane' and not simply dividing the world up into opposites or excluding the elements that refuse to cohere with the dominant discourse. Although speculative, Deleuze and Guattari's theoretical ideas echo these concerns and provide a radical language through which to express some of the New West's multiple identities and its endless capacity to develop and change through the processes of interaction and relation. Their language suggests both the potential and the dangers inherent in this rhizomatic New West for it is a place of extremes, of paradox – what William Kittredge calls 'a double-hearted dreamland' (Kittredge, 1996: 133) – where opposites collide, where surprise and banality, kitsch and creativity, real and imagined exist side by side. However, as Deleuze and Guattari argue, this is a 'model that is perpetually in construction or collapsing, and of a process that is perpetually prolonging itself, breaking off and starting up again ... the furniture we are forever rearranging' (Deleuze and Guattari, 1992: 20–1), and, ultimately, it is within this capacity for paradox that the New West resides and abides. Surely, this is the new, rhizomatic cultural order Rubén Martinez articulates with his poetic double-vision of a New West 'crossing every border ever held sacred', where

History is on fast forward
it's the age of synthesis
which is not to say
that the Rainbow Coalition is
heaven on earth and let's party.
... All kinds of battles are yet to come
(race and class bullets and blood);
choose your weapons
just know that everyone is everywhere now
so careful how you shoot

('Manifesto', 1989, in Martinez, 1992: 134–5)

Bibliography and Further Reading

(*The edition indicated is that used in the text. First date of publication is given at the end of the bibliographical details.*)

Abbey, E. (1962) *Brave Cowboy*. London: Four Square Books (first pub. 1957).

Abbey, E. (1976) *The Monkey Wrench Gang*. New York: Avon Books (first pub.1975).

Abbey, E. (1984) *Beyond the Wall*. New York: Henry Holt.

Abbey, E. (1992) *Desert Solitaire: A Season in the Wilderness*. London: Robin Clark. (first pub. 1968).

Abram, David (1996) *The Spell of the Sensuous*. New York: Vintage.

Adams, Ansel (1983) *Examples: The Making of 40 Photographs*. Boston: Little, Brown.

Adams, Robert (1975) *The New West: Landscapes Along the Colorado Front Range*. Denver: Colorado Associated University Press.

Adams, Robert (1978) 'Inhabited Nature', *Aperture*, 81, pp. 29–32.

Adams, Robert (1985) 'Towards a Proper Silence: Nineteenth Century Photographs of the American Landscape', *Aperture*, Spring, pp. 4–11.

Alexie, Sherman (1994) *The Lone Ranger and Tonto Fistfight in Heaven*. New York: Harper Perennial. (first pub. 1993).

Alexie, Sherman (1996) *Reservation Blues*. London: Minerva (first pub. 1995).

Allmendinger, Blake (1998) *Ten Most Wanted: The New Western Literature*. London: Routledge.

Anaya, Rudolfo (1995) *The Anaya Reader*. New York: Warner Books.

Anderson, Eric Gary (1999) *American Indian Literature and the Southwest*. Austin: University of Texas Press.

Anderson, Lindsay (1981) *About John Ford*. London: Plexus.

Anzaldúa, Gloria (1987) *Borderlands/La Frontera*. San Francisco: Aunt Lute Books.

Anzaldúa, Gloria (ed.) (1990) *Making Face, Making Soul: Haciendo Caras. Creative and Critical Perspectives by Feminists of Color*. San Francisco: Aunt Lute Books.

Apt Russell, Sharman (1993) *Kill the Cowboy: A Battle of Mythology in the New West*. Reading, MA: Addison-Wesley.

Aquila, Richard (1996) *Wanted Dead or Alive: The American West in Popular Culture*. Urbana and Chicago: University of Illinois Press.

Aranda, Pilar (1990) 'On the Solitary Fate of Being Mexican, Female, Wicked and Thirty-three: An Interview with Writer Sandra Cisneros', *Americas Review*, 18(1), pp. 64–80.

Armitage, S. and Jameson, E. (eds) (1987) *The Women's West*. Norman: University of Oklahoma Press.

Arteaga, A. (ed.) (1994) *An Other Tongue: Nation & Ethnicity in the Linguistic Borderlands*. Durham, NC: Duke University Press.

Asinof, E. (1999) 'John Sayles', at http://www.filmscouts.com/films/lon-sta.asp.

Bakhtin, M. M. (1990a) *The Dialogic Imagination*. Austin: University of Texas Press.

Bakhtin, M. M. (1990b) *Speech Genres and Other Late Essays*. Austin: University of Texas Press.

Bakhtin, M. M. (1997) *Problems of Dostoevsky's Poetics*. Minneapolis: University of Minnesota Press (first pub.1984).

Baltz, Lewis and Blaisdell, Gus (1980) *Park City*. Albuquerque: Artspace.

Banham, Reyner (1982) *Scenes in America Deserta*. London: Thames & Hudson.

Banham, Reyner (1988) 'The Man-mauled Desert', In Misrach, R. (1988) *Desert Cantos*. Albuquerque: University of New Mexico Press.

Baritz, L. (1961) 'The Idea of the West', *American Historical Review*, 66, April, pp. 618–40.

Barthes, R. (1973) *Mythologies*. London: Paladin (first pub. 1957).

Barthes, R. (1975) *S/Z*. London: Jonathan Cape.

Barthes, R. (1990) *The Pleasure of the Text*. Oxford: Blackwell.

Baudrillard, Jean (1988) *America*. London: Verso.

Baudrillard, Jean (1992) 'Simulations', in Easthope, A. and MacGowan, K. (eds), *A Critical and Cultural Theory Reader*. Milton Keynes: Open University Press.

Benjamin, W. (1997) *One-Way Street*. London: Verso (first pub. 1979).

Best, S. and Kellner, D. (1991) *Postmodern Theory*. New York: Guilford Press.

Bhabha, H. (1994) *The Location of Culture*. London: Routledge.

Bolton, R. (ed.) *The Contest of Meaning: Critical Histories of Photography*. Cambridge, MA: MIT Press.

Bowden, C. (1986) *Blue Desert*. Tucson: University of Arizona Press.

Bowden, C. (1993) *Desierto: Memories of the Future*. New York: W.W. Norton.

Bowden, C. (1994a) 'Dead Minds from Live Places', in Temple J Nolte (ed.), *Open Spaces, City Places: Contemporary Writers on the Changing Southwest*. Tucson: University of Arizona Press.

Bowden, C. (1994b) *Frog Mountain Blues*. Tucson: University of Arizona Press.

Bowden, C. (1996) 'Saying Adios', in Hepworth, J. R. and McNamee, G. (eds), *Resist Much, Obey Little: Remembering Ed Abbey*. San Francisco: Sierra Club Books.

Bright, D. (1989) 'Of Mother Nature and Marlboro Men: An Inquiry into the Cultural Meanings of Landscape Photography', in Bolton, R. (ed.) *The Contest of Meaning: Critical Histories of Photography*, Cambridge, MA: MIT Press.

Bruce, C. (ed.) (1990) *Myth of the West*. New York: Rizzoli.

Bruce-Novoa, J. (1994) 'Alvar Nuñez Cabeza de Vaca, 1490?–1556?', in Lauter, P. (ed.) *The Heath Anthology of American Literature, Vol. 1*. Lexington, MA: D. C. Heath.

Bruce-Novoa, J. (1993) 'Shipwrecked in the Seas of Signification: Cabeza de Vaca's *Relación* and Chicano Literature', in Herrera-Sobek, M. (ed.) *Reconstructing a Chicano/a Literary Heritage*. Tucson: University of Arizona Press.

Buck-Morss, S. (1993) *The Dialectics of Seeing: Walter Benjamin and the Arcades Project*. Cambridge, MA: MIT Press.

Burgin, V. (1996) *In/Different Spaces: Place and Memory in Visual Culture*. Berkeley: University of California Press.

Buscombe, E. (ed.) *The BFI Companion to the Western*. London: André Deutsch.

Cameron, I. and Pye, D. (1996) *The Movie Book of the Western*. London: Studio Vista.

Campbell, N. and Kean, A. (1997) *American Cultural Studies*. London: Routledge.

Castillo, Ana (1995) *Massacre of the Dreamers: Essays on Xicanisma*. New York: Plume Books.

Cawelti, John (1996) 'What Rough Beast – New Westerns?', *ANQ: A Quarterly of Short Articles*, 9 (3), pp. 4–15.

Certeau, M. de (1988a) *The Writing of History*. New York: Columbia University Press.

Certeau, M. de (1988b) *The Practice of Everyday Life*. Berkeley: University of California Press (first pub. 1984)

Certeau, M. de (1997) *Heterologies: Discourse on the Other*. Minneapolis: University of Minnesota Press (first pub. 1986)

Chagoya, E. and Gómez-Peña, G. (1996) *Friendly Cannibals*. San Francisco: Artspace Books.

Chandler, Raymond (1971) *Farewell, My Lovely*. Harmondsworth: Penguin (first pub. 1940).

Chudacoff, N. (ed.) (1994) *Major Problems in American Urban History*. Lexington, MA: D. C. Heath.

Churchill, Ward (1998) *Fantasies of the Master Race: Literature, Cinema and the Colonization of American Indians*. San Francisco: City Lights.

Cisneros, Sandra (1991) *The House on Mango Street*. New York: Vintage (first pub. 1989).

Cisneros, Sandra (1992) *Woman Hollering Creek*. New York: Vintage (first pub. 1991).

Comer, Krista (1999) *Landscapes of the New West: Gender and Geography in Contemporary Women's Writing*. Chapel Hill: University of North Carolina Press.

Crang, M. (1998) *Cultural Geography*. London: Routledge.

Cresswell, T. (1996) *In Place, Out of Place: Geography, Ideology and Transgression*. Minneapolis: University of Minnesota Press.

Cronon, W. (1992) 'Nature, History, and Narrative', *Journal of American History*, March, pp. 1347–76.

Cronon, W. (1996) *Uncommon Ground: Rethinking the Human Place in Nature*. New York: W. W. Norton.

Cronon, W., Miles, G. and Gitlin, J. (eds) (1992) *Under An Open Sky: Rethinking America's Western Past*. New York: W. W. Norton.

Davidov, J. Fryer (1998) *Women's Camera Work: Self/Body/Other in American Visual Culture*. Durham, NC: Duke University Press.

Davis, Mike (1990) *City of Quartz: Excavating the Future of Los Angeles*. London: Verso.

Davis, Mike (1993) 'Dead West: Ecocide in Marlboro Country', *New Left Review*, 200, July/August, pp. 49–73.

Davis, Mike(1995) 'Beyond Blade Runner: Urban Control The Ecology of Fear', *Mediamatic* (on-line journal), 8 (2–3), pp. 1–12.

Davis, Mike (1998a) 'Las Vegas Versus Nature', Rothman, H. K. (ed.) (1998b) *Reopening the American West*, Tucson: University of Arizona Press.

Davis, Mike (1998b) *The Ecology of Fear: Los Angeles and the Imagination of Disaster*. New York: Metropolitan Books.

Dawson, R. et al. (1993) *Ansel Adams/New Light: Essays on his Legacy and Legend*. San Francisco: Friends of Photography.

Deleuze, G. and Guattari, F. (1992) *A Thousand Plateaus: Capitalism and Schizophrenia*. London: Athlone Press (first pub. 1988)

Deleuze, G. and Parnet, C. (1987) *Dialogues*. London: The Athlone Press.

Deverall, W. (1996) 'Fighting Words: The Significance of the American West in the History of the United States', in Milner, C. A. (ed.) *A New Significance: Re-envisioning the History of the American West*, New York: Oxford University Press.

Didion, Joan (1973) *Play It As It Lays*. Harmondsworth: Penguin (first pub. 1971).

Didion, Joan (1985) *Slouching Towards Bethlehem*. Harmondsworth: Penguin (first pub. 1968).

Didion, Joan (1994) *Sentimental Journeys* London: Flamingo.

Dingus, R. (1982) *The Photographic Artifacts of Timothy O'Sullivan*, Albuquerque: University of New Mexico Press.

Docker, J. (1994) *Postmodernism and Popular Culture*. Cambridge: Cambridge University Press.

Doig, Ivan (1978) *This House of Sky: Landscapes of a Western Mind*. San Diego and New York: Harcourt Brace Jovanovich.

Doig, Ivan (1993) *Heart Earth: A Memoir*. New York: Atheneum.

Drinnon, R. (1990) *Facing West: The Metaphysics of Indian Hating and Empire Building*. New York: Schocken Books (first pub. 1980).

Dunne, J. Gregory (1974) *Vegas*. London: Quartet.

Durham, J. (1993) *A Certain Lack of Coherence: Writings on Art and Cultural Politics*. London: Kala Press.

Eagleton, T. (1992) *Walter Benjamin: Towards a Revolutionary Criticism*. London: Verso.

Eco, Umberto (1993) 'The City of Robots', in Docherty, T. (ed.), *Postmodernism*. Hemel Hempstead: Harvester Wheatsheaf.

Egan, T. (1998) *Lasso the Wind: Away to the New West*. New York: Alfred A. Knopf.

Ellis, B. Easton (1994) *The Informers*, London: Picador.

Emmert, S. (1996) *Loaded Fictions: Social Critiques in the Twentieth Century Western*. Moscow: University of Idaho Press.

Erdrich L. (1984) *Love Medicine*. London: André Deutsch.

Etulain, R. (ed.) *Writing Western History: Essays on Major Western Historians*, Albuquerque: University of New Mexico Press.

Evernden, N. (1996) 'Beyond Ecology: Self, Place, and the Pathetic Fallacy', Glotfelty, C. and Fromm, H. (eds), *The Ecocriticism Reader*. Athens: University of Georgia Press.

Fanon, F. (1980) *The Wretched of the Earth*. Harmondsworth: Penguin (first pub. 1961).

Fernlund, K. J. (1998) *The Cold War American West 1945–1989*. Albuquerque: University of New Mexico Press.

Findlay, J. M. (1992) *Magic Lands: Western Cityscapes and American Culture After 1940*. Berkeley: University of California Press.

Fitzgerald, F. Scott (1976) *The Great Gatsby*. Harmondsworth: Penguin (first pub. 1925).

Forresta, M. et al. (1992) *Between Home and Heaven: Contemporary Landscape Photography*. Washington, DC: Smithsonian Institute.

Foucault, M. (1980) *Power/Knowledge: Selected Interviews and Other Writings, 1972–77.* New York and London: Harvester Wheatsheaf.

Foucault, M. (1986) 'Of Other Spaces', *Diacritics,* Spring, pp. 2–27.

Foucault, M. (1993) *Language, Counter-Memory, Practice: Selected Essays and Interviews.* Ithaca, NY: Cornell University Press (first pub. 1977).

Francaviglia, R. and Narrett, D. (eds) (1994) *Essays on the Changing Images of the Southwest.* College Station: Texas A. & M. University Press.

Frayling, C. (1981) *Spaghetti Westerns: Cowboys and Europeans From Karl May to Sergio Leone.* London: RKP.

Freeman, Judith (1996) *A Desert of Pure Feeling.* New York: Vintage.

Fusco, Coco (1995) *English is Broken Here: Notes on Cultural Fusion in the Americas.* New York: New Press.

Gallagher, C. (1993) *America Ground Zero.* Cambridge, MA: MIT Press.

Gibson, W. (1993a) *Burning Chrome.* London: HarperCollins (first pub. 1986).

Gibson, W. (1993b) 'Disneyland with the Death Penalty', *Wired,* 1(4) (on-line), http://www.wired.com/wired/archive/1.04/gibson/html.

Gibson, W. (1993c) *Virtual Light.* New York: Viking.

Gilpin, Laura (1949) *The Rio Grande, River of Destiny: An Interpretation of the River, the Land, and the People.* New York: Duell, Sloan & Pearce.

Gilroy, P. (1994) *The Black Atlantic: Modernity and Double Consciousness.* London: Verso.

Giroux, H., Lankshear, C., McLaren, P. and Peters, M. (eds) (1996) *Counternarratives: Cultural Studies and Critical Pedagogies in Postmodern Studies.* London: Routledge.

Glotfelty, C. (1996) 'Terry Tempest Williams' Ecofeminist Unnatural History', in Tchudi, S. (ed.), *Change in the American West: Exploring the Human Dimension.* Reno: University of Nevada Press.

Glotfelty, C. and Fromm, H. (eds) (1996) *The Ecocriticism Reader.* Athens: University of Georgia Press.

Golden Taylor, J. et al. (1987) *A Literary History of the American West.* Fort Worth: Texas Christian University Press.

Gómez-Peña, G. (1988) 'Documented/Undocumented', in Simonsson, R. and Walker, S. (eds), *The Graywolf Anthology Five: Multiculturalism Literacy.* St Paul, MN: Graywolf Press.

Gómez-Peña, G. (1993) *Warrior For Gringostroika.* St Paul, MN: Graywolf Press.

Gómez-Peña, G. (1996) *The New World Border.* San Francisco: City Lights.

Gooding-Williams, R. (ed.) (1993) *Reading Rodney King, Reading Urban Uprising.* London: Routledge.

Gregory, D. (1994) *Geographical Imaginations.* Oxford: Blackwell.

Gressley, G. M. (ed.) (1997) *Old West/New West,* Norman: University of Oklahoma Press.

Grossman, J. (ed.) (1994) *The Frontier in American Culture.* Berkeley: University of California Press.

Gugelberger, G. (ed.) (1996) *The Real Thing: Testimonial Discourse and Latin America.* Durham, NC: Duke University Press.

Gunn Allen, Paula (1992) *The Sacred Hoop.* Boston: Beacon Press.

Gunn Allen, Paula (1997) '*Cuentos de la Tierra Encantada*: Magic and Realism in the Southwest Borderlands', in D. Wrobel and M. Steiner (eds), *Many Wests: Place, Culture, and Regional Identity*. Lawrence: University Press of Kansas.

Hales, P. (1988) *William Henry Jackson and the Transformation of the American Landscape*. Philadelphia: Temple University Press.

Hall, S. (ed.) (1997) *Representation*. London: Sage.

Hall, S. and Du Gay, P. (eds) (1996) *Questions of Cultural Identity*. London: Sage.

Haraway, D. (1991) *Simians, Cyborgs, and Women: The Reinvention of Nature*. London: Free Association Press.

Haslam, G. (1987) 'Introduction', in Golden Taylor, J. et al. (eds) *A Literary History of the American West*. Fort Worth: Texas Christian University Press.

Hepworth, J. R. and McNamee, G. (eds) (1996) *Resist Much, Obey Little: Remembering Ed Abbey*. San Francisco: Sierra Club Books.

Hess, A. (1993) *Viva Las Vegas: After Hours Architecture*. San Francisco: Chronicle Books.

Hicks, D. Emily (1991) *Border Writing*. Minneapolis: University of Minnesota.

Holquist, M. (1991) *Dialogism*. London: Routledge.

Holthaus, G. (1997) *Wide Skies*. Tucson: University of Arizona Press.

Holthaus, G., Limerick, P. Nelson et al. (eds) (1991) *A Society to Match the Scenery: Personal Visions of the Future of the American West*. Boulder: University of Colorado Press.

Hurtado, A. L. and Iverson, P. (eds.) (1994) *Major Problems in American Indian History*. Lexington, MA: D. C. Heath.

Jackson, J. Brinckerhoff (1960) in *Landscape*, 10, Fall, pp. 1–2.

Jackson, J. Brinckerhoff (1984) *Discovering the Vernacular Landscape*. New Haven, CT: Yale University Press.

Jackson, J. Brinckerhoff (1990) 'Of Houses and Highways', *Aperture*, 120, Spring.

Jackson, P. (1995) *Maps of Meaning*. London: Routledge.

Jameson, F. (1984) 'Periodizing the Sixties', in Sayres, S. et al. (ed.), *The 60s Without Apology*. Minneapolis: University of Minnesota Press.

Jameson, F. (1986) *The Political Unconscious: Narrative as Socially Symbolic Act*. London: Routledge.

Jameson, F. (1991) *Postmodernism, or the Cultural Logic of Late Capitalism*. London: Verso.

Jeffrey, J. Roy (1979) *Frontier Women: The Trans-Mississippi West 1840–1880*. New York: Hill & Wang.

Jenkins, K. (1991) *Rethinking History,*. London: Routledge.

Jenshel, L. (1992) *Travels in the American West*. Washington, DC: Smithsonian Institute.

Johnson, M. K. (1996) *The New Westerners: The West in Contemporary American Culture*. Lawrence: University of Kansas Press.

Jordan, T. (1992) *Cowgirls: Women of the American West*. Lincoln: University of Nebraska Press (first pub. 1982.)

Jordan, T. (1994) *Riding the White Horse Home: A Western Family Album*. New York: Vintage (first pub. 1993).

Josephy, A. (1971) *Red Power: The American Indians' Fight for Freedom*. Lincoln: University of Nebraska Press.

Jussim, E. and Lindquist-Cock, E. (1985) *Landscape as Photograph*. New Haven, CT: Yale University Press.

Kanellos, N. (ed.) *Hispanic American Literature: A Brief Introduction*. New York: HarperCollins.

Kellner, D. (1995) *Media Culture*. London: Routledge.

Kittredge, W. (1987) *Owning It All*. St Paul, MN: Graywolf Press.

Kittredge, W. (1993) *Hole in the Sky: A Memoir*. New York: Vintage (first pub. 1992).

Kittredge, W. (1996) *Who Owns the West?* San Francisco: Mercury House.

Klein, Lee K. (1997) *Frontiers of Historical Imagination: Narrating the European Conquest of Native America, 1890–1990*. Berkeley: University of California Press.

Klett, Mark (1990) 'The Legacy of Ansel Adams', *Aperture*, 120, Summer, pp. 72–3.

Klett, Mark (1992) *Revealing Territory*. Albuquerque: University of New Mexico Press.

Klett, Mark et al. (1984) *Second View: The Rephotographic Survey Project*. Albuquerque: University of New Mexico Press.

Kolodny, A. (1975) *The Lay of the Land: Metaphor as Experience and History in American Life and Letters*. Chapel Hill: University of North Carolina Press.

Kolodny, A. (1984) *The Land Before Her: Fantasy and Experience of the American Frontiers, 1630–1860*. Chapel Hill: University of North Carolina Press.

Kolodny, A. (1992) 'Letting Go Our Grand Obsessions: Notes Towards a New Literary History of the American Frontiers', *American Literature*, 64(1), March, pp. 1–18.

Kuletz, V. (1998) *The Tainted Desert*. New York: Routledge.

Lauter, P. (ed.) *The Heath Anthology of American Literature, Vol. 1*. Lexington, MA: D. C. Heath.

Lefebvre, H. (1991) *The Production of Space*. Oxford: Blackwell.

Leopold, Aldo (1970) *A Sand County Almanac*. New York: Ballantine (first pub. 1949).

Limerick, P. Nelson (1987) *The Legacy of Conquest: The Unbroken Past of the American West*. New York: W. W. Norton.

Limerick, P. Nelson (1990) 'The Rendezvous Model of Western History', in Udall, S. et al. (eds), *Beyond the Mythic West*, Salt Lake City: Peregrine Smith Books.

Limerick, P. Nelson (1993) 'What Raymond Chandler Knew and Western Historians Forgot', in Meldrum, B. H. (ed.), *Old West – New West*. Moscow: University of Idaho Press.

Limerick, P. Nelson (with Klett, M.) (1992) 'Haunted By Rhyolite', *American Art*, 6(4), pp. 18–39.

Limerick, P. Nelson, Milner, C. A. and Rankin, C. E. (eds) (1991) *Trails: Toward a New Western History*. Lawrence: University of Kansas Press.

Lipsitz, G. (1990) *Time Passages*, Minneapolis: University of Minnesota Press.

Lipsitz, G. (1994) *Dangerous Crossroads: Popular Music, Postmodernism and the Poetics of Place*. London: Verso.

Long, Haniel (1975) *The Marvellous Adventures of Cabeza De Vaca*. London: Picador (first pub. 1939).

Lopez, B. (1992) *The Rediscovery of North America*. New York: Vintage.

McCarthy, Cormac (1993) *All The Pretty Horses*. New York: Vintage (first pub. 1992).

McCarthy, Cormac (1995) *The Crossing*. London: Picador (first pub. 1994).

McCarthy, Cormac (1998) *Cities of the Plain*. London: Picador.

McCracken, R. D. (1997) *Las Vegas: The Great American Playground*. Reno: University of Nevada Press.

Mahon, M. (1992) *Foucault's Nietzchean Genealogy: Truth, Power, and the Subject*. New York: SUNY.

Marcus, Greil (1995) *The Dustbin of History*. London: Picador.

Martinez, R. (1992) *The Other Side: Fault Lines, Guerilla Saints and the True Heart of Rock 'n' Roll*. London: Verso.

Massey, D. (1994) *Space, Place and Gender*. Cambridge: Polity Press.

Massey, D. and Jess, P. (eds) (1995) *A Place in the World*. Oxford: Open University Press.

Matsumoto, V. and Allmendinger, B. (eds) (1999) *Over the Edge: Remapping the American West*. Berkeley: University of California Press.

Maxwell-Brown, R. (1996) 'Courage without Illusion', in Milner, C. A. (ed.) *A New Significance: Re-envisioning the History of the American West*. New York: Oxford University Press.

Meinig, D. W. (1972) 'American Wests: Preface to a Geographical Interpretation', *Annals of the Association of American Geographers*, 62, pp. 159–84.

Meinig, D. W. (ed.) (1976) *The Interpretation of Ordinary Landscapes: Geographical Essays*. New York: Oxford University Press.

Meldrum, B. H. (ed.) (1993) *Old West – New West*. Moscow: University of Idaho Press.

Merchant, C. (ed.) (1993) *Major Problems in American Environmental History*. Lexington, MA: D. C. Heath.

Merchant, C. (1995) *Earthcare: Woman and the Environment*. London: Routledge.

Mills, S. (1997) *The American Landscape*. Edinburgh: Keele University Press.

Milner, C. A. (ed.) (1989) *Major Problems in the History of the American West*. Lexington, MA: D. C. Heath.

Milner, C. A. (ed.) (1996) *A New Significance: Re-envisioning the History of the American West*. New York: Oxford University Press.

Milner, C. A., O'Connor, C. and Sandweiss, M. (eds) (1994) *The Oxford History of the American West*. London and New York: Oxford University Press.

Misrach, R. (1988) *Desert Cantos*. Albuquerque: University of New Mexico Press.

Misrach, R. (1990) *Bravo 20: The Bombing of the American West*. Baltimore, MD: Johns Hopkins University Press.

Misrach, R. (1992) *Violent Legacies: Three Cantos* (Interview with Melissa Harris). New York: Aperture.

Mitchell, W. J. T. (ed.) *Landscape and Power*. Chicago: University of Chicago Press.

Mohl, R. A. (ed.) (1990) *Searching for the Sunbelt: Historical Perspectives on the Region*. Knoxville: University of Tennessee Press.

Moraga, C. and Anzaldúa, G. (eds) (1983) *This Bridge Called My Back*. New York: Kitchen Table Press.

Morris, G. L. (ed.) (1994) *Talking Up A Storm: Voices of the New West*. Lincoln: University of Nebraska Press.

Morrison, T. (1987) 'The Site of Memory', in *Inventing the Truth: The Art and Craft of Memoir*. Boston: Houghton Mifflin.

Muñoz, C. (1989) *Youth, Identity, Power*. London: Verso.

Nabhan, G. and Klett, M. (1994) *Desert Legends: Re-storying the Sonoran Borderlands*. New York: Henry Holt.

Nadel, A. (1997) *Flatlining on the Field of Dreams: Cultural Narratives in the Films of President Reagan's America*. New Brunswick, NJ: Rutgers University Press.

Nash, R. Frazier (ed.) (1990) *American Environmentalism: Readings in Conservation History*. New York: McGraw-Hill.

Nash Smith, H. (1950) *Virgin Land: The American West as Symbol and Myth*. Cambridge, MA: Harvard University Press.

Newman, K. (1990) *Wild West Movies*. London: Bloomsbury.

Norris, S. (1994) *Discovered Country: Tourism and Survival in the American West*. Albuquerque: Stone Ladder Press.

O'Grady, J. P. (1998) 'Living Landscape: An Interview with Gary Snyder', *Western American Literature*, Fall, 33(3), pp. 275–91.

Owens, L. (1992) *Other Destinies: Understanding the American Indian Novel*. Norman: University of Oklahoma Press.

Owens, L. (1998) *Mixedblood Messages: Literature, Film, Family, Place*. Norman: University of Oklahoma Press.

Phillips, S. et al. (eds) (1996) *Crossing the Frontier: Photographs of the Developing West, 1849 to the Present*. San Francisco/SFMOMA: Chronicle Books.

Pratt, M.-L. (1995) *Imperial Eyes: Travel Writing and Transculturation*. London: Routledge (first pub. 1992).

Pye, D. (1996) 'Genre and History' in Cameron, I. and Pye, D., *The Movie Book of the Western*. London: Studio Vista..

Quantic, D. Dufra (1997) *The Nature of Place: A Study of Great Plains Fiction*. Lincoln: University of Nebraska Press.

Raban, J. (1996) *Bad Land: An American Romance*. London: Picador.

Ray, R. B. (1985) *A Certain Tendency of the Hollywood Cinema, 1930–1980*. Princeton, NJ: Princeton University Press.

Regan, M. (1996) 'Piercing the Heart', *Tucson Weekly*, 14–20 March, at http://www.desert.net/tw/03–14–96/reviewl.html.

Reisner, M. (1986) *Cadillac Desert: The American West and Its Disappearing Water*. New York: Penguin.

Rich, A. (1987) *Blood, Bread and Poetry: Selected Prose 1979–85*. London: Virago (first pub. 1986).

Rich, A. (1993) *Adrienne Rich's Poetry and Prose*. New York: W. W. Norton.

Riebsame, C. et al. (eds) (1997) *An Atlas of the New West*. Boulder: University of Colorado Press.

Riley, G. (1988) *The Female Frontier: A Comparative View of Women on the Prairie and the Plains*. Lawrence: Univerity Press of Kansas.

Riley, G. (1992) *A Place to Grow: Women in the American West*. Arlington Heights, TX: Harlan Davidson.

Riley, G. (1999) *Women and Nature: Saving the 'Wild' West*. Lincoln: University of Nebraska Press.

Ringholz, R. C. (1996) *Paradise Paved: The Challenge of Growth in the New West*. Salt Lake City: University of Utah Press.

Robbins, W. G. (1994) *Colony and Empire: The Capitalist Transformation of the American West*. Lawrence: University Press of Kansas.
Robertson, J. O. (1980) *American Myth, American Reality*. New York: Hill & Wang.
Robinson, F. G. (1993) *Having It Both Ways: Self-Subversion in Western Popular Classics*. Albuquerque: University of New Mexico Press.
Robinson, F. G. (ed.) (1998) *The New Western History: The Territory Ahead*. Tucson: University of Arizona Press.
Robinson, M. (1993) 'My Western Roots', in Meldrum, B. H. (ed.), *Old West – New West*. Moscow: University of Idaho Press..
Rosaldo, R. (1993) *Culture and Truth: The Remaking of Social Analysis*. London: Routledge (first pub. 1989).
Rose, Wendy (1994) *Bone Dance: New and Selected Poems, 1965–1993*. Tucson: University of Arizona Press.
Rothman, H. K. (1998a) *Devil's Bargains: Tourism in the Twentieth Century American West*. Lawrence: University Press of Kansas.
Rothman, H. K. (ed.) (1998b) *Reopening the American West*. Tucson: University of Arizona Press.
Rugoff, R. (1995) *Circus Americanus*. London: Verso.
Rushdie, S. (1992) *Imaginary Homelands*. London: Granta.
Rutherford, J. (ed.) (1990) *Identity, Community, Culture, Difference*. London: Lawrence & Wishart.
Said, E. (1993) *Culture and Imperialism*. London: Vintage.
Saldívar, J. D. (1997) *Border Matters: Remapping American Cultural Studies*. Berkeley: University of California Press.
Saldivar-Hull, S. (1999) 'Women Hollering Transfronteriza Feminisms', *Cultural Studies*, 13(2), pp. 251–62.
Sandweiss, M. (1987) 'Laura Gilpin and the Tradition of American Landscape Photography', in Norwood, V. and Monk, J. (eds), *The Desert Is No Lady: Southwestern Landscapes in Women's Writing and Art*. New Haven, CT: Yale University Press.
Sarup, M. (1993) *An Introductory Guide to Post-Structuralism and Postmodernism*. London: Harvester Wheatsheaf.
Sayles, J. (1996) Interview, Cannes, at http://www. filmscouts.com/films/lon-sta.asp.
Schama, S. (1995) *Landscape and Memory*. London: HarperCollins.
Sedgewick, J. (1995) 'Californification', *GQ Magazine*, May, p. 243.
Shepard, S. (1981) *True West*. London: Faber & Faber.
Sherow, J. E. (1998) *A Sense of the American Wets: An Environmental History Anthology*. Albuquerque: University of New Mexico Press.
Silko, L. Marmon (1977) *Ceremony*. New York: Penguin.
Silko, L. Marmon (1996) *Yellow Woman and a Beauty of the Spirit: Essays on Native American Life Today*. New York: Simon & Schuster.
Siporin, O. (1996) 'Terry Tempest Williams and Ona Siporin: A Conversation', *Western American Literature*, 31(2), August, pp. 99–113.
Slotkin, R. (1973) *Regeneration Through Violence: The Mythology of the American Frontier 1600–1860*. Middletown, CT: Wesleyan University Press.
Slotkin, R. (1985) *The Fatal Environment: The Myth of the Frontier in the Twentieth Century*. New York: Harper Perennial.

Slotkin, R. (1993) *Gunfighter Nation: The Myth of the Frontier in Twentieth Century America*. New York: Harper Perennial (first pub. 1992).

Slovic, S. (1992) *Seeking Awareness in American Nature Writing*. Salt Lake City: University of Utah Press.

Snyder, Gary (1969) *Earth House Hold*. New York: New Directions.

Snyder, Gary (1974) *Turtle Island*. New York: New Directions.

Snyder, Gary (1990) *The Practice of the Wild*. New York: North Point Press.

Snyder, Gary (1995) *A Place in Space: Ethics, Aesthetics and Watersheds*. Washington, DC: Counterpoint.

Snyder, J. (1981) *American Frontiers: The Photographs of Timothy O'Sullivan, 1876–1874*. New York: Aperture.

Snyder, J. (1994) 'Territorial Photography', in Mitchell, W. J. T. (ed.), *Landscape and Power*. Chicago: University of Chicago Press.

Soja, E. W. (1989) *Postmodern Geographies: The Reassertion of Space in Critical Social Theory*. London: Verso.

Soja, E. W. (1996) *Thirdspace: Journeys to Los Angeles and Other Real-and-Imagined Places*. Oxford: Blackwell.

Solnit, R. (1990) 'Reclaiming History: Richard Misrach and the Politics of Landscape Photography', *Aperture*, 120, Summer, pp. 30–5.

Solnit, R. (1993) 'Unsettling the West: Contemporary American Landscape Photography', *Creative Camera*, December/January.

Solnit, R. (1994) *Savage Dreams: A Journey into the Landscape Wars of the American West*. New York: Random House.

Solnit, R. (1996) 'Scapeland', in Tucker, A. Wilkes (ed.), *Crimes and Splendors: The Desert Cantos of Richard Misrach*. Boston: Bulfinch Press..

Solnit, R. (1998) 'California is the world capital of amnesia . . .', *Creative Camera*, August/September, pp. 30–7.

Stegner, W. (1987) *The American West as Living Space*. Ann Arbor: University of Michigan Press.

Steiner, S. (1970) *La Raza: The Mexican Americans*. New York: Harper Colophon.

Storey, J. (1993) *An Introductory Guide to Cultural Theory and Popular Culture*. Hemel Hempstead: Harvester Wheatsheaf.

Strinati, D. (1995) *An Introduction to Theories of Popular Culture*. London: Routledge.

Stupich, M. (1993) 'Portfolio', in Dawson, R. et al. *Ansel Adams/New Light: Essays on His Legacy and Legend*. San Francisco: Friends of Photography.

Tallack, D. (1991) *Twentieth Century America*. London: Longmans.

Tasker, Y. (1998) *Working Girls: Gender and Sexuality in Popular Cinema*. London: Routledge.

Tatum, S. (1998) 'Topographies of Transition in Western American Literature', *Western American Literature*, v, February, xxxii, pp. 310–52.

Teague, D. (1997) *The Southwest in American Literature and Art*. Tucson: University of Arizona Press.

Temple, J. Nolte (ed.) (1994) *Open Spaces, City Places: Contemporary Writers on the Changing Southwest*. Tucson: University of Arizona Press.

Thompson, H. S. (1983) *Fear and Loathing in Las Vegas*. London: Paladin (first pub. 1972).

Toelken, B. (1996) 'New Awareness for an Old Significance', in Milner, C. A. (ed.), *A New Significance: Re-envisioning the History of the American West*. New York: Oxford University Press.

Tompkins, J. (1992) *West of Everything: The Inner Life of Westerns*. New York: Oxford University Press.

Tosches, N. (1995) 'Introduction', in Tronnes, M. (ed.), *Literary Las Vegas*. London: Mainstream.

Trachtenberg, A. (1982) *The Incorporation of America*. New York: Hill & Wang.

Trachtenberg, A. (1989) *Reading American Photographs*. New York: Hill & Wang.

Tronnes, M. (ed.) (1995) *Literary Las Vegas*. London: Mainstream.

Truettner, W. (ed.) (1991) *The West As America: Reinterpreting Images of the Frontier, 1820–1920*. Washington, DC: Smithsonian.

Tucker, A. Wilkes (ed.) (1996) *Crimes and Splendors: The Desert Cantos of Richard Misrach*. Boston: Bulfinch Press.

Turner, F. (ed.) (1977) *The North American Indian Reader*. New York: Viking/Penguin.

Turner, F. Jackson (1989) 'The Significance of the Frontier in American History', in Milner, C. A. (ed.) *Major Problems in the History of the American West*. Lexington, MA: D. C. Heath.

Udall, S., Limerick, P. N. et al. (eds) (1990) *Beyond the Mythic West*. Salt Lake City: Peregrine Smith Books.

Urrea, L. A. (1993) *Across the Wire: Life and Hard Times on the Mexican Border*. New York: Anchor Books.

Urrea, L. A. (1998) *Nobody's Son: Notes from an American Life*. Tucson: University of Arizona Press.

Venturi, R. (1966) *Complexity and Contradiction in Architecture*. New York: MOMA.

Venturi, R., Scott Brown, D. and Izenour, S. (1996) *Learning from Las Vegas*. Cambridge, MA: MIT Press (first pub. 1972).

Virilio, P. (1991) *The Lost Dimension*. New York: Semiotext(e).

Vizenor, G. (1993) *Narrative Chance: Postmodern Discourse and Native American Literatures*. Norman: University of Oklahoma Press.

Vizenor, G. (1994) *Manifest Manners: Postindian Warriors of Survivance*. Hanover, NH: Wesleyan University Press.

Watson, L. (1996) *Montana 1948*. London: Pan Books (first pub. 1993).

Weaver, J. (1997) *That the People Might Live: Native American Literatures and Native American Community*. New York: Oxford University Press.

West, C. (1993) *Keeping the Faith*. London: Routledge.

West, E. (1989) *Growing Up With the Country*. Albuquerque: University of New Mexico Press.

West, E. (1995) *The Way West: Essays on the Central Plains*. Albuquerque: University of New Mexico Press.

White, H. (1978) *Tropics of Discourse: Essays in Cultural Criticism*. Baltimore, MD: Johns Hopkins University Press.

White, R. (1991a) 'Trashing the Trails', in Limerick, P. Nelson, Milner, C.A. and Rankin, C. E. (eds) (1991) *Trails Toward a New Western History*. Lawrence: University of Kansas Press.

White, R. (1991b) *It's Your Misfortune and None of My Own: A New History of the American West*. Norman: University of Oklahoma Press.

Wiley, P. and Gottlieb, R. (1982) *Empires of the Sun: The Rise of the New American West*. New York: G. P. Putnams.

Williams, P. and Chrisman, L. (eds) (1993) *Colonial Discoure and Post-Colonial Theory: A Reader*. Hemel Hempstead: Harvester Wheatsheaf.

Williams, R. (1965) *The Long Revolution*. Harmondsworth: Penguin (first pub. 1961).

Williams, R. (1968) *Culture and Society, 1780–1950*. Harmondsworth: Penguin (first pub. 1958).

Williams, T. Tempest (1992) *Refuge: An Unnatural History of Family and Place*. New York: Vintage (first pub. 1991).

Williams, T. Tempest (1995a) *An Unspoken Hunger: Stories from the Field*. New York: Vintage (first pub. 1994).

Williams, T. Tempest (1996) 'Richard Misrach's Bravo 20: The Bombing of the American West', in *Perpetual Mirage: Photographic Narratives of the Desert West*. New York: Whitney Museum of Modern Art.

Williams, T. Tempest (1997) *Pieces of White Shell: A Journey in Navajoland*. Albuquerque: University of New Mexico Press (first pub. 1984).

Williams, T. Tempest and Frank, M. (1995) *Desert Quartet: An Erotic Landscape*. New York: Pantheon Books.

Wills, Garry (1988) *Reagan's America*. New York: Penguin.

Wills, Garry (1997) *John Wayne's America: The Politics of Celebrity*. New York: Simon & Schuster.

Wilson, A. (1992) *The Culture of Nature: North American Landscape from Disney to the Exxon Valdez*. Oxford: Blackwell.

Wood, R. (1986) *Hollywood from Vietnam to Reagan*. New York: Columbia University Press.

Worster, D. (1985) *Rivers of Empire: Water, Aridity and the Growth of the American West*. New York: Pantheon Books.

Worster, D. (1990) 'Transformation of the Earth: Toward an Agroecological Perspective in History', *Journal of American History*, 76(4), March, pp. 1087–106.

Worster, D. (1992) *Under Western Skies: Nature and History in the American West*. Oxford: Oxford University Press.

Worster, D. (1994) *An Unsettled Country: Changing Landscapes of the American West*. Albuquerque: University of New Mexico Press.

Wrobel, D. M. and Steiner, M. C. (eds) (1997) *Many Wests: Place, Culture, and Regional Identity*. Lawrence: University Press of Kansas.

Yates, S. (ed.) (1985) *The Essential Landscape: The New Mexico Photographic Survey*. Albuquerque: University of New Mexico Press.

Young, R. (1995) *White Mythologies: Writing History and the West*. London: Routledge.

Zakin, S. (1995) *Coyotes and Town Dogs: Earth First! and the Environmental Movement*. New York: Penguin.

Zukin, S. (1991) *Landscapes of Power: From Detroit to Disney World*, Berkeley: University of California Press.

Index